FROM WATERGATE TO WHITEWATER

The Public Integrity War

Robert N. Roberts
and
Marion T. Doss, Jr.

PRAEGER

Westport, Connecticut
London

Library of Congress Cataloging-in-Publication Data

Roberts, Robert North.
    From Watergate to Whitewater : the public integrity war / Robert
N. Roberts and Marion T. Doss, Jr.
      p. cm.
    Includes bibliographical references and index.
    ISBN 0–275–95597–4 (alk. paper)
    1. Political ethics—United States. 2. Political corruption—
United States. 3. Clinton, Bill, 1946– . I. Doss, Marion T.,
1936– . II. Title.
JK468.E7R558 1997
172'.0973—dc21   96–53616

British Library Cataloguing in Publication Data is available.

Library of Congress Catalog Card Number: 96–53616
ISBN: 0–275–95597–4

First published in 1997

Praeger Publishers, 88 Post Road West, Westport, CT 06881
An imprint of Greenwood Publishing Group, Inc.

Printed in the United States of America

The paper used in this book complies with the
Permanent Paper Standard issued by the National
Information Standards Organization (Z39.48–1984).

10 9 8 7 6 5 4 3 2 1

Contents

Contents

Part III: The Public Ethics Firestorm

Preface

The public, in the years following the Watergate scandal, has grown increasingly cynical about the integrity of public officials and the ability of government to solve difficult local, state and national problems. Despite great optimism that Watergate would mark the beginning of a new era of integrity in government, the opposite has occurred. Watergate, instead, ushered in an era of unprecedented public integrity carnage.

The carnage had little to do with legitimate concern over the condition of public service ethics. It had much more to do with the trend in American politics that saw movement conservatives and new progressives battle over the role of government in American society. Movement conservatives fought to dismantle the administrative state. New progressives struggled to preserve the responsibility of government for dealing with a vast array of problems facing American society.

This book argues that the public integrity war has made it next to impossible for the public and the media to distinguish between legitimate character issues and those motivated by ideology. Furthermore, the public integrity war will likely continue as long as movement conservatives and new progressives continue their struggle to convince the majority of the American public to accept their respective visions of government.

Acknowledgments

This book is dedicated to the following: the American people, whose love of liberty has championed democracy and made government servant rather than master; an early public integrity warrior, James Madison of Virginia, who gave us the Constitution and the Bill of Rights; to the Virginia university that bears his name, James Madison University, a highly spirited community of teachers, scholars and diverse support personnel working to expand and share knowledge; to our visionary and intrepid president, Dr. Ronald E. Carrier, whose pragmatic leadership over the past quarter century has allowed JMU to flourish and has raised it to national attention as a widely respected and highly nurturing public university; and to an inspiring educator, Dr. William R. Nelson, professor of political science and law, mentor without peer and respected friend.

Introduction

On May 28, 1996, a Little Rock, Arkansas, Federal Court jury convicted Arkansas Governor Jim Guy Tucker and Susan and James McDougal on multiple fraud charges.[1] The Whitewater investigation, at that moment, ceased being a political witch-hunt. Prior to the verdict, the Clinton White House and supporters of President Clinton had conducted an all-out campaign to discredit the independent counsel investigation of Kenneth Starr.[2] The convictions gave Kenneth Starr a new mandate to pursue his Whitewater investigation.

The *Washington Post*, on February 6, 1995, published an opinion piece by Meg Greenfield entitled "Right and Wrong in Washington: Why Do Our Officials Need Specialists to Tell the Difference?"[3] Greenfield, editor of the *Washington Post* editorial page and long-time Washington observer, reminded Washington that "having all those ethics boards is not the same as having ethics."[4] Greenfield wondered why Washington public officials had become so dependent upon ethics specialists to distinguish between right and wrong. "What has been reached in our age is the idea of ethics not as an intrinsic and understood and codifiable aspect of human behavior, but rather as one of many highly technical side concerns."[5]

Greenfield argued that Washington had lost its moral compass. No one seemed any longer to understand the difference between right and wrong. "What we once were assumed to know ourselves if we affected to be upstanding people, and could always count on parents, pastors and cops to call briskly to our attention [if] we didn't . . . is now believed to be beyond our own power of comprehension."[6]

This book attempts to explain how this situation has come to pass. To-day's public integrity war is the result of growing divisions over the appropriate role of government in American society. Critics of big government, on one side of the political spectrum, see public corruption scandals as evidence of the moral bankruptcy of big government. Supporters of big government, on the other hand, see these scandals as the result of special interests exercising too much power in the political system. Both critics and supporters of government have come to regard ethics scandals as support for their visions of the role of government in American society.

The roots of the modern public integrity war can be traced back to colonial times and to the struggle for independence. Throughout much of American history there has been a struggle between those advocating a greater role for government and those fearful that a larger government will lead to tyranny and oppression. Watergate, however, ushered in a new phase of this struggle. Movement conservatives and new progressives turned to public integrity attacks as a means of persuading Americans to join their political movements. Likewise, new progressive and movement conservative supporters have come to view attacks on their leaders as attacks on their movements. Neither movement can afford to throw overboard a leader who strays from the straight and narrow.

This book also argues that Bill Clinton's political survival ironically can be traced directly to the public integrity war. Despite nearly four years of allegations of impropriety on the part of Bill Clinton and Hillary Rodham Clinton, and numerous other high-level Clinton administration officials, Bill Clinton's political base has remained loyal. A decade earlier, supporters of Ronald Reagan reacted in much the same way with respect to attacks leveled against members of that administration.

The book, finally, argues that as long as movement conservatives and new progressives battle for political power, the public integrity war will continue to intensify. Innocent public servants will find themselves targets of unjustified attacks. Unethical public servants will find it possible to characterize themselves as martyrs in the public integrity war. This integrity war has made it next to impossible for the public to distinguish between villains and victims.

POLITICAL SOUND BITES

In July 1995, in one of his weekly radio talks to the nation, President Bill Clinton announced that he had asked John Gardner, founder of the citizens' lobby Common Cause, and presidential historian Doris Kearns Goodwin to work with him to establish a bipartisan commission on political reform.[7] Clinton argued that a "bipartisan commission could cut the knot that is strangling change. The panel would follow the approach that has worked on other critical issues. It would be comprised of distinguished citizens and would recommend broad changes in the rules which cover lobbyists and in how we finance political campaigns."[8] A month earlier, President Clinton and Speaker of the House Newt Gingrich had shaken hands in New Hampshire, apparently agreeing on the need to establish a political reform commission.[9] Nothing ever came of that agreement.

On August 4, 1995, in an Oval Office announcement, President Clinton again challenged Speaker Gingrich to join him in the establishment of a bipartisan political reform commission. Clinton cast the Republican opposition as protectors of the status quo and as enemies of political reform.[10] President Clinton announced that he had directed the attorney general to prepare an executive order "that would bar Executive Branch employees from meeting with any lobbyist who does not fully disclose his or her activities to the public."[11] If lobbyists want to have access to federal officials, they would have to disclose "who they are, what they're working on, how much they're spending and what policy they are pushing or trying to block."[12] According to Clinton, the executive order would "bring the sunlight of full disclosure to the lobbying process in Washington."[13]

A product of insider Arkansas politics, Clinton had draped himself in the mantle of political reform: "From the reform victories of the turn of the century progressives to the changes that followed Watergate . . . moments of natural renewal have always called forth people of goodwill, regardless of party, who were willing to do what it takes to change things for the better. This is part of our national history, and it must be part of our common ground."[14]

Lobby reform had again caught on as a solution for the American public's growing distrust of politics as usual in Washington. Resistance to lobbying reform collapsed, and President Clinton signed into law the measure on December 20, 1995.[15] This law required lobbyists to register with Congress "and disclose the identity of their clients, the issues on which lobbying is being done, and roughly how much is being paid for it."[16] Within a few days of the signing of the law, Washington returned to normal.

Meanwhile, Senator Alfonse D'Amato of New York continued his Whitewater probe. A long line of witnesses paraded before his committee. Testimony provided the nation with a fascinating insight into the internal workings of the White House and Arkansas politics, but little else. The Republican members of the committee attempted to characterize Bill Clinton as the boss of a corrupt political machine. The White House, at the same time, kept up a barrage of criticism against the hearings.

Two years of Whitewater hearings had no impact on public opinion. Those individuals who already believed the nation had made a mistake by electing Clinton president saw the hearings as vindication of their viewpoint. Clinton loyalists, on the other hand, viewed the hearings as a political witch-hunt. The report of the committee, issued in late June 1996, constituted an indictment of the Clinton White House for its efforts to protect the Clintons from disclosures that might do serious damage to the presidency. The White House, as expected, rejected in total the findings of the committee. The media and the public continued to shake their heads in confusion.

MOVEMENT CONSERVATIVES AND NEW PROGRESSIVES: CLASH OF VISIONS AND VALUES

Throughout American history, presidents and members of their administrations have faced allegations of improper and illegal conduct.[17] After the Second World War, the growing power of movement conservatives and new progressives guaranteed that allegations of improper conduct by high-level public officials would receive much closer scrutiny.

The term *movement conservatives* refers to those people who argue that big government constitutes the most serious problem facing the nation. Movement conservatives blame the growth of the administrative state for destroying individual initiative, for putting in place policies and programs hostile to traditional American families, and for attempting to limit the role of religion in American society.

New progressives, on the other side of the political aisle, argue that powerful special interests exert far too much control over the political process. They feel that average Americans need a government to stand up for their interests and make a difference in their lives. The industrial revolution, according to this line of reasoning, changed the nation forever. The country ceased being a Jeffersonian agrarian nation of small towns and farmers. Powerful private interests acquired the ability to control the political process through legal or illegal means. Government, more often than not, did the bidding of special interests rather than acting in the public interest.

The chapters that follow tell the story of how fighting corruption in government evolved from an attempt to rid government of bad individuals into an ideological battle for the hearts of the American people. New progressives have seen ethics reform as a way to prevent powerful special interests from rolling back progressive measures. Movement conservatives have viewed ethics reform as a way to equate corruption with big government, leading to demands to dismantle the welfare state. Each side believes it holds the moral high ground. Each believes that the vision and values of its foe threaten the very foundation of the nation. Neither movement understands that the issue of ethics in government simply is not great enough to sway voters to shift their allegiance.

Political philosophy has become entwined with perceptions of public integrity. "The war for the soul of American democracy continues," states the Public Integrity Research Corporation.[18] "Beyond the politics of the Beltway lie the real battlegrounds in the states, counties, and towns of

America. It is a grass roots struggle against big government statist, socialist utopian, and we-know-best elites in government and the dominant media."[19]

In March 1992, the *Los Angeles Times* published an opinion piece by progressive writer Elaine Crulla Kamerck. Written during the middle of the campaign for the 1992 Democratic nomination for president, Kamerck questioned the progressive credentials of Bill Clinton:

> Then came the stories of the Clintons' involvement in a failed land deal, which would have been unremarkable except the developer ended up the owner of a failed savings and loan.
>
> This was followed by stories about Hillary Clinton's law firm doing business with the state. In New York or Los Angeles she could have had her pick of law firms that did no state business. In a state with the population smaller than that of Los Angeles that's impossible. And this week we heard stories about Bill Clinton's close relationship with a chicken-processing magnate who dumps waste into Arkansas streams and another businessman who won state contracts under the Clinton Administration even while his other business was cocaine.
>
> In all of these stories there is no smoking gun. You sometimes have to read them more than once to figure out that Clinton himself had done nothing illegal. What does emerge, however, from their cumulative weight is a picture of a state that resembles, in some ways, a Third World country. Mind-numbing, mostly rural poverty exists alongside a handful of extremely rich people who form a small and interconnected elite. The Clintons have been at the center of that elite for a decade.[20]

Of course, once Clinton obtained the Democratic nomination for president, progressive concerns about his Arkansas background quickly gave way to the goal of recapturing the White House.

THE MYTHS OF THE PUBLIC INTEGRITY WAR

Many scholars and political observers expected Watergate to usher in a golden age of ethics in government. But the opposite result occurred: Watergate touched off a period of unmitigated public ethics carnage.

Since Watergate, there has been a desperate search to understand the public integrity war. Political scientists, historians and political commentators have various theories to explain the expanding ethics bloodbath, each theory positing a solution for the perceived crisis. However, these theories overstate the impact of events that have occurred since Watergate and underestimate the impact of long-term political trends on the nation's morbid post-Watergate preoccupation with government ethics.

The Feeding Frenzy Model

Investigative journalists have little difficulty finding the latest example of a five-hundred dollar toilet seat or the impermissible gift received by this or that public official. And among more than 18 million public employees, there are certain to be periodic instances of unethical conduct. When the media focus almost exclusively on the negative aspects of government and on the conduct of public officials, the public mind must certainly get the impression that government is performing poorly. If the media exercised greater self-restraint, the public would entertain a much higher regard for government and public officials.

Professor Larry Sabato of the University of Virginia, in the early 1990s, developed the "feeding frenzy" model to describe the behavior of the media, turning minor indiscretions of public officials into national stories. Sabato, writing in his book *Feeding Frenzy*, admonished the media for spending so much time covering the private lives of public figures and ignoring significant scandals, such as the 1980s collapse of the savings and loan industry.[21] "Ever since Watergate," wrote Sabato:

government scandals have been paraded across the television set in a roll call so lengthy and numbing they are inseparable in the public consciousness, all joined at the Achilles' heel.[22] The sad conclusion is inescapable: the press has become obsessed with gossip rather than governance; it prefers to employ titillation rather than scrutiny; as a result, its political coverage produces trivialization rather than enlightenment. And the dynamic mechanism propelling and demonstrating this decline in news standards is the "feeding frenzy."[23]

According to Sabato, the media have the professional responsibility and ability to distinguish between real scandals involving serious misuse of official authority and news-making reports exposing the skeletons in the closets of all public officials.[24] Sabato's feeding frenzy model received tremendous attention from the media and among political commentators. While the American public certainly had a low opinion of public officials, it had an even lower opinion of the media. To combat this poor image, the media undertook an unprecedented amount of soul searching and self-criticism. Reasoned public discourse would most likely return if the media simply exercised greater self-restraint.

Sabato, like many other political observers of the early 1990s, greatly overstated the impact of media reports about ethical lapses by public officials on public opinion. The 1992 presidential election provided a perfect test for this feeding frenzy model. Character questions plagued Bill Clinton throughout the primary and presidential campaigns. Clinton, despite these questions, received strong support from a base composed of the Democratic Party and independent progressives. Unlike Gary Hart in 1988, Clinton understood that character mattered, but that ideology mattered even more. The feeding frenzy model simply overstated the impact of media reporting on the political process.

Revenge and the Counterculture Model

The counterculture model has turned out to be the strangest explanation developed to explain the public's preoccupation with ethics in government after the Watergate scandal. Throughout the 1980s, officials in the Reagan administration came under sharp attack for their apparent insensitivity to ethical standards. These scandals forced numerous Reagan officials to leave government under a cloud, but they did little to weaken public confidence in Ronald Reagan as president.

The counterculture model explained these attacks on public figures as coming from "refugees from the 1960s" who subsequently assumed positions of power in the media or in various left-wing public interest groups. According to this model, the Vietnam antiwar movement gave birth to a generation of men and women with absolutely no respect for established institutions or for individuals who reached positions of power and respect by playing by the rules. Consequently, these counterculture "refugees" had little need for traditional institutions either inside or outside of government.[25]

Suzanne Garment, in her 1991 book *Scandal: The Crisis of Mistrust in American Politics*, argued that the Vietnam War had convinced many young people who grew up during that time that "the presidency itself had become corrupt in the deepest sense. The corruption was so outrageous and threatening that it demanded the almost undivided attention and steady anger of the citizenry."[26] These refugees, greatly disappointed with their failure to overthrow the establishment, turned their frustration against establishment figures both inside and outside of government. According to Garment:

Yet despite the visible differences, the activists who form such a prominent part of today's anti-corruption campaign harken back to the 1960s in fundamental attitudes. The unforgiving stance adopted by the new crusaders reflects not simply an aversion to crime but the same radical opposition to conventional authority, the same denial of its legitimacy, and the same sort of drive for political power that we saw in the streets of Chicago more than two decades ago. Moreover, today's ethics police practice scorched earth warfare of a sort readily recognizable from Vietnam days. They are not content to throw the book at a political figure who becomes their target; instead, they spend great effort figuring out how to hit him or her with the whole library.[27]

Garment's model of the post-Watergate political scene seemed a reasonable explanation for the intensity of attacks against public officials.[28] But the 1992 presidential campaign and the subsequent Whitewater scandal did serious damage to the counterculture explanation. If counterculture journalists controlled the liberal media, such as the *New York Times* and *Wash-*

ington Post, why would they report so extensively about candidate Clinton's character problems during the campaign? Even though the network news organizations paid little attention to Whitewater after Clinton's 1992 election victory, major newspapers such as the *New York Times* simply refused to let Whitewater die. Conservative news operations such as the *Wall Street Journal* and the *American Spectator* devoted even more attention to an expansion of how the Clintons conducted public and private business in Arkansas. No one could honestly argue that reporters working for the *American Spectator* or the *Wall Street Journal* saw as their mission to tear down the establishment.

The Good-Government Reform Model

The good-government reform model—in sharp contrast to the feeding frenzy and counterculture explanations—argued that corruption is rampant in government. Special interests yearly pour millions of dollars into political campaigns. Those wishing to run for state or national office must spend tremendous amounts of time raising money if they expect to run a competitive political campaign. Likewise, appointed public servants find themselves subject to attempts by special interests to influence their official actions.

To restore public trust in government, the good-government reform model argued, citizens must demand that special interests and public officials comply with strict codes of conduct and fully disclose their attempts to influence public officials. "The Watergate scandal," wrote Michael Josephson, founder of the Josephson Institute for Ethics, "provided the impetus for scores of new laws and reams of regulations which have permanently changed the landscape of public service and dramatically improved the integrity of government."[29] But these Watergate-inspired political reforms, from the perspective of the good-government reform movement, have fallen far short of cleaning up the nation's political system.

Common Cause, the so-called citizen's lobby, in 1990 celebrated its twentieth anniversary.[30] The most influential good-government reform lobby, Common Cause has come to symbolize post-Watergate good-government reform. "The accountable and fair exercise of power on behalf of citizens," wrote Fred Wertheimer, president of Common Cause, "is at the core of our political system. And it's at the core of what Common Cause has been fighting for, with our coalition allies, since our founding."[31] According to this model, public distrust in government is the natural result of a corrupt political system. But before average citizens can assume their rightful place in the political system, Congress and the state legislatures need to enact much stricter campaign finance, lobbying reform and public ethics laws.

Good-government reform has had a remarkable series of successes. Public financial disclosure by high-level public officials is now commonplace. Federal, state and local employees typically must comply with strict codes of conduct regulating on- and off-the-job conduct that might create the appearance of impropriety. Tough restrictions have been placed on lobbying by former government officials. Yet the successes of the good-government reform movement have done very little to restore public trust in government.

The Institutional Breakdown Model

Benjamin Ginsberg and Martin Shefter, in their thought- provoking book *Politics by Other Means: The Declining Importance of Elections in America*, argue that as the power of political parties declined and political deadlock set in, Republicans and Democrats turned to revelation, investigation, and prosecution (RIP) to accomplish what they could not accomplish at the polls.[32] Both parties, according to Ginsberg and Shefter, increasingly relied upon the RIP strategy to gain political advantage, a less risky strategy than attempting to break the deadlock by mobilizing citizens who participate in the political process. They explained:

> In contrast to the immediate gains that can be realized today by using revelations and investigations to drive opponents from office, the path of mobilization would entail major risks for both parties. For the Republicans, expansion of the electorate could threaten the advantage they currently enjoy in the arena of presidential elections. As for the Democrats, whatever the potential benefits to the party as a whole, an influx of millions of new voters would create serious uncertainties for current officeholders at the local, state, and congressional levels.[33]

Despite the fact that Ginsberg and Shefter make a compelling argument for their institutional collapse model and partisan use of ethics allegations to immobilize their opponents, they tend to underplay the fact that Watergate did not start the public integrity war. Watergate did, however, help to provide the public integrity bureaucracy with badly needed resources to enforce existing restrictions against corrupt activities by local, state and federal officials. "How did our politics reach the point where public officials now regularly seek to secure the imprisonment of their political opponents?" ask Ginsberg and Shefter.[34] They explain that this development "dates from Watergate and reflects the intensification of partisan warfare that has occurred in the United States over the past quarter century."[35] As the book details, the public integrity war began long before Watergate.

Modern public integrity scandals may make life difficult for those public officials who come under scrutiny. But political scandals have done little to shift the political balance of power between movement conservatives and new progressives. The fear of becoming embroiled in a political scandal, nevertheless, has shrunk the number of distinguished citizens willing to volunteer for public service.

BATTLE FATIGUE AND THE SEARCH FOR HEROES

On May 24, 1996, the *Washington Post* reported a *Washington Post-ABC News* poll showing Bill Clinton holding a commanding lead among registered voters against Republican Bob Dole. Fifty-five percent of those polled said Bill Clinton deserved a second term as president.[36] Besides questioning registered voters on their preference for president, the poll asked: "If you had to choose, which of the two qualities is more important in a president: someone who has the highest personal character or someone who understands the problems of people like you?"[37] Seventy-seven percent of those polled responded that it was more important that a president understand their problems than have the highest personal character. By mid-June 1996, however, polls showed a significant narrowing of the gap between Bob Dole and Bill Clinton. Clinton had not lost any of his core support, but independent voters appeared much less committed to a Clinton second term than they had been a few months earlier.

The late Joseph Campbell, in his writings and commentary, explained the importance of myth in the evolution and survival of a culture.[38] More important, he stressed the importance of heroes to the health of a culture: "A hero is someone who has given his or her life to something bigger than oneself."[39] The profoundly moral objective of heroism, argued Campbell, is to give hope to a culture: "The moral objective is that of saving a people, or saving a person, or supporting an idea. The hero sacrifices himself for something—that's the morality of it."[40]

Campbell, however, recognized that cultures have not expected their heroic figures to be saints. Odysseus, the hero of Homer's *Odyssey*, never came close to achieving sainthood. Homer provided a magnificent picture of his strengths and weaknesses. James Madison, more than two hundred years ago, wrote "If men were angels, no government would be necessary."[41] Madison understood that government would attract both honorable and dishonorable individuals.

In summary, the public integrity war is the story of how the nation has come to confuse political philosophy with public integrity and how fringe political factions have manufactured a crisis in public service ethics.

NOTES

1. R. H. Melton and Michael Haddigan, "Three Guilty in Arkansas Fraud Trial," *Washington Post*, May 29, 1996, p. A1.

2. See Margaret Carlson, "Washington Diary; Star Wars," *Time*, May 6, 1996,

p. 20; Fred Barnes, "Shooting Starr," *Weekly Standard*, April 15, 1996, pp. 11–12.

3. Meg Greenfield, "Right and Wrong in Washington: Why Do Our Officials Need Specialists to Tell the Difference?" *Washington Post*, February 6, 1995, p. A7.

4. Ibid.

5. Ibid.

6. Ibid.

7. White House, Office of the Press Secretary, Saturday Radio address by the President to the nation, the Oval Office, July 22, 1995. URL: http://library.whitehouse. gov/retrieve.cgi?dbtype=audio&id=79&query=bipartisan+commission

8. Ibid.

9. Speaker of the House Newt Gingrich and President Bill Clinton had attended a gathering of senior citizens in Claremont, New Hampshire. Frank McConnel, a retired steel worker, stated that politics had become polluted by special interests and that too often the voice of the people was shut out. McConnel proposed the creation of a bipartisan commission to write reforms.

10. Jonathan D. Salant, "Clinton Order," *Congressional Quarterly Weekly Report*, August 5, 1995, p. 2334. See also "Clinton Looks to Heighten Scrutiny of Lobbyists," *Inside Politics*, CNN, Program 904, August 4, 1995.

11. White House, Office of the Press Secretary, Remarks of the president on political reform, August 4, 1995, p. 2 (hereafter cited as White House, Remarks, 8/4/95). Texas A&M White House Archives. gopher://ftp.tamu.edu:701020-15154-1.data/politics/1995/reform.0804

12. Ibid.

13. White House, Remarks, 8/4/95, p.1.

14. Ibid.

15. Helen Dewar and Michael Weisskopf, "House Gives Final Approval to Lobbyist Disclosure Bill," *Washington Post*, November 30, 1995, p. A1; John F. Harris, "Law Aspiring to Shed Light on Lobbyists Leaves Some Gray Areas," *Washington Post*, December 20, 1995, p. A4.

16. Dewar and Weisskopf, p. A15; Harris, p. A4.

17. See Comer Van Woodward, ed. *Responses of the President to Charges of Misconduct* (New York: Delacorte Press, 1974).

18. Public Integrity Research Corporation. URL: http://www.pihome.com:80/pirc/pirc1.html, January 20, 1997.

19. Ibid. Headquartered in Gilbert, Arizona, this tax-exempt organization was established by Richard F. Mauzy to conduct "investigation, research and analysis of issues, laws, and policies affecting the integrity and effectiveness of public officials, institutions and policy."

20. Elaine Crulla Kamerck, "A Third World State Muddles Clinton's Path." *Los Angeles Times*, March 26, 1992, p. B7.

21. Larry J. Sabato, *Feeding Frenzy* (New York: Free Press, 1991).

22. Ibid., p. 5.

23. Ibid., p. 6.

24. See Howard Kurtz, *Media Circus: The Trouble with America's Newspapers* (New York: Times Books, 1992).

25. Suzanne Garment, *Scandal: The Crisis of Mistrust in American Politics* (New York: Random House, 1991), p. 31.

26. Ibid.

27. Ibid., pp. 8–9.

28. For a discussion of first-term Reagan administration ethics scandals, see Thomas Riehle, "Scandals, etc. from A to Z," *National Journal*, January 14, 1984, pp. 92–93.

29. Michael Josephson, "The Ethics of Politics: The Best of Times, The Worst of Times," *Ethics* 13/14 (1991): 39.

30. For a retrospective of the role Common Cause played in supporting political reform from 1970 to 1990, see "Common Cause 1970–1990," *Common Cause Magazine*, Fall 1992.

31. Fred Wertheimer, "20 Years: Common Cause: Advancing Honesty and Fairness in Our Political System," *Common Cause Magazine*, Fall 1992, p. 2.

32. Benjamin Ginsberg and Martin Shefter, *Politics by Other Means: The Declining Importance of Elections in America* (New York: Basic Books, 1990), p. 26.

33. Ibid., p. 193.

34. Ibid., p. 433.

35. Ibid., pp. 433–34.

36. Richard Morin and Mario A. Brossard, "Dole's Resignation Doesn't Resonate with Voters, Poll Suggests," *Washington Post*, May 24, 1996, p. A12.

37. Ibid.

38. Joseph Campbell, *The Power of Myth with Bill Moyers*, ed. Betty Sue Flowers (New York: Doubleday, 1988).

39. Ibid., p. 123.

40. Ibid., p. 127.

41. James Madison, "Number 51, The Social Foundations of Political Freedom." In *The Federalist Papers, Alexander Hamilton, John Jay, James Madison*, ed. Andrew Macke (New York: Washington Square Books, 1964), p. 122.

PART I

THE GATHERING STORM

The seeds of the modern public integrity war were sown long before the Watergate scandal of the 1970s. Throughout American history various political and social movements have held starkly different visions of American society. The Founding Fathers recognized that political factions could rip the new nation apart. They devised a blueprint for national government that was designed to force divergent factions to compromise if they wished to share power. Throughout American history, however, various movements have allowed ideology to cloud their judgment. Instead of constituting a virtue, compromise has been regarded as an unpardonable sin.

Political movements throughout most of the nineteenth century found that allegations of political corruption did little to weaken public support. This fact helped to provide an environment that permitted political corruption to thrive through most of nineteenth-century America. Reformers, by the end of the nineteenth century, however, would make a persuasive case that public corruption threatened the democratic foundations of the nation.

Chapter 1

The Moral Foundations of
Public Service

Political ethics experts point to the Watergate scandal as having triggered the current preoccupation with government ethics.[1] In fact, the storm clouds had begun gathering many decades earlier. Much of the battle over ratification of the Constitution, fought between the Federalists and the Anti-Federalists, focused on sharp differences of opinion regarding states' rights and individual civil liberties. "Federalism was a fram of mind, a set of attitudes that included belief in a strong activist central government,"[2] a movement that feared the prospect of states' striking out on their own more than a national government's imposing its will on the states.

The Anti-Federalists, on the other hand, feared that the national government would assert supremacy over the states. They demanded strict limitations on the power of that national government. And this debate did not end with ratification of the Constitution and the Bill of Rights.

Besides this ongoing debate over the relationship between the federal and state governments, the colonial period of American history saw the evolution of a model of the ideal public servant. This model stressed private-sector achievements and the willingness of successful citizens to take on public responsibilities and then return to their private lives. Historian Daniel J. Boorstin, in his book *Hidden History,* helps to explain the impact of our early national political figures on our political system: "In no other country has the hagiography of politics been more important. The lives of our national saints have remained vivid and contemporary."[3]

THE PURITAN ETHIC

It's been almost four hundred years since the first colonists reached the shores of North America, and some people tend to forget that many of those colonists came to carve out communities free of the corruption and authoritarian state control that had circumscribed their lives in Europe. In their quest for a moral society, New England Puritans "banned the theater, religious music, sensuous poetry and the observance of Christmas."[4] Puritanism, despite certain excesses, "inspired moral and intellectual traits that have persisted distinctively in American culture to the present day."[5] Puritans considered public service an obligation, not an opportunity for personal advancement or enrichment.

GOVERNMENT BY GENTRY

From New England to Georgia, it was assumed that members of communities would select only morally upright people to serve in positions of authority. The colonists based their faith on the fact that they limited recruitment to members of the upper class. Many upper-class families taught their children that civic responsibility and public service were important and that they had a moral obligation to help the communities and the colonies that had provided them the opportunity to prosper. Public service, to a large degree, became the responsibility of the upper classes.

The gentry of Virginia took this responsibility particularly seriously. "Just as the owner of a large plantation had thrust on him tasks of management which he could not escape—he had to lay out orchards, decide on the time to plant and to cut the tobacco, find raw materials for shoes and clothing," wrote historian Daniel Boorstin, "so he had political duties which he could not shirk."[6] Members of the gentry served without pay and had to cover out of their own pockets the expenses associated with travel to seats of government.

Although the gentry during the colonial period believed that it had responsibility to take on leadership positions in government, colonial society still placed sharp restrictions on who could actively participate in the political process. Colonial society generally limited political participation to white males who owned property. Poor whites, women, slaves and minorities, as a general rule, did not have a right to vote or to hold public office. This fact, however, does not lessen the achievements of a generation of public servants who risked all in the hope of carving a new nation out of the wilderness. That succeeding generations of Americans look back to the nation's early leaders is the best evidence of their impact on American political thought and on our view of public service.

CONSTITUTIONAL HEROES: 1789–1829

The Revolutionary War freed the colonies from English control, but did not end the debate over the role of the national government. The Constitution was drafted and adopted, in large measure, as the result of the failure of the Articles of Confederation to bring some modicum of order to the demands of governing thirteen very different colonies. The Constitution, however, provided early presidents little guidance on how to staff the new national government. That new national government could not function as long as it relied upon the willingness of members of the gentry to take a few days off each month to handle the nation's business. The new nation needed a permanent bureaucracy to conduct the public business of the new nation. And with the need for a permanent bureaucracy came the potential for public officials to use their positions to line their own pockets or to help their friends outside of government.

The early presidents, to their great credit, set high standards for members of the new government.[7] George Washington, for instance, made "fitness of character" an important criterion for those whom he appointed to his administration. Fitness of character meant that the individuals were well respected in their communities. The fact that the young national government conducted relatively few activities that brought federal officials into direct contact with citizens played an even more important role in limiting the amount of corruption involving federal employees. Administrative historian Leonard D. White writes:

External circumstances favored high official standards. The pressures on officials were light. The general government had relatively few contacts with citizens. It dispensed few favors and interfered with no established ways of life. Conversely, citizens had little to ask of government. They were usually content to be let alone.[8]

Supporters of a more active federal government could not dispute the fact that, as the federal government took on more responsibilities, the opportunities for those inside and outside of government to profit from the activities of government would multiply. After throwing off the yoke of "corrupt" colonial governments imposed by the British Crown, the country would not respond favorably to disclosures of profiteering by federal officials. Those opposed to giving the national government more power would certainly use any scandals as evidence that corruption would rot from within such a powerful national government.

Concern over corruption in government did not mean that early-nineteenth-century America regarded anything inherently wrong with government and the private sector working closely together to solve problems faced by the nation. To the contrary, private-public cooperation fit the prevailing view of the limited role of government in American society. Possible conflicts of interest, consequently, raised few eyebrows at this time in American history.

For instance, George Washington's secretary of the treasury, Alexander Hamilton, faced the monumental problem of placing the United States on a sound financial footing. Hamilton's first step involved creating a system to finance the debt of the United States. Congress, at the insistence of Hamilton, chartered the Bank of the United States. This new national bank refinanced the national debt by selling securities to private investors. Those given the opportunity to invest, assuming the survival of the nation, had the opportunity to make fortunes.[9]

Besides being the architect of the system for financing the debt of the new nation, Hamilton used his position as secretary of the treasury to aid private business associates. Prior to becoming secretary, Hamilton helped establish the Society for Useful Manufacturers. While serving as secretary of the treasury, he persuaded the Bank of New York to make low-interest loans to this group. The Bank of New York served as a depository bank for large amounts of federal funds.[10] If a secretary of the treasury engaged in this type of conduct today, he or she would certainly face the prospect of a congressional inquiry and perhaps an independent counsel investigation into possible criminal conduct.

A much more serious problem for defenders of the national government grew directly out of the authority of Congress to appropriate funds. The growth of the national economy during the first half of the nineteenth century meant that Americans could afford to import goods from Europe and other parts of the world. A large increase in tariff revenues gave Congress money to spend. Private interests began to see the federal treasury as an important source of revenue. Private citizens looked to Congress to compensate them for any losses they incurred as the result of actions taken by the national government.

Large and small businesses, as well as private citizens, found it increasingly difficult to deal with Congress and federal departments and agencies. As the nation expanded westward, the distances increased between Washington and where businesses operated and where citizens lived. A group of enterprising individuals, some of whom worked for federal agencies and departments, quickly learned that private citizens would pay good money to those who knew their way around Washington and had the ability to open the right doors. Even if these public entrepreneurs, in fact, had little influence over members of Congress or clerks in major federal agencies and departments, the public came to believe otherwise. A congressional investigation in 1818 revealed that a small number of federal clerks had violated department regulations by accepting payments from private citizens for helping them pursue claims for money owed to them by federal agencies.[11]

These early disclosures, however, did little to tarnish the reputation of a young national government. Still, the early years made it clear that as the national government grew larger and distributed more benefits, public integrity problems would multiply. The Founding Fathers had successfully laid the foundations for a viable national government, but greatly underestimated the willingness of private citizens and private enterprise to look to Washington for help. Even if the Founding Fathers could have anticipated this trend, little evidence exists that they would have supported detailed codes of conduct to regulate official behavior or new criminal laws to punish those public officials who put private interests ahead of the public interest. In fact, strong evidence exists that they believed the best guarantee for honest and responsible government rested with keeping political power in the hands of an elite whose personal values assured honest government.[12]

Members of the country's early political elite believed that the character of those entering government determined whether or not they would violate the public trust. But by the second decade of the nineteenth century, the winds of political change began to sweep the nation. Demands increased to permit a larger cross-section of adult males to vote. Ownership of property gradually ceased to be a prerequisite of political participation. National political parties gradually emerged from regional factions. Public service eventually ceased to be the domain solely of the gentry.

During the remainder of the nineteenth century, the transformation of the nation's political system resulted in an influx of individuals who had their own vision of public service. Besides, the nation now placed much heavier demands on local, state and national governments to assist with the nation's economic expansion. The Civil War resulted in vast public expenditures by the federal government directed at keeping the Union intact. The industrial revolution gave birth to corporate giants who were willing to use their wealth to purchase the loyalty of public officials at all levels of government. Local, state and even the federal government proved totally unprepared for this assault on the legitimacy of government. To many, the country appeared headed toward the same level of moral decay that the colonists had cited as a reason for breaking away from England.

The speed of change that transformed the country from an agrarian outpost into a world industrial power left the nation little time to think about finding ways to control massive levels of public corruption. The constitutional heroes of the nation had succeeded in laying the foundation for honest government. But they greatly underestimated how easily a new generation of public servants could turn that foundation into a quagmire of corruption and self-interest.

NOTES

1. Michael Josephson, "The Ethics of Politics: The Best of Times, The Worst of Times," *Ethics* 13/14 (1991): 39.

2. "Federalist Party," *1997 Grolier Multimedia Encyclopedia.*

3. Daniel Boorstin, *Hidden History* (New York: Harper & Row, 1987), p. 81.

4. Thomas H. Johnson, *The Oxford Companion to American History* (New York: Oxford University Press, 1966), p. 666.

5. Ibid.

6. Daniel J. Boorstin, *The Americans: The Colonial Experience* (New York: Random House, 1958), p. 111.

7. See C. Van Woodward, *Responses of the President to Charges of Misconduct* (New York: Delacorte Press, 1974). George Washington, pp. 1–22; John Adams, pp. 23–29; Thomas Jefferson, pp. 31–44; James Madison, pp. 45–46; James Monroe, pp. 46–53; John Quincy Adams, pp. 55–59.

8. Leonard D. White, *The Jeffersonians* (New York: MacMillan, 1959), p. 413.

9. Van Woodward, p. 6.

10. Ibid., p. 9.

11. White, p. 416.

12. Hubert G. Locke, "Ethics in American Government: A Look Backward," *Annals of the American Academy of Political and Social Science* 537 (January 1995): 18.

Chapter 2

Barbarians at the Gate: 1828–1883

The period 1828 through 1883 saw a collapse in public service ethics.[1] Large numbers of federal, state and local public officials seemed willing to trade their honor for an opportunity to line their pockets. Powerful private interests found they had little trouble buying the loyalty of public officials. The flood of corruption scandals, however, had little impact on the political landscape of the nation. Instead of there being a grassroots public uprising against corrupt government, the public adapted remarkably well to rampant graft and influence peddling by a significant cross-section of government employees and officials. It took decades for various reform movements to build sufficient power and permanence to begin restoring public service as an honorable profession and to put into place administrative reforms vital to reducing the ability of officials to use their positions to supplement their salaries.

No single factor adequately explains the collapse of public service ethics during the middle decades of the nineteenth century. The growth of national political parties, fed by millions of immigrants, blurred the line between public and political service. Political parties could purchase the political loyalty of millions of new arrivals simply by helping them to find housing and jobs and to obtain their citizenship papers. Congress, at the urging of special interests and the public, expanded the responsibilities of federal departments. The more money Congress appropriated as federal revenues increased, the more opportunities multiplied for unscrupulous public servants and private citizens to line their pockets with public funds.

Societal changes also contributed to the development of a more permissive moral environment. Those living in larger, impersonal cities, with the exception of the very rich, found urban existence a constant struggle. Disease, tainted food, crime, and hazardous working conditions greeted new arrivals to cities such as Boston, New York and Philadelphia. Critics feared that the sinful conditions of these urban centers would infect the rest of American society.[2] Thomas Jefferson and other political philosophers argued that "most vices could not take root in country soil."[3] The strongest defenders of democratic values, Jefferson maintained, were those who earned their living from the land. But the warnings of Jefferson and other critics of urban growth fell on deaf ears.

TO THE VICTORS BELONG THE SPOILS

The growth of the spoils system, without question, played the most important role in the erosion of ethical standards in government. Demands for a more democratic government, brought about by a severe economic recession in the 1820s, made possible a bloodless political revolution.[4]

The political aristocracy had lost its monopoly on political power and a new generation of public servants assumed control. Many newcomers saw partisan politics and public jobs as avenues of upward mobility. The new spoils system challenged the dominant vision of public service. It put an end to the "quasi-monopoly of office holding enjoyed by the class of gentlemen who had been called to official position since the foundation of the Republic."[5] Andrew Jackson, elected to the presidency in 1828, did not invent the spoils system. However, Jackson gave the spoils system legitimacy by proposing the theory of rotation in office as a way to provide a cross-section of Americans the opportunity for public service.[6]

Civil service historian Paul Van Riper has explained that, under the spoils system, civil servants "received not only a livelihood and an opportunity to serve, but also often an opportunity for personal gain."[7] Public service, for those not born to the upper class, became an important means of upward mobility. Political loyalty, not blood, constituted the price of admission.

Political parties quickly became addicted to the spoils system. Parties needed spoils appointments to reward loyal workers who organized thousands of newly enfranchised voters—voters who looked to political parties for help with an assortment of daily problems and who paid for party services with their votes.[8] Political machines expected those provided with public jobs to kick back part of their salary and to work actively for the election of the party's candidates.[9]

This new class of public servants "brought to office a set of expectations far different from those who intended" to spend a lifetime in public service or from those members of the upper class who spent brief periods in the public sector and then returned to their private occupations.[10] Spoils appointees, with less secure futures, sometimes decided to break the law to build themselves a nest egg as a hedge against a change in their political fortunes.

The fact that large numbers of public servants remained honest did not alter the fact that public service had lost the prestige it had prior to the late 1820s.

PUBLIC PLUNDER

National and state governments, during this period, spent larger and larger amounts of public funds on projects designed to boost the economic development of individual states and of the country at large. New York, for example, completed construction of the Erie Canal in 1826, which for a time made New York City "the principal gateway to the farther West."[11] Other states followed New York's example by constructing canals "or lending their credit to canal corporations."[12] States funded numerous public works projects to make sure that they were not put at a competitive disadvantage.

The 1803 Louisiana Purchase provided the country with a vast new tract of land for settlement. Federal land offices spread across the country to manage land sales. "Opportunities for collusion were frequent; pressure by speculators was great," wrote Leonard White, "and agents of the land offices were almost irresistibly drawn into speculation themselves, sometimes with government funds."[13] Congress annually appropriated large sums for river dredging and harbor construction.[14] Lobbyists for tariffs, steamship subsidies and railroad land grants swarmed over Congress, seeking preferential treatment for their clients.[15]

Congress and federal executive departments proved to be totally unprepared for the onslaught of lobbyists and influence peddlers.[16] Beginning in the 1820s, private citizens employed the services of so-called claims agents to speed their claims against the federal government. Many of these claims involved allegations that federal personnel destroyed private property while on public business. Numerous claims, for example, resulted from the Mexican American War of 1840. Until the 1850s, federal law required Congress to appropriate money to pay any claim. Claims agents told their clients that because of their access to members of Congress or officials in federal departments, they had the ability to get Congress to act on their individual claims. The fact that some federal employees hung out shingles as claims agents made the practice look even more suspicious.

A number of highly publicized examples of well-connected individuals obtaining large congressional claims settlements embarrassed Congress. To control the controversy, Congress, in 1853, prohibited federal employees from receiving payments for representing private clients with respect to claims pending before the federal government.[17] Congress, with the passage of the 1853 statute, attempted to restore public confidence in the impartiality of the legislative process. The statute, in fact, did little to stop the downward slide in public service ethics.

This book does not attempt to chronicle all of the local, state and federal public corruption scandals of the nineteenth century.[18] The corruption, it should be noted, did not remove pressure on government to assume new responsibilities. However, the scandals did cause increasing alarm on the part of the elite, who had lost political power to political machines. If public corruption became entrenched in American political culture, the power of political machines would certainly continue to grow and the opportunity to return civic-minded individuals to positions of power would fade.

The Civil War, without question, produced an unprecedented level of federal graft.[19] Contractors sold the War Department millions of dollars in substandard goods. War Department officials received payments from contractors to help them obtain military contracts. Despite the fact that congressional investigations and newspaper reports detailed the extent of the corruption, the years immediately following the Civil War saw only half-hearted efforts to improve the management of federal departments to prevent the recurrence of similar types of scandals.

The situation went from bad to worse. The industrial revolution made possible the growth of powerful private organizations able to control large segments of the national economy and capable of purchasing the loyalty of powerful political figures at all levels of government. Millions of immigrants flooded into already crowded cities. City governments struggled to maintain basic services. Although the vast majority of public servants remained honest, a significant number took advantage of the turmoil to line their pockets.

A decline in ethical standards seemed to impact all aspects of American life. "It could be found in state and municipal governments, in business and finance and transportation, and even in the professions. There was almost everywhere a breakdown of old moral standards, and to many it seemed that integrity had departed from public life," stated historians Morison and Commager.[20]

Everything, however, seemed to dictate against reversal of the downward slide in ethical standards. Political parties demonstrated little interest in doing away with the spoils system. Local, state and federal government agencies proved no match for the robber barons of an era that came to symbolize the transformation of the nation into a world economic power.

The 1872 Crédit Mobilier scandal, for example, saw a front corporation of the Union Pacific Railroad give members of Congress large blocks of stock to deter Congress from investigating diversions of profits from the Union Pacific.[21] Secretary of the Navy George Roberson, without a reasonable explanation, "managed to accumulate a fortune of several hundred thousand dollars during his tenure of office."[22] Again, congressional investigations in 1874 uncovered the activities of the Whiskey Ring in St. Louis, which "systematically defrauded the government of millions of dollars in taxes on distilled whiskey."[23] Treasury officials allegedly cooperated with the scheme. Powerful railroad interests bought the loyalty of state legislatures. The Tweed ring in New York City, like the political machines in many other cities, took a percentage of all business conducted by the City of New York.[24]

ADMINISTRATIVE INCOMPETENCE

Historian Mark Summers, in *The Era of Good Stealing*,[25] separated fact from lore regarding the impact of scandals on the nation's political system. "With certain exceptions," stated Summers, "corruption was scattered rather than systematic: individual men on the make rather than 'business as usual.' "[26] The scandals, however, pointed out serious limitations in the ability of government to perform expanded responsibilities: "The boss, the organized lobby, the swindling contractors, all owed their rise to the fact that a small, limited government with popularly elected officials could no longer do all the tasks that were expected of it either efficiently or competently."[27] Improvements in the management of public programs failed to keep up with demands for public goods and services.

Attempts to improve the administration of public programs collided head-on with the spoils system. "Once the government desks were doled out," wrote Summers, "patronage had only begun its distribution of favors to favorites: advertising and printing jobs for struggling party presses, construction and repair work for friendly contractors, frontier trading concessions for New York firms."[28] Advocates of the spoils system, however, turned out to be masters of public relations. Critics of spoils, they argued, exaggerated the extent of corruption and wanted only to revert to an era where members of the upper class had a monopoly on government positions. Men with humble beginnings would then no longer have the same opportunity to serve their local communities or the nation.

Instead of supporting major administrative reform, including limits on spoils appointments, defenders of the spoils system and the status quo frequently joined with reform-minded individuals to support new laws governing the conduct of public officials. Congress, after each new scandal, enacted another new law to deal with the most recent type of abuse of the public trust. These laws did little to improve the quality of public administration or attract to government service individuals with high moral standards. Rule-driven ethics became a cost-effective substitute for radical reform of the management of public institutions.[29] In this manner, the majority of twentieth-century public ethics rules had their origins during the second half of the nineteenth century.

Congress, for instance, in 1853 passed an act to prevent frauds upon the Treasury of the United States. Congress enacted the law as the result of an allegation that Secretary of the Treasury Thomas Corwin, while serving in the Senate, helped a private citizen to pursue a fraudulent claim against the Mexican Claims Commission.[30] The law prohibited any officer of the United States, including members of Congress, from receiving any compensation for helping private citizens pursue claims against the United States.[31]

The act of June 11, 1864, prohibited officers and employees of the federal government, including members of Congress, from receiving compensation for any services in relation to proceedings in which the United States is a party. Congress enacted the prohibition after allegations that government officials received payments to help private individuals and companies obtain War Department contracts made necessary by the Civil War.

The resurgence of the Democratic Party during the early 1870s put even greater pressure on the Grant White House and on the Republican-controlled Congress to take some steps against public corruption. Section 5 of the act of June 1, 1872, making appropriations to the Post Office Department, prohibited former officers and employees of executive branch agencies and departments from assisting in the prosecution of claims against the United States. Stories of former federal officials assisting private parties in pursuing claims against the federal government embarrassed Congress and the Grant administration.

The 1874 elections saw the Democratic Party regain control of the House for the first time since the Civil War. Democrats immediately set out to "cleanse the government and to furnish campaign material for the impending presidential contest."[32] The investigations did not implicate Grant in any impropriety, but close associates of Grant found themselves effectively run out of government. Secretary of War William W. Belknap, for example, resigned in 1876, after evidence surfaced that he had sold Indian-post traderships. His resignation short-circuited an effort by Congress to impeach him.[33]

The rise of the Democratic Party helped to restore states' rights as a respectable political doctrine. *States' rights* meant stopping the federal government from interfering in the affairs of state governments. The most fervent critics of an activist government argued that "no public work could be achieved without plunder."[34] Southern Democrats, still reeling from the carnage of the Civil War and Reconstruction, proved effective in fanning the flames of antigovernment sentiment.

The decades immediately following the Civil War saw many states amend their constitutions sharply to restrict the authority of the state and localities to raise and spend money. Many states fixed the salaries of legislators and other officials by state constitutions or statutes, making it next to impossible to raise them. States also amended their constitutions sharply to limit the amount of money the state or local governments could borrow. Other states forbade "the state's use of resources to aid corporations."[35] "Reform was not what should be done through government, but to it."[36]

The overall level of public corruption clearly contributed to the antigovernment backlash that followed the Civil War. The antigovernment reformers, in the long run, proved just as corrupt as those whom they replaced. Ideology, not a legitimate concern for public service ethics, motivated Democratic critics of Republican rule.

RESTORATION OF MORAL GOVERNMENT

While the Democratic and Republican parties battled for control of the national government and the privilege of distributing the spoils of victory, two very distinct reform movements took root. In the farmlands of the Midwest, the decades following the Civil War saw the birth of an agrarian revolt against the abuse of economic and political power by the new industrial giants. This revolt, in the 1880s, gave birth to a new political party that demanded radical steps by government to protect the American people from the brutal practices of industrial giants who behaved as if they had a license to roam the country wreaking economic havoc on small business and working men, women and children.[37] Long before the populist movement became a major force in national politics, liberal reformers saw civil service reform as the only effective way to check the rising tide of public corruption.

Civil service historians have detailed the torturous history of civil service reform.[38] The most vocal supporters of civil service reform came from upper-class northeastern families. "Most of them were lawyers, editors, clergymen, professors, and businessmen," stated civil service historian Ari Hoogenboom, "whose interests were mercantile and financial rather than industrial."[39] The movement, which had its origins in the 1850s, looked to Great Britain for a solution to America's government ethics crisis.

Great Britain, in 1855, had established a British Civil Service Commission.[40] Yet it took considerable time for the British system to end the practice of appointments on the basis of political affiliation. In fact, it wasn't until 1870 that the British civil service system required open, competitive exams.[41] Over time, the British civil service system evolved into an elite system that recruited individuals drawn from the British upper classes.

In America, reformers representing mainly the older established New England families had also established the goal of an "honest civil service manned with officers drawn largely from their own ranks."[42] Despite the fact that Thomas Jenckes introduced the first civil service reform law into Congress in December 1865, it took until the early 1870s for the momentum behind civil service reform to broaden beyond this small group of upper-class New England reformers.

A split in the Republican Party during the early 1870s played a major role in building this broader base of support for civil service reform.[43] Civil War scandals and scandals during the first Grant administration led these Republicans to "lose faith in their old organization as an instrument for good government."[44] They saw extending the right to vote as paving the way for the growth of a spoils system. Large numbers of voters seemed all too willing to exchange their votes for benefits distributed by party machines. Liberal reformers developed a clear agenda regarding "what could be done to cure" the Republic "of corruption."[45] Historian Summers has noted: "In this they were starkly different from rural Democrats or old conservative divines, for they saw themselves not as the mere keepers of an old and dying order of morals, but as the voice of the future, the heirs of the war's better spirit, the destroyers of a degenerate past."[46] Few would openly admit, however, that they supported stripping the right to vote from the uneducated and unpropertied.

Liberal reformers had an almost religious belief in the use of scientific judgment to restore public faith in government. They developed a utopian vision of government. Civil service reform would stamp out the evil that brought terrible shame to the entire country.[47]

The resurgence of the Democratic Party in the late 1860s and early 1870s, as noted, panicked the Grant White House and the Republican-controlled Congress. They feared that the Democratic Party would use public corruption scandals to discredit Republican leadership. In March 1871, with the presidential election approaching, Congress passed legislation giving President Grant the authority to "set up a commission that would write rules for government hiring and promotion."[48] The new Civil Service Commission stood Washington on its head. During the fall of 1871, the commission wrote rules requiring "competitive examinations, a reclassification of offices, promotions based on department experience, a ban on political assessments, and boards of examiners chosen by the Commission itself."[49] It appeared as if civil service reformers had won a glorious victory. But the sparks of victory proved short-lived. President Grant succeeded in dousing the Democratic challenge and Republicans retained control of Congress. Despite the best efforts of the commission to implement reforms, Congress gradually extinguished the commission by refusing to appropriate funds for its operation.[50] By March 1875, the civil service system had effectively shut down.

SCALING THE PARAPETS

Neither the fledgling populist movement nor the liberal Republican supporters of civil service reform came anywhere near to achieving their goals during the 1860s, 1870s and early 1880s. Yet the next three decades saw remarkable progress in raising ethical standards in the federal government. The movement's efforts paved the way for unprecedented growth in the role of government in American society. The success of good government reform movements, however, did not end the public integrity war. This period, quite the contrary, witnessed the beginning of a much more ideologically driven public integrity war.

NOTES

1. See Anne Fell, "Heroes, Rogues and Milestones," *Ethics: Easier Said Than Done* 13/14 (1991): 52–54; Hubert G. Locke, "Ethics in American Government: A Look Backward," *Annals of the American Academy of Political and Social Science* 537 (January 1995): 19–21; Leonard D. White, *The Jacksonians* (New York: Macmillan, 1954), pp. 411–36; Leonard D. White, *The Republican Era* (New York: Henry Holt, 1948), pp. 365–85; C. Van Woodward, *Responses of the President to Charges of Misconduct* (New York: Delacorte Press, 1974), pp. 61–185.

2. White, *The Jacksonians*, p. 412.

3. Daniel J. Boorstin, *The Lost World of Thomas Jefferson* (New York: Henry Holt, 1948), p. 147.

4. Locke, pp. 19–20.

5. White, *The Jacksonians*, p. 419.

6. Frederick Mosher, *Democracy and Public Service*, 2nd ed. (New York: Oxford University Press, 1982), p. 65.

7. Paul Van Riper, "Spoils as Dysfunctional and Functional." In *People in the Public Service*, eds. Robert Golembiewski and Michael Cohen (Itasca, IL: F.E. Peacock, 1976), p. 560.

8. Fell, p. 52.

9. Ibid.

10. White, *The Jacksonians*, p. 420.

11. Samuel Eliot Morison and Henry Steele Commager, *The Growth of the American Republic*, 2 vols. (New York: Oxford University Press, 1962), p. 1:498.

12. Ibid.

13. White, *The Jacksonians*, p. 421.

14. Ibid., p. 414.

15. Ibid., p. 415.

16. Robert Roberts, *White House Ethics* (Westport, CT: Greenwood Press, 1988), pp. 9–10.

17. Ibid.

18. For a comprehensive discussions of early American political scandals, see George Charles Benson, *Political Corruption in America* (Lexington, MA: Lexington Books, 1978); Nathan Miller, *Stealing From America: A History of Corruption from Jamestown to Reagan* (New York: Paragon House, 1992); Shelly Ross, *Fall from Grace: Sex, Scandal, and Corruption in American Politics from 1702 to the Present* (New York: Ballantine Books, 1988); Mark W. Summers, *The Plundering Generation: Corruption and Crisis of the Union 1849–1861* (New York: Oxford University Press, 1987); C. Van Woodward, pp. 61–185.

19. See Albert Shannon, *The Organization and Administration of the Union Army: 1861–1865* (Gloucester, MA: Peter Smith, 1965).

20. Morison and Commager, p. 2:71.

21. Ibid., p. 2:69.

22. Ibid., p. 2:70.

23. Ibid.

24. Ibid., p. 2:71.

25. Mark Wahlgren Summers, *The Era of Good Stealing* (New York: Oxford University Press, 1993), p. x.

26. Ibid.

27. Ibid.

28. Ibid., pp. 92–93.

29. For an excellent discussion of the use of rule-driven ethics in public administration, see Harry W. Reynolds, Jr., "Educating Public Administrators about Ethics," *Annals of the American Academy of Political and Social Science* 537 (January 1995): 126–28.

30. Congress had established the Mexican Claims Commission to indemnify citizens of the United States against losses to the Mexican Government which resulted from the Mexican War.

31. Roberts, *Ethics*, pp. 9–12.

32. Morison and Commager, p. 270.

33. Ibid., pp. 2:70–71.

34. Summers, *Good Stealing*, p. 134.

35. Ibid., p. 135.

36. Ibid.

37. Morison and Commager, pp. 2:333–339.

38. See Carl Russell Fish, *The Civil Service and the Patronage* (New York: Russell & Russell, 1963); Ari Hoogenboom, *Outlawing the Spoils: A History of the Civil Service Reform Movement 1865–1883* (Urbana: University of Illinois Press, 1961).

39. Hoogenboom, p. 21.

40. Hoogenboom, p. 17; see also Paul P. Van Riper, *History of the United States Civil Service* (Evanston, IL: Row, Peterson, 1958).

41. Hoogenboom, p. 17.

42. Ibid., p. 21.

43. John G. Sproat, *"The Best Men": Liberal Reformers in the Gilded Age* (Chicago: University of Chicago Press, 1982), pp. 64–65.

44. Ibid., p. 64.

45. Ibid., p. 169.

46. Ibid.

47. Mosher, *Democracy and Public Service*, p. 68.

48. Ibid., p. 100.

49. Ibid., p. 101

50. Ibid., p. 103.

Chapter 3

The Public Service Counterrevolution: 1883–1930

We often forget how rapidly public confidence in government returned after decades of despair over public service ethics. Toward the close of the nineteenth century and during the early decades of the twentieth century, a combination of forces made possible an astonishing restoration of public faith in public service and government.[1] The civil service, municipal reform and progressive reform movements succeeded in forcing structural and major administrative changes in the way government conducted public business.

The restoration of public faith, however, would certainly have failed without the emergence of a new generation of national, state and local leaders who rebelled against the hedonistic values of post–Civil War America. "The coarse, materialistic civilization that emerged in the United States during the years after the Civil War," wrote historian Richard Hofstadter, "produced among cultivated middle-class young men a generation of alienated and homeless intellectuals."[2] Without the influx of a generation of idealists who believed that government could have a positive role in American society, these reform movements certainly would have failed. Much like the constitutional heroes a century before, this new generation of civic-minded individuals viewed public service as a calling, not simply as an opportunity to line their pockets. It included men such as Oliver Wendell Holmes, Jr., Henry Cabot Lodge, Theodore Roosevelt and Woodrow Wilson.[3]

Woodrow Wilson wrote in 1887 that "the poisonous atmosphere of city government, the crooked secrets of state administration, the confusion, sinecurism, and corruption ever and again discovered in the bureaux at Washington forbid us to believe that any clear conceptions of what constitutes good administration are as yet widely current in the United States."[4] The decades following Wilson's indictment of government saw burgeon the scientific study of government and public administration. Large numbers of Americans came to view public service as a worthwhile career. Reformers hoped that their initiatives would shield the new generation of public servants from ideological and partisan pressures. This would free members of the new meritocracy to discover more efficient ways to solve the problems facing communities, states and the nation. Reformers, by the end of the period, knew that the country did not intend to return to a time when an elite group of public servants controlled the nation's public agenda.

CIVIL SERVICE REFORM AND THE BIRTH OF THE ADMINISTRATIVE STATE

The civil service reform movement, according to David Rosenbloom, "articulated a new—or arguably restorative—vision of government."[5] Reformers saw civil service reform as a way to drive unethical individuals out of government. The country could no longer afford to leave government to amateurs who lacked the personal integrity to be entrusted with public responsibilities.

The 1883 passage of the Pendleton Act represented the high-water mark of the nineteenth-century civil service reform movement. Civil service reform advocates, despite the dismantling of the 1871 Grant Civil Service Commission, never had lost faith. Reformers worked in New York City and in other large cities to build support for their movement. The establishment of the National Civil Service Reform League, in 1881, played a major role in increasing pressure on Congress and the White House.[6] Meanwhile, the assassination of President Garfield by a disgruntled office seeker forced Congress to act to calm mounting public outrage.[7]

The Pendleton Act, as passed by Congress, fell far short of the goals set by civil service reformers.[8] Congress refused to return to an era of a closed civil service system. Instead, the statute permitted entry at all levels, required job-related examinations, and applied the new rules to only some 14,000 positions, or to about 12 percent of the federal workforce.[9] The act did, however, give the president authority to extend the new rules "to other parts of the service at his discretion."[10] The Jacksonian movement had broken class control over public service. American society had undergone much too radical a change to permit a return to the vision of public service prior to 1829 and the Jacksonian revolution.[11] Technical expertise gradually replaced political loyalty as the primary qualification for public service.

Technical Competence and the Marketplace

Civil service reformers hoped to surround public servants with a moat that would prevent outside forces from undermining their exercise of expertise. Had government remained relatively uninvolved in regulating various parts of the nation's economy, or had it not expanded its role as the distributor of a wide assortment of public goods and services, this tactic might have worked. The defensive failed because the public demanded a much more activist national government in the years just preceding the First World War. There was no practical way to prevent public officials from coming into contact with the agents of special interests. Despite this fact, pressure increased to put into place a much more extensive breastwork of ethics rules to protect public confidence in the impartiality of public officials. Rule-driven ethics gradually replaced character-driven ethics as the primary method of maintaining public confidence in the emerging meritocracy.[12]

Nineteenth-century civil service reformers could not have anticipated the growth of private-sector employment opportunities for individuals with public-sector expertise. They failed to anticipate the explosion in special interests with the resources necessary legally to buy access to decision makers at all levels of government. Civil service reform, in the long run, could not prevent a violent clash between defenders of laissez-faire economics and those who demanded government protection from economic servitude.

PUBLIC INTEGRITY SKIRMISHES AND THE AGE OF REFORM

The populist and progressive movements of the late nineteenth century, much like the civil service reform movement, provided a theoretical justification for replacing patronage appointees with professional public servants. The populist and progressive movements, unlike civil service reform, touched a responsive chord in the hearts and minds of millions of Americans who faced an increasingly difficult time dealing with the dislocations caused by the industrial revolution. The movements provided disillusioned Americans with hope that government would intervene on their behalf.

Both movements sought to protect or restore the Yankee-Protestant vision of American life.[13] That vision gave every American an opportunity to move up the social and economic ladder through sacrifice and hard work. Tyrannical corporations and scheming political bosses had destroyed opportunities for individual initiative and had used their power to prevent government from dealing with social wrongs. "The competitive process," wrote Hofstadter, "seemed to be drying up. All of society was felt to be threatened—not by economic breakdown, but by moral and social degeneration and the eclipse of democratic institutions."[14] The vast majority of Americans, unless government intervened, would become interchangeable cogs in one vast industrial machine. Both movements, according to Richard Hofstadter, "wanted economic success to continue to be related to character, wanted the economic system not merely to be a system for the production of sufficient goods and services but to be an effective system of incentives and rewards."[15]

Because of the distrust populists and progressives had for traditional political parties, the movements looked for ways to take power out of the hands of politicians and place it in the hands of impartial experts and nonpartisan citizens. The period from the late 1880s through the early 1920s saw many populist and progressive reform proposals adopted at the local, state and federal levels. These included (1) the Australian or secret ballot; (2) direct primaries; (3) initiative, referendum and recall; (4) municipal home rule; (5) civil service reform; (6) city manager form of government; (7) tax reform and (8) independent regulatory agencies.[16]

At the federal level, the movements had a number of major successes. Congress, in 1887, established the Interstate Commerce Commission and gave it responsibility for setting rates for railroads and other types of interstate transportation.[17] Indeed, federal regulatory agencies proliferated after the turn of the century.[18] The states, in 1913, ratified the Seventeenth Amendment, which required the popular election of U.S. Senators. The same year saw the states ratify the Sixteenth Amendment, which authorized Congress to impose and collect a federal income tax. Moreover, Congress also enacted antitrust legislation with the idealistic goal of improving the operation of private economic markets.[19]

What's Good for Big Business Is Bad for America

The emphasis placed on the control of big business distinguished the populist and progressive movements from the civil service reform movement. Members of the business community had strongly backed civil service reform. But populists and progressives received little support from American business and industry. Big business, to the contrary, vigorously fought populist and progressive reform proposals. A Supreme Court, dominated by former corporate lawyers, struck down state laws regulating wages, hours and working conditions on the grounds that such laws violated the due process clause of the Fourteenth Amendment.[20]

By 1890, a dozen railroads, for example, employed over 100,000 workers.[21] The federal government, in comparison, employed 20,000 civilian employees in Washington, D.C. Forty thousand service members constituted the combined strength of the Army, Navy and Marines.[22] Fear that these large private enterprises threatened the survival of democracy in America pervaded the reform movements of the era.

Support for the populist and progressive movements did not mean that the public supported large new public programs to deal with poverty or other social problems of the era. A certain level of nostalgia permeated the era of reform. The country longed to return to a simpler time. If a larger and more intrusive government were required to accomplish this objective, the benefits seemed to outweigh the costs.

An Uneasy Alliance: The Press and Political Reform

Long before the populist and progressive movements, the press played a major role in mobilizing public opinion to support various causes. "The newspaper," for example, "became useful as an active tool for mobilizing public opinion in the cause of the Revolution."[23] Federalists and Anti-Federalist alike made persuasive arguments for their respective positions. The Federalists, however, had a clear advantage in terms of the number of newspapers supporting ratification of the Constitution.[24] This advantage may have made the difference in persuading the states to ratify the new Constitution.

After 1828, the rise of national political parties and the spoils system intensified efforts by politicians to exert control over the press. Political parties needed to find more effective methods of communicating their platforms to larger and larger numbers of voters. Political parties and their leaders learned how to use patronage and other inducements to keep the support of the press. Newspapers received lucrative government printing contracts. Parties provided patronage appointments to the friends and associates of editors and publishers of newspapers.[25] Over time, the press became a tool of partisanship, as newspaper editors and owners established closer ties to politicians in order to survive.[26] Media historian Warren Francke wrote:

The short history of political affiliation by the press describes partisan newspapers, characterized by designated presidential organs, loyally serving elected officials and party leaders from the founding years toward the mid-nineteenth century. The watchdog function was divided: editors howled at the opposition and defended their own.[27]

Beginning in the middle of the eighteenth century, the press became less dependent upon political parties for financial assistance. The growing readership of newspapers provided newspapers and magazines with a steady revenue stream that helped to free major newspapers and magazines from financial dependence on political machines. This financial independence brought with it a certain degree of editorial independence.[28]

The Civil War also helped to free the press from partisan political control. Throughout the Civil War, the press had aggressively reported allegations of fraud and corruption. Large metropolitan newspapers covered the war extensively and brought the brutality of war home to their readers.

Journalism gradually evolved into a respected profession,[29] as commercial, not political, concerns increasingly drove the press to publish stories directed at attracting the largest possible readership.[30] These forces transformed the press and opened the way for a new generation of reporters prepared to take on the establishment.

Without the active support of the press, the populist and progressive movements would have withered on the vine. The press publicized the agenda of these reform movements and included numerous stories supporting the argument that government could no longer sit idly by while segments of the public suffered.

In the process of building support for reform, the press of the progressive era opened Pandora's box. To build support for reform, the press needed to dramatize the failure of government. This drumbeat of negative stories, however, carried the risk of showing government as the problem and not the solution. However, the muckrakers of the progressive era were willing to take that risk.

The Crusade of the Muckraker

Much of the public support for the progressive movement was a direct result of the writings of "muckrakers." These writers took it upon themselves to inform readers of the seamier side of American life. Most muckrakers viewed themselves as independent representatives of the public interest and were not aligned with any particular political party. President Theodore Roosevelt applied the epithet to describe sociologists, philosophers, historians, economists, journalists and novelists who undertook the crusade for justice in American society.[31] The exposés of the muckrakers awakened the moral conscience of the nation and temporarily overcame the American people's fears of a more activist government.

Muckrakers spent considerable effort disclosing instances where big business bribed legislators to obtain preferential treatment and paid political leaders to protect them from government investigations or regulation.[32] These disclosures forced state legislatures to enact new ethics restrictions to protect the independence and impartiality of public officials.[33]

Regulatory Ethics and the Administrative Process

Strong evidence exists that, even if the progressive movement had not occurred, civil service reform and the improved management of public agencies would have helped to reduce the level of public corruption that had run rampant during much of the nineteenth century. Despite this fact, progressives strongly supported the expansion of rule-driven ethics as the primary method of protecting the independence of public officials.

Progressives, much like supporters of civil service reform, believed tight ethics rules could isolate regulators and other public officials from special interests, who would stop at nothing to influence the behavior of government decision makers. Progressives directed much of their animosity toward the industrial moguls, whom progressives blamed for most of the social and economic ills of the era. The Meat Inspection Act of 1906 is a vivid example of the effort by progressives to shield a new generation of public officials from temptations that might cloud their judgment.

Muckrakers had disclosed the shocking unsanitary and unsafe working conditions in meatpacking plants across the country.[34] Subsequent congressional investigations confirmed this report. In response, the public demanded government action to guarantee the safety of the nation's meat supply. The Meat Inspection Act gave the Department of Agriculture responsibility for implementing a system to eliminate unsanitary conditions in meatpacking plants across the country. Nineteenth-century corruption scandals had taught progressives that many low-paid public employees were quite open to accepting favors and gifts from private sources. Consequently, the Meat Inspection Act also prohibited all Department of Agriculture employees from accepting gifts from meatpacking companies.[35]

Ninety years later, President Clinton's secretary of agriculture, Mike Espy, became the subject of an independent counsel investigation for allegedly accepting gifts from "regulated businesses, including the Arkansas chicken giant Don Tyson."[36] Prior to becoming secretary of agriculture, Mike Espy had served as a member of the House of Representatives. Federal law and House ethics rules had permitted Espy as a congressman to accept small gifts, travel expenses, and entertainment from nonpublic sources.[37] Some observers wondered whether Espy really understood the difference between House and Department of Agriculture gift-acceptance rules.[38]

The Disinterested Public Servant

Progressives saw the disinterested public servant as essential to the implementation of their grand design for a new interventionist national government. Average Americans would never have the ability to match the influence of the powerful economic interests. Public servants, on the other hand, could become guardians of the public trust—but only if well inoculated against moral infections spread by greedy economic interests. Progressives looked everywhere for evidence of big business attempting to destroy the independence of public servants.

The expanding demand for federal assistance, ranging from agriculture to education reform, stretched the resources of federal agencies and departments to the limit. The industrial revolution gave birth to a number of philanthropic foundations funded by the giants of American business and industry. During the early twentieth century, both the Carnegie and Rockefeller foundations began programs whereby these foundations paid the salaries of individuals who provided services to the Interior Department's Bureau of Education.

The Department of Interior, for example, entered into cooperative arrangements "with certain private organizations for the purpose of studying various aspects of education."[39] The Bureau of Education paid these individuals one dollar a year, and the private foundations paid the remainder of their salaries. The bureau "also employed and paid one-dollar a year special collaborators who occupied positions in public or private school systems, to perform only occasional services for the Bureau."[40] Progressive critics of this practice viewed foundation funding of the salaries of federal officials as a subversive effort to purchase the loyalty of public servants. To deal with this threat, Senator George Chamberlain of Oregon supported a ban on nonfederal sources supplementing the salaries of federal officials. The federal government simply should not allow nonfederal sources to pay the salaries of federal employees engaged in public business. He apparently believed that if private sources paid the salaries of federal officials a strong likelihood existed that the officials would use their public positions "to influence the government into endorsing and publicizing the particular educational views of certain private organizations."[41]

These arguments proved persuasive. On March 3, 1917, Congress enacted a new salary supplementation ban. But instead of limiting the ban to Bureau of Education employees, Congress prohibited all executive branch officials and employees from accepting salaries from nonpublic sources.[42]

The legislative effort to guarantee that public servants remain or at least appear disinterested did not stop with the 1917 salary supplementation ban. Throughout the First World War, progressives and their labor allies sharply criticized the Wilson administration's use of on-loan business executives to staff war mobilization agencies.[43] The Wilson administration worked closely with big business and industry. This angered many progressives, who believed that big business had used the war simply as another opportunity to make money.[44] Critics argued that these on-loan executives used their government positions to get their companies large military contracts, even though they failed to point out examples where such conduct had taken place.

If former War Department officials wanted to profit from access to inside information, the First World War provided an unprecedented opportunity. Congress, in an effort to prevent such behavior, in 1919 passed legislation prohibiting former military procurement officials, for two years after leaving the federal government, from using inside information to pursue procurement-related claims against the federal government. The law specifically prohibited former executive branch employees from representing nongovernmental interests in certain matters pending before the employees' former executive branch agency.[45] The two-year ban applied only to individuals who had served in executive branch agencies from April 6, 1917, to July 11, 1919.[46]

Progressive support for the salary supplementation ban and the postemployment claims representation prohibition demonstrated the preoccupation of progressives with protecting the independence of public officials. But the progressive era came to an end long before the movement had an opportunity to implement its reform agenda.

THE UNFINISHED AGENDA

The First World War effectively ended the progressive movement and the era that bears its name. But the movement had succeeded in building the foundation for a new administrative state.[47] The public gained a new respect for government and for public servants. Government had a positive role to play as the nation confronted the challenges of the new century.

Progressives, like most ideologically driven advocates, greatly overestimated their ability to win over the American people in support of radical change. By the end of the progressive era, the vast majority of Americans had accepted the industrial revolution. Big corporations may have exploited Americans, but big government also was in a position to violate their rights. In 1916, Elihu Root, in an address as president of the American Bar Association, stressed the importance of developing a new body of administrative law: "If we are to continue a government of limited powers, these agencies of regulation must themselves be regulated. . . . The rights of the citizen against them must be made plain. A system of administrative law must be developed, and that with us is still in its infancy, crude and imperfect."[48]

Elihu Root's warning did not meet a receptive audience. Nothing seemed likely to stand in the way of the country's success. Civil service reform had turned the tide against political machines. Professional public administration had established a foothold at the national level and spread to the state and local governments. New regulatory agencies, at the federal and state level, seemed to have restored a certain level of economic equilibrium. The abuse of discretion by public officials no longer constituted a pressing national problem.

Although the progressive era proved that government could improve the lives of Americans, it planted the seeds for a violent confrontation between the supporters and opponents of activist government. A powerful ideological movement had taken root that rejected the teachings of Adam Smith and laissez-faire economics. The public did not have to accept a government controlled by political machines that used government to maintain their political power. Defenders of the capitalist juggernaut, however, showed little inclination to withdraw from the battlefield. Because these movements held such starkly different visions of American society, they guaranteed that future clashes would occur.

ETHICAL BACKSLIDING AND THE ERA OF NORMALCY

Prohibition turned out to be the last great victory of the progressive movement. The Eighteenth Amendment, "forbidding the manufacture, sale or transportation of intoxicating liquor,"[49] went into effect in January 1920. Supporters blamed intoxicating liquors for almost every social problem in the nation. Prohibition would usher in a new era of social order and responsibility. But the progressives badly underestimated the difficulty of enforcing prohibition. Criminal enterprises quickly moved in to supply the public with what it could no longer obtain legally. Bootleggers made fortunes. Public officials, particularly at the local level, received a share of the profits in return for agreeing to look the other way. Millions of Americans disobeyed the law.

Between 1920 to 1930, capitalism reasserted its ascendancy. "The sole function of government," said President Hoover, "is to bring about a condition of affairs favorable to the beneficial development of private enterprise."[50] Big business and finance regained their pre-progressive era power. Merger mania swept all parts of the American economy.[51] Private citizens rushed to take advantage of the money to be made in a stock market that seemed destined to go ever up. The idealism of the progressive era evaporated.

Though public corruption between the end of the First World War and the beginning of the Great Depression did not reach the level it had during the latter half of the nineteenth century, ths was still a time of questionable ethics. Municipal political machines, such as New York City's Tammany Hall, regained much of their lost notoriety. Alphonse "Al" Capone moved from New York to Chicago in 1920 and put into place a crime syndicate that ran the city of Chicago for nearly a decade—estimates of his 1927 profits exceed $100 million.[52] (It took federal law enforcement officials and a 1931 federal tax evasion conviction to take Capone out of circulation.)

The federal government did not escape the ethical backsliding, as one of the greatest scandals in federal history—Teapot Dome—demonstrated. In the early 1920s, Secretary of the Interior Albert Fall and Secretary of the Navy Edwin Denby helped Sinclair Oil interests to "gain control of the immensely valuable naval oil reserves" located in California.[53] Nevertheless, Democrats had difficulty capitalizing on the Teapot Dome scandal because the "oil-leasing policy had been inaugurated under a law passed in Wilson's administration."[54] Despite the fact that Teapot Dome received extensive press coverage and resulted in lengthy congressional investigations, the public yawned at the scandal. The glamor had worn off political reform. The public seemed preoccupied with enjoying the good life.

Critics of government, however, proved unsuccessful in rolling back most of the reforms of the progressive era. Professional public administration continued to grow. Civil service systems spread from the federal to state and local levels. Regulatory agencies consolidated their positions as mediators of disputes between the public and private sectors.[55] The early skirmishes of an ideologically driven public integrity war had ended in a stalemate. The public demanded better local, state and federal services, but balked at higher taxes or bigger government. If government could operate like business, it could provide more services at lower cost. It would take the Great Depression and the Second World War to give supporters of big government the opportunity to fully implement their vision of the administrative state.

NOTES

1. Hubert G. Locke, "Ethics in American Government: A Look Backward," *Annals of the American Academy of Political and Social Science* 537 (January 1995): 20–21.

2. Richard Hofstadter, *The American Political Tradition & the Men Who Made It* (New York: Vintage Books, 1948, 1973), p. 266.

3. Ibid.

4. Woodrow Wilson, "The Study of Administration," *Political Science Quarterly* 2 (June 1887): 201, cited in James W. Fesler, *Public Administration: Theory and Practice* (Englewood Cliffs, NJ: Prentice-Hall, 1980), p. 14.

5. David H. Rosenbloom, "The Evolution of the Administrative State and Transformation of Administrative Law." In *Handbook of Regulation and Administrative Law*, eds. David H. Rosenbloom and Richard D. Schwartz (New York: Marcel Dekker, 1994), p. 4.

6. Ari Hoogenboom, *Outlawing the Spoils: A History of the Civil Service Reform Movement 1865–1883* (Urbana: University of Illinois Press, 1961), p. 211.

7. Locke, p. 21.

8. Paul P. Van Riper, "Americanizing a Foreign Invention: The Pendleton Act of 1883." In *Classics of Public Personnel Policy*, ed. Frank J. Thompson (Oak Park, IL: Moore, 1979), p. 4.

9. Samuel Eliot Morison and Henry Steele Commager, *The Growth of the American Republic*, 2 vols. (New York: Oxford University Press, 1962), p. 2:320.

10. Ibid.

11. Van Riper, p. 13.

12. For a discussion of the use of rule- and character-driven ethics in maintaining ethics in government, see Harry W. Reynolds, Jr., "Educating Public Administrators about Ethics," *Annals of the American Academy of Political and Social Science* 537 (January 1995): 126–31.

13. Richard Hofstadter, *The Age of Reform: From Bryan to F.D.R.* (New York: Vintage Books, 1960), p. 9.

14. Ibid.

15. Ibid., p. 11.

16. Morison and Commager, p. 2:466.

17. Rosenbloom, p. 7.

18. Two examples are the Federal Reserve Board (1913) and the Federal Trade Commission (1914).

19. Rosenbloom, pp. 7–8.

20. Craig R. Ducat and Harold W. Chase, *Constitutional Interpretation*, 5th ed. (St. Paul, MN: West Publishing Company, 1992), pp. 522–25.

21. Alfred D. Chandler, Jr. "Government Versus Business: An American Phenomenon." In *Business and Public Policy*, ed. John T. Dunlop (Cambridge: Harvard University Press, 1980), p. 3.

22. Ibid.

23. Richard Davis, *The Press and American Politics: The News Mediator* (New York & London: Longman, 1992), p. 45.

24. Ibid., p. 49.

25. Ibid., p. 57.

26. Ibid.

27. Warren Francke, "The Evolving Watchdog: The Media's Role in Government Ethics," *Annals of the American Academy of Political and Social Science* 537 (January 1995): 113.

28. Ibid., p. 65.

29. Ibid., pp. 71–72.

30. Ibid., p. 70.

31. Morison and Commager, p. 2:452.

32. Arthur Link, *Progressivism* (Arlington Heights, IL: Harlan Davidson, 1983), p. 31.

33. Ibid.

34. Richard L. Watson, Jr., *The Development of National Power: The United States 1900–1919* (Boston: Houghton Mifflin, 1976), p. 126.

35. The most recent version of the statute is found at 21 U.S.C. section 662 (1994).

36. John F. Harris, "Clinton Defends Ethics Record," *Washington Post*, March 4, 1995, p. A10.

37. For a discussion of congressional gift acceptance rules during the late 1980s, see June E. Edmondson, "And Gifts and Travel for All: A summary and explanation of the Ethics Reform Act of 1989," *Federal Bar News & Journal* 37 (September 1990): 404.

38. See "Espy Undoing: Law of 'The Jungle' Era," *Chicago Tribune*, October 9, 1994, p. 1:25; "Poor Tutor," *Houston Chronicle*, August 30, 1994, p. A12; "Where Mr. Espy Got His Bad Habits," *St. Louis Post-Dispatch*, September 9, 1994, p. C6.

39. Frederick W. Ford, Acting Assistant Attorney General, Office of Legal Counsel. *Memorandum for the Attorney General, Re: Conflict of Interest Statute*, December 10, 1964, p. 119.

40. Ibid.

41. Ibid., p. 119.

42. Robert Roberts, *White House Ethics* (Westport, CT: Greenwood Press, 1988), pp. 22–23.

43. Ibid., pp. 28–32.

44. See Robert D. Cuff, *The War Industries Board: Business-Government Relations during World War I* (Baltimore, MD: Johns Hopkins University Press, 1973).

45. Ibid., p. 79.

46. Ibid., pp. 79–80.

47. Rosenbloom, pp. 9–10.

48. Kenneth Culp Davis, *Administrative Law: Cases-Text-Problems* (St. Paul, MN: West, 1977), p. 7.

49. Morison and Commager, p. 2:632.

50. Ibid., p. 2:633.

51. Ibid., p. 2:637.

52. Thomas H. Johnson, *The Oxford Companion to American History* (New York, Oxford University Press, 1966), p. 145.

53. Ibid, p. 621; also see Roberts, pp. 25–27.

54. Morison and Commager, p. 2:622.

55. Peter Woll, *American Bureaucracy*, 2d ed. (New York: W.W. Norton, 1977), pp. 48–49.

Chapter 4

Peace in Our Time: The Rise and Fall of Administrative Legitimacy: 1930–1960

The Great Depression and the Second World War provided advocates of an expanded role of government in American society an unprecedented opportunity to put their theories into practice. Long-term economic recovery, New Dealers argued, required aggressive federal intervention to deal with massive market failures. Private business, industry and finance appeared helpless to do anything about a national calamity. "The New Deal," wrote political scientist Peter Woll, "led directly to an acceptance of the responsibility of government for economic regulation by both political parties."[1] The calamitous events of the era between 1929 and the end of the Second World War seemingly assured big government a permanent place in American society.[2]

New federal agencies spent billions of dollars on programs designed to pull the nation out of the Great Depression. The Second World War forced the national government to spend sums beyond anyone's wildest imagination to combat the greatest threat to the nation's survival in its history. The combination of vastly accelerated public expenditures and mountains of New Deal federal regulations created record opportunities for public officials to use their positions for personal gain and to help private interests outside of government. Yet "no scandal produced the conviction, indictment, or even the forced resignation of a member of the White House staff or any other major New Deal administrator."[3] Relatively few instances of profiteering by federal officials or government contractors surfaced during or after the Second World War.[4]

But serious public management problems lurked below the surface. Corrupt political machines continued to operate freely in many large cities and state capitals. Politics often played a role in the allocation of relief funds received from Washington.[5] Special interests pulled out all the stops to make sure New Deal officials understood their perspective. Small and large business increasingly complained of heavy-handed conduct by federal officials implementing New Deal programs. Many in business regarded the "administrative process [as] antibusiness, designed to curtail fundamental freedoms."[6] They demanded the enactment of measures designed to limit administrative discretion.

THE TYRANNY OF THE MERITOCRACY

Despite growing reports of the abuse of administrative discretion by federal agencies, through the 1930s the Roosevelt White House fought efforts to require federal agencies, departments and independent regulatory agencies to comply with uniform rules of administrative procedures. The Roosevelt White House believed such rules "would unnecessarily cripple the government's many agencies."[7] Many New Dealers saw administrative reform as a strategy to tie the hands of government officials and prevent government from rapidly dealing with the nation's problems.

The Roosevelt White House did take steps to protect public trust in the impartiality of New Deal officials, however. The increased regulatory responsibility of New Deal agencies meant that many more federal employees had access to information that could make them fortunes if used for speculative purposes. Congress, as previously discussed, had since the early nineteenth century enacted a series of unrelated conflict-of-interest statutes.[8] None of these statutes restricted the financial investments of employees and family members.[9]

And so, between 1935 and 1937, the Roosevelt White House ordered the Civil Service Commission to study the issue of prohibiting federal employees from speculating in stock.[10] "I have given much consideration to the general problem of speculation in stocks and commodities in the Government service," wrote Franklin Roosevelt.[11] "It is my thought that if I could prescribe regulations for all of the officers and employees of all branches of the Executive Branch of the Government, the Congress might follow the good example with legislation relating to the Judiciary and the Legislature."[12] In 1937, the White House issued a directive prohibiting federal employees from purchasing or selling "corporate stocks or bonds or commodities for speculative purposes."[13]

The Civil Service Commission and Roosevelt White House recognized how difficult the directive would be to enforce. The directive, however, served an important symbolic purpose. It reminded federal employees and officials that increased power meant increased scrutiny of their conduct.

Burying the Hatchet and War Mobilization

In the 1930s, big business and New Deal agencies did little to hide their dislike of each other. The Second World War put to the test the ability of big business and government to put aside their differences. During the First World War, the Wilson White House had worked closely with the leaders of business and industry to mobilize the nation for war.[14] But the Wilson White House paid a price for this collaboration.

Progressive leaders and organized labor denounced Wilson for giving big business and industry so much authority over war-mobilization activities. They compared this policy to allowing foxes to run wild in the chicken coop.[15] Woodrow Wilson had few reservations about the partnership; however, many in the Roosevelt administrative had serious reservations about giving big business such a prominent role in war planning.[16] To do so would demonstrate a lack of confidence in career military and civilian personnel and their government organizations.[17]

The Roosevelt White House, in the end, left primary responsibility for war-mobilization planning with the War Department. The entry of the United States into the Second World War ended any reservations the White House had about allowing mobilization agencies to recruit thousands of private-sector experts and executives.[18] Like their counterparts who had served during the First World War, Second World War executives served without pay or for a dollar a year—their private employers continued to pay their regular salaries. Because of these arrangements, the press soon came to refer to these individuals as "dollar-a-year men."

The War Production Administration (WPA), at the insistence of the Roosevelt White House, put in place a rudimentary conflict-of-interest clearance system. The WPA required dollar-a-year and without-compensation men to disclose financial holdings and to undergo extensive background checks.[19] War-mobilization agencies assigned dollar-a-year and without-compensation men to responsibilities that did not require them to make decisions or recommendations that had a direct impact on their private-sector employers. Congress finally tightened a number of conflict-of-interest laws to prevent on-loan executives from assisting private parties pursue war-related claims against the government.[20] One law even barred former federal officials, for a period of two years after leaving federal service, from "assisting with the prosecution of private claims against the federal government if the claim involved a subject matter of their former employment."[21]

The Second World War private-public partnership worked remarkably well. The dollar-a-year and without-compensation executives rendered exceptional service to their country. Little evidence surfaced that they used their positions for personal gain or for the benefit of their private employers.[22] The success of the war effort, however, did little to mollify critics of

New Deal policies and programs. Big government and abuse of power continued to go hand in hand.

CRACKS IN THE ARMOR

In 1941, the Attorney General's Committee on Administrative Procedure had recommended major changes in how administrative agencies conduct public business.[23] The Roosevelt White House, however, continued to oppose the legislation. The passage of the Administrative Procedure Act (APA) of 1946 represented an effort by Congress to deal with growing criticism of the administrative state. It established a "basic legal framework for much of the federal administrative process."[24] The APA established statutory rules to provide the public with greater opportunity to participate in rule making and to clarify the role of the courts in reviewing administrative decisions.[25]

The APA, however, did little to end criticism of New Deal programs and big government. A growing vocal minority still regarded the New Deal as the first-mile marker on a road leading the nation into socialism. Defenders of the administrative state at the same time blamed eroding support for New Deal–type programs and government regulation on powerful special interests, who would stop at nothing to roll back the progress of the last two decades. Nothing could prevent a head-on collision between the new progressives and movement conservatives of the postwar years. Ethics in government became the battleground for these radically different views of government.

The Truman Scandals and the Loss of Faith

Over recent years, historians have portrayed Harry Truman as a heroic figure in American history and in the history of the American presidency.[26] The 1992 biography *Truman*, by David McCulloch, has helped to transform Truman into one of the more revered presidents in American history.[27] However, earlier historians, largely because of public integrity scandals that ripped the Truman administration, painted a much less favorable picture of the Truman presidency.[28] Members of the so-called Missouri, or Truman, gang, according to Truman critics, used their close relationship with the president to line their own pockets.

"Never was there such a large, weirdly assorted, and variegated crew, and never one which ran so instinctively and unerringly to the banal and second rate," stated Robert Allen and William Shannon in their 1950 book, *The Truman Merry-Go-Round*.[29] "But the worst thing about the Truman gang," noted Allen and Shannon, "is their complaisance, their sense of self-satisfaction, and their utter lack of any sense of moral commitment, personal urgency, or intellectual fervor."[30] The so-called Truman scandals sent shock waves through the progressive wing of the Democratic Party and gave new hope to conservatives that New Deal big government had begun to rot from within.[31] Many who had poured their hearts and souls into defending the New Deal and fighting the Second World War felt betrayed.

It is beyond the scope of this book to detail the Truman scandals.[32] The vast majority involved allegations of influence peddling. During the early 1950s, for example, the Reconstruction Finance Corporation came under scrutiny for allegedly steering loans to politically well-connected individuals.[33] The Truman White House saw the allegations as a partisan effort to discredit New Deal policies and programs.

To the astonishment of the Truman White House, progressive Democrats pressed the investigation. Senator J. William Fulbright, an Arkansas Democrat, led the congressional investigation.[34] The Truman White House found it impossible to understand why a loyal Democrat, like Senator Fulbright, pursued an investigation certain to provide critics of Democratic policies and programs with powerful ammunition. Long before Harry Truman recognized the seriousness of the scandals, Senator Fulbright understood that even minor scandals could seriously erode public trust in government.

The Bureau of Internal Revenue scandal turned out to be even more damaging to the Truman presidency. The bureau had a long history of problems. Civil service reform had failed to reach the bureau. Presidents still filled many of the key Internal Revenue positions with political appointees. Rumors increased during the early 1950s that Bureau of Internal Revenue tax collectors accepted cash to "fix" tax delinquencies.[35] These rumors led to a full-scale investigation by the Treasury Department, the Justice Department, and Congress. These investigations uncovered instances of bureau employees' accepting bribes, of employees' avoiding payment of their own taxes, and of poor management practices at all levels within the bureau.[36] Once the extent of the problems became widely known, the Truman White House and Congress moved quickly to reorganize the tax collection system to prevent the recurrence of such untoward conduct.[37]

The Loss of Innocence

Time and time again, the Truman White House asked the public to look at the progress the country had made under Democratic leadership. Taken in the context of all the good being done by government, the public should not allow critics to use a few isolated instances of mismanagement as justification for abandoning the progress. When President Truman, on September 27, 1951, sent a message to Congress addressing ethical standards in the federal government, he left little doubt as to how he felt about the allegations: "To my mind the most disturbing feature of the charges and rumors stirred up by these attempts is their effect on the confidence of the American people in their Government. . . . This is a terrible distortion of the true facts about our Government. It would be tragic if our citizens came to believe it."[38]

Truman made his way to Washington as a senator from Missouri through the good graces of the powerful political machine of Thomas Pendergast. Ironically, as chairman of the Special Committee to Investigate the Defense Program looking for evidence of profiteering by defense contractors, Truman had established a national reputation as a "crusader for honesty and efficiency in expenditure of public funds."[39]

President Truman and many within his administration failed to appreciate just how bureaucratic the Washington establishment had become. Big and small businesses, as well as private citizens, found it a nightmare to deal with those federal agencies responsible for numerous programs and regulatory activities. New growth opportunities emerged for well-connected individuals to sell their knowledge to private citizens and businesses. A growing group of lobbyists in the postwar years solicited clients seeking government contracts, legislative favors and help in cutting through the mountains of bureaucratic red tape.[40] "The five-percenters," Cabell Phillips wrote, "used the pitch that they [knew] the ropes in Washington, [had] 'drag' in the important departments and bureaus, and [could] bypass all the tedious bureaucratic channels by getting a sympathetic hearing directly with the man at the top."[41]

A Rescue Mission

The scandals led the Senate to authorize a special investigation into the ethical climate in government.[42] The Senate gave Senator Paul Douglas, Democrat from Illinois, responsibility for conducting the investigation. In 1951, Douglas held hearings on the state of federal public service ethics. The subsequent committee report, titled "Proposals for Improvement of Ethical Standards in the Federal Government, including Establishment of a Commission on Ethics,"[43] put forward an ambitious agenda for restoring public confidence in government. The report blamed greedy special interests for the slump in public service ethics. Douglas also recognized that with big government came new opportunities for corruption:

The abuse of discretion or the exploitation of power are most serious chiefly where the Government is dispensing valuable rights and privileges, constructing extensive public works, spending vast sums for military supplies and equipment, making loans, granting direct or indirect subsidies, levying taxes, and regulating the activities of privileged monopolies or economic practices in which there is public interest.[44]

The report laid out a blueprint for protecting public trust in the administrative state. To rebuild public trust in government, the Douglas report recommended the dismissal of federal employees for (1) using confidential government information in personal or business transactions; (2) accepting valuable gifts, favors or services "from any person or organization with which the official or employer transacts business with the government"; (3) discussing "future employment outside the government with a person or an organization with which there is pending official business"; (4) divulging "valuable commercial or economic information of confidential character to unauthorized persons" and (5) becoming "unduly involved, for example, through luncheons, dinners, parties, or other social engagements with persons outside the Government with whom they do official business."[45] The recommendations were consistent with a vision of government held by the new progressives. Enemies of the administrative state lurked everywhere, and the government needed to take emergency steps to protect itself.

On September 27, 1951, as previously noted, President Truman sent a "Message to Congress on Ethical Standards in the Executive Branch." The message proved to be ironic. Throughout his presidency, Truman defended the integrity of his administration. Yet the "Message to Congress" recommended that Congress pass sweeping legislation requiring public financial disclosure for "all presidential appointees, elected federal officials, military aides, and certain other federal officials earning more than $10,000 a year."[46] Politics had forced Truman to act. Members of the Democratic Party knew that Republicans would use the "mess in Washington" to try to convince voters that Washington needed a housecleaning.

Congressional Republicans made sure that the Truman ethics initiatives did not pass, so that Democrats would not receive credit for restoring public trust in government. After all the uproar, the Truman scandals ended with a whimper. Harry Truman decided not to run for a full second term in 1952. Dwight David Eisenhower, a national hero, ran for president as a Republican, and the American people swept Eisenhower into the White House and elected large numbers of Republicans to Congress.

Efforts by the Republican Party to make the "mess in Washington" a major campaign issue had failed.[47] The Republican platform promised "to put an end to corruption, to oust the crooks and grafters, to administer tax laws fairly and impartially, and to restore honest government to the people."[48] The Republican National Committee, for example, in 1952 published a fierce attack against Democratic leadership. The committee titled its report *Crook & Crony Government: The Story of Democrat Fraud and Graft.*[49] Most historians agree that Eisenhower would have won the presidency if he had accepted the Democratic nomination. The report became a mere footnote in presidential campaign history.

EQUAL OPPORTUNITY SCANDALS AND THE REPUBLICAN MANDATE

Republicans interpreted the election results as a mandate to dismantle the welfare state. "Many Republicans looked forward," according to historians Morison and Commager, "to a complete reversal of Democratic policies which (their platform asserted) led toward socialism and the wrecking of the free enterprise system."[50] Some twenty years of Democratic control of the White House had not extinguished the intense hatred of the national government among a significant minority of the American people.

The cold war provided conservatives with a new weapon to use against big government. The growing power of Soviet Russia and the intervention of Communist China in the Korean War offered conservatives the opportunitiy to argue that a powerful national government would lead to socialism and would soon destroy the democratic institutions of the country.

Although the American people voted for change, the Republican Party soon received the message loud and clear that the change did not include ending most of the federal programs put in place during the preceding two decades. Farmers wanted to keep their farm price supports. Veterans demanded continuation of benefits for education, housing and health care. States lobbied hard for increased federal funding of highway construction. Political obscurity awaited anyone who proposed even tampering with Social Security. The deepening cold war forced the federal government to continue to spend billions on national defense. Members of the Eisenhower administration also learned that ethics scandals could do as much damage to the Eisenhower presidency as they had done to the Truman presidency.

The Truman scandals had taught Washington reporters a great deal about honest graft and conflicts of interests. Groups fiercely opposed to Republican plans for the nation did not head for the hills and wait for a counterrevolution. To the contrary, progressives proved willing to scrutinize the financial affairs of their nominees to uncover information that they might use to raise questions regarding the suitability of an individual for public service.

Despite adequate warnings of the modified ethics climate in Washington, many high-level Eisenhower appointees turned out to be totally unprepared for what they found awaiting them. Through the eight years Dwight Eisenhower served as president, high-level Eisenhower appointees faced an endless stream of allegations of impropriety.[51] Most ended up not being particularly serious. A number of high-level Eisenhower nominees, however, left government under a cloud. Although these scandals did not reduce the popularity of President Eisenhower, the Eisenhower White House had to spend countless hours dousing ethics fires. Critics of the Eisenhower administration succeeded in using the scandals to portray Republicans as friends of powerful special interests. By the end of the decade, a conflict-of-interest hysteria gripped Washington.

Like the Truman White House before it, the Eisenhower White House believed politics motivated almost all the allegations of impropriety made against members of the administration. Liberal critics used allegations to slow or stop the adoption of administration policy initiatives. Yet as with the Truman scandals, modern historians rarely mention the Eisenhower scandals in their analyses of the Eisenhower presidency.

A Model Scandal

The Dixon-Yates controversy is the model for the modern public integrity scandal. It is a textbook example of how to use a conflict-of-interest allegation to derail a policy initiative.[52] It took a 1961 United States Supreme Court decision to finally lay the controversy to rest.[53]

This scandal had its origin in the ongoing debate over the appropriate role of government in American society. The city of Memphis for a number of years had operated its own power company. Congress, at the urging of the Roosevelt administration in 1933, created the Tennessee Valley Authority (TVA), with "power to acquire, construct, and operate dams in the Tennessee valley, manufacturing nitrate and fertilizer, generate and sell electric power, inaugurate flood control, withdraw marginal lands from cultivation, develop the river for navigation, and in general advance the economic and social well-being of the people living in the said river basin."[54] The TVA became the source of cheap power to municipalities throughout the region.

During the 1952 campaign, President Eisenhower promised not to sell off the TVA. Candidate Eisenhower did, however, make it clear that he believed the private sector should meet the future power needs of the country.[55] Years earlier, Memphis had entered into a long-term agreement with the TVA to provide its future power needs. By the early 1950s, the TVA realized that without a significant increase in its power-generating capacity, it faced serious problems meeting its commitments to supply power.

President Truman had asked Congress to appropriate funds to increase the generating capacity of the TVA. When the Eisenhower administration took over, it made clear that it strongly opposed the TVA's expanding its role as the major source of power for the area. Private power companies complained bitterly that they had no way of competing with the TVA while federal funds subsidized its operations. If the government could come up with a way for the private sector to meet the power needs of growing communities in the TVA service region, it might pave the way for a new era in public-private partnerships.

To accomplish this goal, in early 1953 the Bureau of the Budget enlisted the services of Adolphe Wenzell, vice president and director of First Boston

Corporation, a large underwriting firm specializing in utility financing, as an unpaid consultant to examine the costs and benefits of TVA power production.[56] The subsequent report submitted by Wenzell to the Bureau of the Budget "expressed strong opposition to any further increase in government-generated power, and recommended the sale of the TVA system to private company."[57] Wenzell's recommendation went far beyond anything anticipated by the bureau: when the bureau asked Wenzell to conduct his study, it knew that Wenzell and First Boston arranged the financing for the construction of private generating facilities across the country. It apparently never crossed the minds of bureau officials that First Boston might profit if the federal government began phasing out federal power production.

In early 1954, the Atomic Energy Commission (AEC) announced that it had entered into an agreement with a consortium of private power companies to meet its future power needs. This agreement freed up power from the TVA to meet its contract obligations with the city of Memphis and other communities and ended the need for the TVA to expand its generating capacity. When the public policy lobby heard the news, it became convinced that the action constituted the first step in dismantling the TVA. By the Eisenhower administration, public power had accumulated strong support across the country.

Senator Lester Hill (D. Ala.), a vocal supporter of the TVA, responded with anger to the agreement. On the floor of the Senate, Senator Hill announced that one Adolphe Wenzell, a vice president and director of First Boston Corporation, had advised the Bureau of the Budget on the Dixon-Yates contract. The power consortium, Senator Hill announced, gave First Boston the contract to arrange the financing for the project.[58]

Subsequent investigations led to charges and countercharges of conflicts of interest, coverups and partisan character assassination. Critics of Republican policies used the scandal as evidence that big business had gotten its hooks into the Eisenhower administration. Political expediency forced the Eisenhower White House to throw the AEC consortium project overboard. President Eisenhower himself announced cancellation of the contract in July 1955.[59] The power consortium—the Mississippi Valley Generating Company—immediately sued the federal government for wrongful termination of the contract, and the Court of Claims found in favor of Mississippi Valley to the amount of $1,870,000.

The totally unexpected Supreme Court decision in *United States* v. *Mississippi Valley Generating Co.*, 364 U.S. 520 (1961), gave supporters of modern conflict-of-interest regulation a tremendous victory. Even though the Justice Department declined to prosecute Wenzell for a violation of criminal law, the Supreme Court reversed the holding of the Court of Claims and found that Wenzell's involvement with the contract gave the federal government grounds to terminate because Wenzell had violated the federal self-dealing conflict-of-interest statute.[60] The fact that the Justice Department never prosecuted Wenzell for violating the statute did not seem to trouble the majority of the High Court. First Boston had received the contract to arrange financing for the Mississippi Valley Generating Company's power plant. Wenzell had an indirect interest in the Atomic Energy Commission's entering into the contract with Mississippi Valley Generating. Justice Earl Warren, in language that warmed the hearts of even the most fervent conflict-of-interest hawks, stated:

The statute does not specify as elements of the crime that there be actual corruption or that there be any actual loss suffered by the Government as a result of the defendant's conflict of interest. This omission indicates that the statute is thus directed not only at dishonor, but also at conduct which tempts dishonor. This broad proscription embodies a recognition of the fact that an impairment of impartial judgment can occur in even the most well-intentioned men when their personal economic interests are affected by the business they transact on behalf of the Government.[61]

The decision handed advocates of a dramatic expansion of rule-driven ethics the authority to implement their vision of political reform.

THE WALKING WOUNDED

The Dixon-Yates scandal did not end the ethics problems of the Eisenhower administration. Toward the end of Eisenhower's presidency, the Sherman Adams affair caused Eisenhower great discomfort. Adams, former governor of New Hampshire, came to Washington to serve as a personal assistant to Eisenhower.[62] Early 1958 saw a flurry of newspaper stories detailing contacts he had with the Civil Aeronautics Board on behalf of an airline facing revocation of its operating license.[63] The Administrative Procedure Act prohibited such ex parte contacts with respect to adjudicatory proceedings of a federal regulatory agency.

Adams might have survived had it not been for new revelations by the House Special Subcommittee on Legislative Oversight that Adams permitted "New England industrialist Bernard Goldfine" to pick up $1,642.28 in hotel bills from the Sheraton-Plaza in Boston.[64] A house investigator testified at a public hearing that he had information that Goldfine received "preferred treatment before at least two of the regulatory commissions as a result of his close association."[65] Adams subsequently issued a statement admitting he had accepted hotel accommodations from Goldfine and had made inquiries to regulatory agencies on behalf of Goldfine.[66] But Adams denied any relationship between the favors he received and the contacts made on behalf of Goldfine.

The Eisenhower White House learned the hard lesson that rarely does all the damaging information come out at once. Newspapers soon reported that Adams had accepted a "$700 vicuna coat and a $2,400 oriental rug" from Goldfine.[67]

On June 17, 1958, Adams reported to the caucus room of the Old House Office Building to answer questions from the congressional investigatory committee. Six hundred spectators and reporters watched the unprecedented proceedings. Throughout the hearing, Adams denied any wrongdoing or impropriety. Toward the end of the hearing, Adams conceded that if he had the opportunity to turn back the clock he "would have acted a little more prudently."[68] Partisan politics sealed the fate of Sherman Adams. The September Maine general election saw the Republican Party suffer a political disaster.[69] Republicans across the country read the election victory as the direct result of the Sherman Adams affair, and Adams resigned his White House position on September 22, 1956.

The vast majority of Eisenhower historians pay little attention to the Eisenhower era public ethics controversies. But at least one historian has taken a much less sympathetic view of the administration's ethics record. "From the campaign slush fund of Vice-Presidential candidate Richard Nixon to the vicuna coat and oriental rug of Presidential Assistant Sherman Adams, the story was much the same," wrote historian David A. Frier. "It was a story of an Administration characterized by moral pronouncements and amoral responses to many of the crucial ethical problems of the fifties."[70]

The public integrity war had entered an important new phase. The 1960s would provide an excellent test of the theory that a bureaucratic solution existed to resolve the public integrity crisis.

NOTES

1. Peter Woll, *American Bureaucracy* (New York: Norton, 1977), p. 50.

2. David H. Rosenbloom, "The Evolution of the Administrative State and Transformation of Administrative Law." In *Handbook of Regulation and Administrative Law*, eds. David H. Rosenbloom and Richard D. Schwartz (New York: Marcel Dekker, 1994), p. 10.

3. C. Van Woodward, *Responses of the President to Charges of Misconduct* (New York: Delacorte, 1974), p. 306.

4. U.S. Congress, House Committee on Merchant Marine and Fisheries, *Investigation of shipyard profits* (Washington, DC: Government Printing Office, 1946).

5. Paul Van Riper, "Spoils as Dysfunctional and Functional." In *People in the Public Service*, eds. Robert Golembiewski and Michael Cohen (Itasca, IL: F.E. Peacock, 1976), p. 321.

6. Kenneth Culp Davis, *Administrative Law: Cases-Texts-Problems* (St. Paul, MN: West, 1977), p. 7.

7. Ibid., p. 8. President Roosevelt vetoed the Walter-Logan bill in 1940.

8. Frederick W. Ford, Acting Assistant Attorney General, Office of Legal Counsel, Memorandum for the attorney general re conflict-of-interest statute, December 10, 1964.

9. For most of the century, federal personnel rules required federal employees to keep their financial affairs in order. This included paying all bills on time. Failure to do so constituted grounds for disciplinary action.

10. Franklin D. Roosevelt, memorandum for the U.S. Civil Service Commission, June 11, 1935, Official File, Franklin D. Roosevelt Library as cited in Robert Roberts, *White House Ethics* (Westport, CT: Greenwood Press, 1988), p. 27.

11. Ibid.

12. Ibid.

13. *Public Papers and Addresses of Franklin D. Roosevelt*, Samuel Irving Rosenman, comp. (New York: Macmillan, 1941), p. 170.

14. Roberts, *Ethics*, pp. 23–25; Also see Robert D. Cuff, *The War Industries Board: Business-Government Relations during World War I* (Baltimore, MD: Johns Hopkins University Press, 1973).

15. Ibid.

16. Roberts, *Ethics*, pp. 28–29.

17. Ibid.

18. U. S. War Production Board, *Policies and Procedures on Dollar-a-Year and Without Compensation Employees of the War Production Board and Predecessor Agencies*, May 1940 to March 1944 (Washington, DC: War Production Board, 1944).

19. Ibid.

20. Ford, p. 80.

21. Ibid.

22. Roberts, *Ethics*, p. 31.

23. Davis, *Administrative Process*, p. 8.

24. Rosenbloom, p. 17.

25. James O. Freedman, *Crisis and Legitimacy: The Administrative Process and American Government* (Cambridge: Cambridge University Press, 1978) pp. 138–39.

26. See David McCulloch, *Truman* (New York: Simon & Schuster, 1992).

27. Ibid.

28. Cabell Phillips, *The Truman Presidency* (New York: Macmillian, 1966), p. 405.

29. Van Riper, p. 406, citing Robert S. Allen and William V. Shannon, *The Truman Merry-Go-Round* (New York: Vanguard Press, 1950), pp. 88–89, footnote 4.

30. Ibid.

31. See Jules Abels, *The Truman Scandals* (Chicago: Regnery, 1956); Andrew J. Dunar, *The Truman Scandals and the Politics of Morality* (Columbia: University of Missouri Press, 1984).

32. Andrew J. Dunar, *The Truman Scandals and the Politics of Morality*, provides the most objective analysis of the public integrity controversies of the Truman presidency.

33. Van Woodward, pp. 332–33.

34. Ibid.

35. McCullough, p. 871.

36. Roberts, *Ethics*, pp. 40–41.

37. McCulloch, p. 871.

38. Harry Truman, Message to Congress, September 27, 1951; see also Roberts, *Ethics*, p. 49.

39. Dunar, pp. 17–18.

40. Roberts, *Ethics*, p. 38.

41. Phillips, p. 405. The term "five-percenter" referred to the fee or commission the lobbyist charged for services rendered.

42. Van Riper, p. 408.

43. U.S. Senate, Committee on Labor and Public Welfare, *Report of the Sub-committee on Labor and Public Welfare on Ethical Standards in Government*, 82nd. Cong. 1st. Sess. 1951.

44. Ibid., p. 11.

45. Ibid., p. 2.

46. Roberts, *Ethics*, p. 49.

47. Dunar, p. 143.

48. Arthur M. Schlesinger, Jr., ed., *History of Presidential Elections. 1789–1968*, 4 vols. (New York: Chelsea House, 1971), pp. 4:3291–92, cited in Dunar, p. 147.

49. *Crook & Crony Government: The story of Democrat fraud and graft: documents and index* (Washington, DC: Republican National Committee, 1952).

50. Samuel Eliot Morison and Henry Steele Commager, *The Growth of the American Republic* (New York: Oxford University Press, 1962), pp. 2:958.

51. For a detailed description of all of the Eisenhower-era public integrity scandals, see David A. Frier, *Conflict of Interest in the Eisenhower Administration* (Ames: Iowa State University Press, 1969).

52. Aaron Wildavsky, *Dixon-Yates: A Study in Power Politics* (Westport, CT: Greenwood Press, 1976).

53. *United States v. Mississippi Valley Generating Co.*, 364 U.S. 520 (1961).

54. Morison and Commager, pp. 2:719–20.

55. Wildavsky, pp. 17–22.

56. Roberts, *Ethics*, p. 63.

57. Ibid.; also see Wildavsky, p. 27.

58. Van Woodward, p. 357.

59. Ibid.

60. 18 U.S.C. 434. Congress in 1962 replaced this statute with Section 208, title 18, *United States Code*.

61. Ibid., pp. 459–550, as cited in Kenneth F. Warren, *Administrative Law in the Political System*, 2d. ed. (St. Paul, MN: West Publishing Co., 1988), p. 229.

62. Van Woodward, pp. 351–53.

63. Frier, pp. 12–13.

64. Ibid., p. 15

65. Ibid.

66. Ibid., p. 20.

67. Ibid.

68. Ibid., p. 25.

69. Ibid., p. 194.

70. Ibid., p. 25.

Chapter 5

Strategic Ethics Initiatives: 1960–1973

The 1960 presidential race pitted Richard Nixon, the stalwart Republican warrior, against John Kennedy, the charismatic Democrat war hero from Massachusetts. The Kennedy strategy, as exemplified by the famous missile gap ploy, aimed at creating an "ethics gap" during the 1960 campaign. Speaking at Wittenberg University in Ohio, on October 17, 1960, Kennedy declared that "no officer or employee of the Executive Branch shall use his official position for financial profit or personal gain, or reveal to others for their advantage confidential information acquired through his position."[1] Kennedy urged Congress to enact "a simple, comprehensive code on conflict of interest," a code that eliminated in existing laws and regulations "duplications, inadvertencies and gaps."[2]

Even though the ethics issue did not have a major impact on the 1960 presidential election, the Kennedy White House followed through with its pledge to put in place a new executive branch ethics management system.[3] The restructuring of the federal ethics management program ushered in a new era in public ethics regulation. Instincts for political survival, not ideology, motivated the Kennedy White House to pursue its ethics reform initiatives.

THE MANAGEMENT OF PROPRIETY

Shortly after taking office, President Kennedy appointed an advisory panel on ethics in government to report back to him on updating the present ethics management program.[4] The panel, interestingly enough, did not find any serious ethical problems in the executive branch. Confusion surrounding the scope of existing prohibitions, not corrupt public officials, constituted the most serious problem. To reduce reliance on difficult-to-enforce criminal sanctions, the panel strongly recommended supplementing criminal restrictions with uniform ethics guidelines issued by the White House.[5] If serious ethics problems existed anywhere in Washington, they existed at the other end of Pennsylvania Avenue, in Congress. Yet President Kennedy's ethics panel declined to recommend tightening any congressional ethics rules.

Armed with this report, the White House, assisted by John Macy, then chairman of the Civil Service Commission, issued uniform ethics rules for high-level presidential appointees and directed federal agencies to update their standards-of-conduct rules for all executive branch employees. President Kennedy, on April 27, 1961, sent Congress a message titled "Ethical Conduct in Government."[6] The message established temporary rules governing: (1) acceptance of gifts, (2) use of inside information for personal purposes, (3) outside employment and (4) financial conflicts of interest for federal employees. The order, like those to follow, focused almost exclusively on financial conflict-of-interest situations that might raise doubts in the public's mind regarding the impartiality of public officials.

Issued in May 1961, Executive Order 10939, "To Provide a Guide on Ethical Standards of Government Officials," set forth new financial conflict-of-interest rules for presidential appointees, nominees and other high-level federal officials. The directive ordered covered officials not to accept anything of value from nonpublic sources if acceptance created either the appearance of or resulted in: "(1) use of public office for private gain, (2) an undertaking to give preferential treatment to any person, (3) any loss of complete independence and impartiality, (4) the making of a Government decision outside official channels, and (5) any adverse effect on the confidence of the public in the integrity of the Government."[7]

The Kennedy ethics directives proved remarkably similar to the proposals put forward in Senator Douglas's 1951 report on ethics in government.[8]

The Kennedy White House, besides issuing sweeping ethics directives, quietly lobbied Congress to update criminal conflict-of-interest statutes. The 1961 Supreme Court *Mississippi Valley Generating*[9] decision, discussed in Chapter 4, gave Congress a strong incentive to update poorly drafted criminal public-corruption and conflict-of-interest statutes. By the early 1960s, federal agencies and departments found it increasingly difficult to persuade certain experts to accept federal positions. Many feared that if they accepted appointments, even on a temporary basis, federal ethics rules would prevent them from returning to the private sector and having future dealings with the federal government.

Ethics militants in Congress, however, did not make life easy for the Kennedy White House. Many still held New Deal–era views of big business.

They had little interest in updating ethics laws to facilitate individuals' moving back and forth between government and the private sector. They felt Congress needed to further tighten ethics laws to prevent powerful special interests from exercising undue influence in public decision making. If this meant that tighter ethics rules might deter certain individuals from accepting public positions, then they believed the government didn't need the services of such individuals.[10]

The Kennedy White House ultimately prevailed. Congress enacted a unified set of public-corruption and conflict-of-interest statutes. These statutes included a number of well-crafted provisions designed to prevent ethics rules from hampering federal recruitment. The ethics militants, at the same time, succeeded in obtaining passage of new ethics rules that significantly expanded the scope of existing prohibitions. The 1962 revision of federal bribery and conflict-of-interest rules guaranteed that future presidential administrations would have to spend more time on the management of public integrity.

The Public Integrity Minefield

To obtain concessions from Congress, the Kennedy White House had promised Congress the establishment of an effective ethics management program in each federal agency. The Kennedy White House hoped that clear guidelines and expert advice would prevent many inadvertent ethics violations. Agencies would also find it much easier to discipline employees for violating administrative ethics rules rather than to prove violations of criminal law.

Rule-driven ethics had a number of advantages over character-focused ethics.[11] Rules could be written down and explained. Ambiguity was eliminated. Investigatory and adjudicatory procedures could be used to resolve disputes over compliance. The Kennedy directives incorporated seven general rules that have become key elements of modern public ethics management.

First, to remain above reproach, the new public servant must not accept things of value from nonpublic sources for the performance of official acts or from sources having a direct interest in the actions or inaction of the official.[12] Even if the source of the gift did not expect anything in return, some members of the public still might think otherwise.[13]

Second, public officials must not take any action with respect to any matter in which they have a financial interest.[14] For example, suppose a public official owns 1,000 shares of Dell, Inc. The public official has responsibility for purchasing twenty desktop computers for his organization. Even though the purchase of twenty desktop computers would have absolutely no impact on the value of Dell stock, and even though Dell makes exceptional desktop computers, as long as the public official owns Dell stock he has absolutely no business purchasing Dell computers for his public organization.

Third, the outside employment activities of public servants must not conflict with their public responsibilities.[15] For example, a public employee might decide to take a part-time job working in the quality control unit of a meatpacking plant. The employee has a full-time government job as a meatpacking plant inspector. Modern conflict-of-interest theory holds that the employee either give up his job as a meat inspector or his part-time job in quality control.

Fourth, public officials must not make use of nonpublic information for personal financial gain. Government agencies collect vast quantities of information. The Federal Reserve Board, for example, makes periodic decisions whether to raise or lower interest rates. If individuals in the financial markets had access to this information in advance of the general public, they could exploit it to enrich themselves at the expense of the latter.[16]

Fifth, former public servants must not use their contacts in government to obtain preferential treatment for private clients.[17] Sixth, public officials must not represent private parties in their dealings with government.[18] And seventh, the public official must not engage in any of the above types of conduct if the conduct creates any appearance of bias or impartiality.[19]

Protection from the Appearance of Impropriety

No major ethics scandals tainted the reputation of the Kennedy administration. But minor ethics controversies made clear to the Kennedy White House that John Macy's Civil Service Commission had not developed a foolproof system for protecting public confidence in the impartiality of the administrative state. These controversies showed the difficulty of enforcing the above rules as the federal government spent increasing amounts of money. The Korth affair foreshadowed ethics controversies to come.

John Kennedy recruited Ford Motor Company president Robert Mc-Namara to serve as secretary of defense.[20] McNamara viewed his primary task as bringing the cost of defense programs under control. This objective required ending the competition between the branches of the armed services for limited resources. As part of this strategy, and against the wishes of the Navy and Air Force, the Department of Defense decided to purchase a single experimental tactical fighter and attack aircraft (TFX) for use by both the Navy and the Air Force. Setting aside individual service concerns, the Defense Department solicited bids for a single airplane. Boeing and General Dynamics were the primary contenders for the potentially lucrative contract.

During the early 1960s, General Dynamics had found itself in serious financial difficulty.[21] As one of the larger employers of the Fort Worth, Texas, area, there would have been a severe fiscal hardship on the local economy and the state of Texas if General Dynamics went under. Consequently, a group of banks provided General Dynamics with $200 million in loans to keep the corporation solvent, with Continental Bank of Fort Worth providing a significant portion of the loan package. General Dynamics badly needed the TFX contract. When the "Air Force Council and System Source Selection Board . . . voted to award the coveted contract to Boeing on the grounds of better design and lower cost"[22] top civilian Defense Department officials rejected these findings and awarded the contract to General Dynamics.[23] While federal law did not require that the contract go to the lowest bidder, a firestorm of controversy quickly erupted over the decision.

In October 1963, newspapers reported that Fred Korth, secretary of the navy, "used official Navy Department stationery, as well as the department's yacht *Sequoia* in [order] to solicit private business."[24] Executive Order 10939 directed all high-level presidential appointees not to engage "in any outside employment or other outside activity not compatible with the full and proper discharge of the responsibilities of his office or position."[25] But it was the conflict-of-interest allegations involving the TFX contract that proved much more damaging to Korth's reputation and ultimately forced his resignation. Prior to becoming secretary of the navy, Korth headed the Continental Bank of Fort Worth. As already noted, Continental had been one of the banks that loaned General Dynamics the funds to keep it operating. At the time, federal law did not require Korth to sell his stock in Continental Bank when he became secretary of the navy. However, when it became known that Korth had not disqualified himself from making the TFX decision, Korth came under intense criticism from Congress.[26] Although Korth denied any wrongdoing with respect to either controversy, the Kennedy White House proved unwilling to subject itself to a long fight to retain Korth in the administration. Korth resigned in October 1963, expressing his desire to return to the private sector.

A 1970 Senate investigation of the overall TFX fiasco determined that Korth had sixteen contacts with General Dynamics officials and only two with representatives of Boeing. Yet the investigation determined that Korth had not played a major role in the decision to award the contract to General Dynamics.[27] For years to come, the TFX would be plagued with cost overruns and technical problems. Congress terminated the program in the late 1960s.

The Brave New World of Public Ethics

Surprisingly few individuals questioned the direction of federal ethics reform. Bayless Manning, who had served as a member of President Kennedy's ethics advisory committee, in 1964 issued a warning about the high cost of public ethics reform. In an article entitled "The Purity Potlatch:

Conflicts of Interest and Moral Escalation,"[28] Manning condemned the growing preoccupation with conflicts of interest and ethics in government: "In the public mind, to receive a gift or to have a conflict of interest has by now been equated with venality; a government official in a position of conflicting interests is a kind of crook."[29] Manning regarded the tightening of public ethics rules as a dangerous moral escalation.[30] No evidence, he argued, shows that these rules do anything to guarantee the good character of public officials.

Many in Washington probably agreed with Manning, but found it impossible to publicly oppose the direction of public ethics reform. The Kennedy administration, however, felt it had to do everything in its power to prevent appearances of impropriety if it hoped to gain public support for a larger role for national government in American society.[31]

Changing of the Guard

The assassination of John Kennedy put in jeopardy the new executive branch ethics program.[32] There was no guarantee that Lyndon Johnson would give the same priority to public integrity management. Johnson had entered the vice-presidency in 1961 after years of service in the House and Senate, where he had not placed political reform at the top of his legislative agenda.[33] Much like Harry Truman, Lyndon Johnson had worked his way up via a political machine. Johnson entered Congress poor; by the time he became vice president, his family assets had grown to close to $20 million.[34] Biographer Robert Caro, in *The Years of Lyndon Johnson: Means of Assent*, concluded that "the birth and early years of the Johnson financial empire illuminate very clearly the subtle means by which favoritism and influence are exercised, and their effect on other individuals and on the body politic as a whole."[35] Much of the Johnson family wealth came from the purchase of radio and television stations while he served in Congress.[36] The Bobby Baker affair, early in the 1960s, put a spotlight on weak congressional ethics rules and raised serious questions regarding Lyndon Johnson's integrity.

In the late 1950s, Bobby Baker became the right-hand man to then Senate Majority Leader Lyndon B. Johnson. Access to the majority leader gave Baker immense power and prestige. But his world crumbled in 1963, when a vending machine company filed a civil suit against him. Having failed to win a vending machine contract, the company alleged that Baker used his influence to obtain a vending contract for a company in which he held a financial interest.[37] Subsequent investigation revealed that Baker had made $2 million from his law practice while serving as Lyndon Johnson's assistant. Much of the money came from groups and individuals who paid Baker's firm to lobby on their behalf. "A federal court, in January 1967, convicted Baker of tax evasion, theft and conspiracy to defraud the government."[38] Baker, throughout a lengthy investigation and prosecution, never implicated Lyndon Johnson in any of his criminal activities.[39] But the Bobby Baker scandal and other ethics controversies surrounding its members during the 1960s forced Congress to take a hard look at the rules governing the conduct of its members.

Public Integrity and the Great Society

John Macy, chairman of the U.S. Civil Service Commission during the Kennedy and Johnson administrations, wrote in his 1971 book *Public Service: The Human Side of Government* that "the public servant must serve the citizens in the full glare of public scrutiny. In accepting his public responsibility, he must recognize that he accepts a special code of conduct and a special set of ethical standards."[40] Besides complying with applicable statutes and regulations, Macy argued, the public servant "must avoid any behavior that creates the appearance of violation of the code or the standards or will undermine the confidence of the public in his impartiality, objectivity, and integrity."[41] Macy succeeded in persuading the Johnson White House to keep the Kennedy ethics initiatives alive. After a Civil Service Commission review of executive branch ethics regulations during late 1964,[42] Johnson ordered a major expansion of the ethics management activities of the Civil Service Commission.[43]

The Johnson White House understood that a major public ethics scandal could severely disrupt public support for the Great Society initiatives and Vietnam War expenditures. The gift-giving practices of major defense contractors gave the Johnson White House reason to worry.[44]

Accordingly, the General Accounting Office (GAO) aggressively began to audit the billing practices of defense contractors for inappropriate charges. The audits raised serious questions about whether an arms-length relationship existed between defense contractors and officials of the Army, Navy, Air Force, Marines, and Department of Defense.[45] The audits alleged that defense contractors provided gifts and entertainment to federal employees and then deducted those expenses from gross income as a business expense.[46] The GAO investigation revealed numerous instances of Defense Department personnel having accepted items such as "hunting trips, golf outings, meals, cocktails, tickets to sporting events, etc."[47] Defense Department directives at that time clearly prohibited personnel from accepting most gifts, lodging and entertainment from defense contractors.

A conflict-of-interest controversy involving Assistant Secretary of Commerce Herbert W. Klotz finally persuaded the Johnson White House of the necessity for additional conflict-of-interest safeguards.[48] An allegation that Klotz had relied on inside information to purchase stock options for Texas Gulf Sulphur Company created a minor furor. Prior to the purchase of the stock, Texas Gulf had discovered some $2 billion worth of zinc, copper and silver deposits near Timminis, Ontario.[49] The Securities and Exchange Commission (SEC) alleged that a number of company officers had taken options to purchase thousands of shares of company stock before the company announced the find. After the company announced the find, the officers of the company supposedly exercised these options and made a killing in the market.

Assistant Secretary Klotz had purchased Texas Gulf stock options after a friend who had received inside information strongly urged him to make the purchase. Klotz denied that his friend provided him with any specific information.[50] The value of the Klotz shares went from $29.70 for the options to some $70 shortly after the announcement of the find.[51] In late April 1965, Klotz tendered his resignation to President Johnson. Media reports indicated that Johnson had demanded his resignation, yet it was Secretary of Commerce O'Connor who had announced the resignation.[52]

Expanding the federal ethics management program made strong political sense. The Great Society called for a large expansion of federal programs and in the distribution of federal funds nationwide. Opportunities to use federal positions for financial gain would certainly increase.

BUREAUCRATIC ETHICS

Early in May 1965, President Johnson issued a new standards-of-conduct executive order.[53] The order went far beyond anything previously attempted by the federal government. It marked a major escalation in the war against appearances of impropriety.

First, President Johnson replaced existing ethics orders with a new order that covered all executive branch employees and officials. Executive Order 11222, "Prescribing Standards of Ethical Conduct for Government Officers and Employees," established a series of broad obligations related to assuring the objectivity and impartiality of federal decision making. The order, most important, directed all executive branch employees to avoid any action that "might result in, or create the appearance of (1) using public office for private gain; (2) giving preferential treatment to any organization or person; (3) impeding government efficiency or economy; (4) losing complete independence or impartiality of action; (5) making a government decision outside official channels; or (6) affecting adversely the confidence of the public in the integrity of the Government."[54]

Second, the order required each federal agency and department to establish a formal ethics program headed by a designated agency ethics official (DAEO). The DAEO, not the Civil Service Commission, had primary responsibility for enforcing the new standards-of-conduct rules. The order made no provision for the Civil Service Commission to conduct independent investigations of allegations of rule violations. Agencies had responsibility to "craft the model regulation to fit their own needs."[55]

Third, and highly controversial, the Johnson White House decided to require presidential nominees to file confidential financial disclosure statements. The confidential disclosure provisions of the order also gave the Civil Service Commission authority to order other federal employees to file confidential disclosure statements. Although John Macy and the Civil Service Commission strongly supported confidential financial reporting for high-level federal officials, not everyone found confidential disclosure a major improvement in ethics regulation.

Prior to the issuance of the order, the White House had asked Justice E. Barrett Prettyman, senior circuit judge of the U.S. Court of Appeals, to look over the order. Prettyman did not like what he read and leveled his harshest criticism against those provisions of the order requiring employees and officials to avoid even appearances of impropriety. "The Order," wrote Prettyman, "contains many expressions which are usually frightening to the normal well-meaning person, traps for the unwary, and escape hatches for the intentional malefactor."[56] Prettyman saw the confidential financial reporting provisions of the order as violating the privacy rights of employees and members of their family.[57] This criticism forced the White House and the Civil Service Commission to redraft some provisions, but had little impact on the tone and substance of the directive.

The financial disclosure provisions of the executive order dramatically changed the nature of federal conflict-of-interest management. The order required top appointees to file financial disclosure statements with the chairman of the Civil Service Commission, who reviewed them for conflicts of interest and worked with the appointee to resolve conflicts.[58] Although the high-level disclosure system experienced few problems, a quarrel was fueled by agency decisions to require tens of thousands of other federal employees to file confidential disclosure statements.[59] The controversy forced the Civil Service Commission to scale back the scope of disclosure requirements for lower-level employees.

The Kennedy and Johnson administrations succeeded in avoiding major public integrity scandals. Thus, the 1960s saw a lull in the public integrity war, and the 1964 Johnson election landslide seemed to indicate little support for movement conservatives.

THE POLITICS OF POLARIZATION AND RESUMPTION OF HOSTILITIES

The 1964 landslide defeat of Barry Goldwater convinced supporters of an activist federal government that a reactionary fringe had captured the Republican Party. Few believed that in four short years anything could threaten progressive control of Congress and the presidency. Yet by the end of the 1960s, the nation's political climate had undergone a radical change. Opposition to the Vietnam War, race riots across the country, the sexual

revolution, a geometric rise in illegal drug use, advanced decay of the nation's urban centers, and a perceived collapse of the American educational
system aroused the nation's silent majority, who seemed prepared to accept
drastic actions to keep the nation from flying apart.

Other Americans, at the same time, pushed for even more radical changes
in the political, social and economic systems of the country in order to
guarantee all citizens equal opportunity, a clean environment and a share
of the nation's wealth. Women and minorities still occupied a dispropor-
tionate share of low-paying jobs or had difficulty finding gainful employment. The politics of polarization gradually replaced the politics of
consensus. Movement conservatives and new progressives rushed to fill the
perceived political vacuum.

The 1968 election campaigns saw rioting in the streets of Chicago during
the Democratic nomination convention and heard Richard Nixon promising to get the nation out of Vietnam and to restore order to the nation's
streets. While Nixon won the presidency, the Democratic Party remained
in firm control of Congress. New progressives viewed the 1968 victory of
Richard Nixon as a disaster. To them, Nixon represented everything wrong
with the political process.

The Nixon campaign made masterful use of ideology to dismantle the
New Deal Democratic coalition. Nixon had organized his campaign around
the theme that the national government had grown too large and powerful
and that the federal government needed to return power to the states.

Faced with a Democratic Senate, the Nixon White House spent long
hours working with presidential nominees to discover conflicts of interest
that might cause confirmation problems.[60] Indeed, the Nixon White House
proved remarkably successful in avoiding major disputes regarding the
qualifications of appointments to high-level positions.

Nixon historians have forgotten that the Nixon Justice Department and
the U.S. attorneys whom he appointed ushered in a new era in the federal
pursuit of corrupt state and local government officials. By the early 1970s,
federal law enforcement agencies and prosecutors had become major players in the public integrity war.[61] The Nixon administration deserves some
credit for helping to open the door to greater federal involvement in the
fight against corrupt public officials.

OVER THE BRINK

James Madison, in "Federalist 51" warned the nation about the danger
of strong factions: "In a society, under the forms of which the stronger
faction can readily unite and oppress the weaker, anarchy may as truly be
said to reign, as in a state of nature where the weaker individual is not
secured against the violence of the stronger."[62]

The 1970s would see the full force of the public integrity war. The Nixon

White House turned the power of the federal government against anyone it viewed as a political threat. Then Watergate gave new progressives a golden opportunity to implement their vision of political reform. However, Watergate also provided movement conservatives with strong evidence that big government inevitably leads to the abuse of power.

NOTES

1. "Kennedy Promises," *Congressional Quarterly Weekly Report*, January 13, 1961, p. A41.

2. Ibid.

3. For a description of the modern executive branch ethics management program see Deanne C. Siemer, "Enforcement of the Federal Ethics Laws as Applied to Executive Branch Personnel," Issues and Opinion Paper Prepared for the Working Conference on Ethics in Government, Administrative Conference of the United States, Washington DC, March 1, 1988, pp. 13–23. In *Sourcebook on Governmental Ethics for Presidential Appointees* (Washington DC: Office of the Chairman Administrative Conference of the United States, 1988).

4. Robert Roberts, *White House Ethics* (Westport, CT: Greenwood Press, 1988), pp. 78–79.

5. Ibid.

6. John F. Kennedy, Message from the president to the Congress relative to ethical conduct in the government, April 27, 1961, House Document No. 145, 87th Cong., 1st sess.

7. Roberts, *Ethics*, p. 84.

8. Stuart C. Gilman, "Presidential Ethics and the Ethics of the Presidency," *Annals of the American Academy of Political and Social Science* 537 (January 1995): 71.

9. *United States v. Mississippi Valley Generating Co.*, 364 U.S. 520, 81 S.Ct 294, 5 L. Ed. 2d 268 (1961).

10. Roberts, *Ethics*, pp. 93–94.

11. For an excellent discussion of the difference between rule-driven ethics and character-focused ethics, see Harry W. Reynolds, Jr., "Educating Public Administrators about Ethics," *Annals of the American Academy of Political and Social Science* 537 (January 1995): 126–31.

12. Robert Roberts, "Regulatory Bias and Conflict of Interest Regulation," In *Handbook of Regulation and Administrative Law* eds. David H. Rosenbloom and Richard D. Schwartz (New York: Marcel Dekker, 1994), p. 493.

13. Ibid.

14. Ibid. p. 492.

15. Ibid. p. 494.

16. Ibid. p. 495.

17. Ibid. p. 84.

18. Ibid. p. 494.

19. Robert N. Roberts, "Lord, Protect Me From The Appearance of Wrongdoing," In *Public Personnel Policy: The Politics of Civil Service*, ed. David H. Rosenbloom (Port Washington, NY: Associated Faculty Press, 1985), pp. 177–192.

20. Prior to becoming Secretary of Defense, McNamara served as president of the Ford Motor Company. See Philip H. Burch, Jr., *Elites in American History: The New Deal to the Carter Administration* (New York: Holmes & Meier, 1990), p. 177.

21. See Richard A. Smith, "How a Great Corporation Got Out of Control," *Fortune*, January 1962, pp. 64–69, 178–84, cited by Burch, p. 220 n.67.

22. Burch, p. 189.

23. For a comprehensive review of the TFX project and contract, see Robert J. Art, *The TFX Decision: McNamara and the Military* (Boston: Little Brown, 1968).

24. David A. Frier, *Conflict of Interest in the Eisenhower Administration* (Ames: Iowa State University Press, 1969), p. 215.

25. Roberts, *Ethics*, p. 84.

26. Ibid.

27. Burch, p. 221, n.75. See U.S. Senate, Committee on Government Operations, *TFX Contract Investigation* (Washington, DC: Government Printing Office, 1970), pp. 37–38, 51.

28. Bayless Manning, "The Purity Potlatch: An Essay on Conflict of Interests, American Government, and Moral Escalation," *Federal Bar Journal* 24 (Summer 1964): 243–49.

29. Ibid., p. 248.

30. Ibid.

31. This book does not attempt to discuss the aspects of the private life of John Kennedy that became public only after his death—specifically, John Kennedy's extramarital affairs while he was president. See Joseph Reeves, *A Question of Character: A Life of John Kennedy* (New York: Free Press, 1991); Shelly Ross, *Fall from Grace: Sex, Scandal, and Corruption in American Politics from 1702 to the Present* (New York: Ballantine Books, 1988); "Politicians and Privacy," *Congressional Quarterly*, April 7, 1992, p. 352.

32. Gilman, p. 71.

33. *Congressional Ethics: History, Facts, and Controversy* (Washington DC: Congressional Quarterly, 1992), p. 146.

34. Robert A. Caro, *The Years of Lyndon Johnson: Means of Ascent* (New York: Alfred A. Knopf, 1982), p. xxix.

35. Ibid.

36. Ibid., pp. 80–118.

37. Ibid., p. 102.

38. Ibid.

39. For a review of the Bobby Baker affair, see Robert Rowe, *The Bobby Baker Story* (New York: Parallax, 1967); G. R. Schreiber, *The Bobby Baker Affair* (Chicago: Regnery, 1964).

40. John W. Macy, Jr., *Public Service: The Human Side of Government* (New York: Harper & Row, 1971), p. 249.

41. Ibid.

42. Ibid., p. 253.

43. Gilman, p. 71.

44. Roberts, *Ethics*, pp. 113–115.

45. Frederick G. Mosher, *The GAO: Quest for Accountability in American Government* (Boulder, CO: Westview Press, 1979), p. 155.

46. Roberts, *Ethics*, p. 113.

47. Arthur Focke, Memorandum for special counsel to the president, April 9, 1965, White House Staff Files, Lyndon Baines Johnson Library, p. 3., cited in Roberts, *Ethics*, p. 115.

48. Frier, p. 217.

49. Ibid.

50. Ibid., p. 218

51. Ibid.

52. Ibid., p. 220.

53. Gilman, p. 71.

54. Ibid.

55. Ibid.

56. Roberts, *Ethics*, p. 120.

57. Ibid.

58. Macy, p. 254.

59. Roberts, *Ethics*, pp. 124–26.

60. Ibid., pp. 131–34.

61. See Charles E. Ruff, "Federal Prosecution of Local Corruption: A Study in the Making of Law Enforcement Policy," *Georgetown Law Journal* 65 (June 1977): 1171–228.

62. James Madison, "Federalist 51," *The Federalist Papers*, ed. Andrew Macke (New York: Pocket Books, 1964), p. 121.

PART II

PUBLIC ETHICS WARRIORS

The 1968 presidential election victory of Richard Nixon marked a turning point in the public integrity war. Nixon believed his critics would do anything in their power to destroy him. Although Nixon's obsession with his political enemies contributed greatly to the evolution of the Watergate scandal, other forces and trends played an equally significant role in fueling a major escalation of the public integrity war.

Critics of the regulatory process, individuals with business backgrounds attempting to gain acceptance in government, an explosion in media reporting and investigations of official misconduct by public officials and the increasing power of the public ethics bureaucracy all made a significant contribution to turning the public integrity war into a conflagration. The flames engulfed every part of the nation's political system. Instead of bringing victory to either the new progressives or movement conservatives, this intensification of the public integrity war hostilities simply convinced more and more Americans that the traditional political system had irrevocably broken down.

Chapter 6

Regulatory Rebels

Richard Nixon's 1968 presidential election victory signaled the beginning of an era of divided national government. Neither party had the ability, or the will, to break the political stalemate. During the 1970s, factions increased their respective influence in both the Democratic and Republican parties. Single-issue interest groups saw their membership rapidly expand as more and more Americans became disillusioned with the two major parties. The environmental, women's, and gay rights movements joined the civil rights movement as major political forces pushing hard from the left side of the political spectrum. At the same time, conservative groups organized grassroots campaigns against tax increases. The pro-life movement, after the landmark 1973 Supreme Court decision in *Roe* v. *Wade*,[1] began a grassroots campaign to overturn the abortion rights opinion. Religious conservatives began to explore the possibility of forging their ranks into a national political force of millions.

Progressive political forces blamed special interests for blocking the popular will of the American public. Frustration with politics as usual, in 1970, led to the establishment of Common Cause, an organization formed to free the political process from addiction to special-interest money. Common Cause argued that campaign finance reform, tougher ethics rules and restrictions on lobbying of public officials would help bring special-interest politics under control.

Of particular concern to Common Cause and to other public-interest groups was the issue of federal regulation. Critics of the regulatory process argued that federal and state regulators no longer exercised independent judgment. Regulatory agencies, according to this line of reasoning, were most responsive to "regulated industry and to their own internal bureaucratic imperatives."[2] Proponents of this theory of regulatory behavior began an aggressive crusade to free regulatory agencies from the control of special interests. Reforming the regulation process became synonymous with public integrity reform.

NEW PROGRESSIVES AND REGULATORY CAPTURE

A year after Senator Paul Douglas's committee issued its landmark report on ethics in government, *The Annals of the American Academy of Political and Social Science* published a volume entitled *Ethical Standards in American Public Life*.[3] The volume included an article by Senator Douglas in which he addressed the most serious ethical problems facing government.[4] Douglas identified the prior employment and subsequent employment of federal officials as two of the most significant ethics problems facing government. "One of the most pressing problems," stated Douglas, "is that the government is employing mature, well-established businessmen, especially in numerous positions in defense agencies which deal directly with the very industries from which they recently came."[5] Despite recognizing the service these individuals provide to the government, Douglas expressed the view that their use created a number of serious ethical hazards for government:

Can they be perfectly fair if cases come before them which directly or indirectly involve the company from which they came? Can they be completely objective in decisions which affect their industry—for example, where the industry favors a policy divergent from public policy? Can their men be completely detached in determining what the public interest requires?[6]

Douglas expressed equally serious concerns with respect to jobs public officials take after leaving government. Douglas urged public officials not to take any private-sector jobs that had anything to do with their official duties. "All agree that in this new employment," commented Douglas, the public official "should not handle specific matters for which he was formerly responsible or which he officially knew about."[7] Long before Ralph Nader popularized the regulatory capture theory, Paul Douglas sounded the alarm over the "revolving door."

The late 1960s and early 1970s saw regulatory critics adopt the theory of regulatory capture to explain why federal and state regulatory agencies seemed to defend the practices of regulated industries and oppose policies designed to help consumers and to improve efficiency of regulated industries.[8] The theory of regulatory capture argued that regulated industries controlled the behavior of regulatory agencies because regulators saw their role as protecting regulated industries from effective oversight:

Over time, [industries] develop channels for obtaining preferential access to the early stages of decision-making, when it is usually easier to affect outcomes. Their pressure tactics are refined, focused, and effective. The long-term personal relationships they nurture with key regulatory personnel are likewise aids to successful lobbying.[9]

Economists developed the theory of regulatory capture during the 1950s and 1960s to explain why regulatory agencies and regulated industries rarely disagreed on important regulatory issues.[10] Theorists argued that regulators acted as "self-interested actors who rationally exchang[ed] policies for votes and resources while forcing the general public to bear the burdens of industry support."[11] Regulators, in other words, protected regulated industries in order to assure the survival of their organizations.

During this period, Ralph Nader became the most visible champion for the theory of regulatory capture.[12] Unlike the economists and political scientists who developed the theory, Nader attached much more sinister motives to the behavior of regulators. One Nader report attributed regulatory failure to "influence peddling, incestuous job interchange with industry, [and] lack of appointment integrity."[13] As Nader argued, regulators recruited from regulated industries did not have the ability to represent the public interest in their deliberations even if they sold off all holdings in regulated companies before beginning their public duties.[14] They were predisposed to favor the policies of regulated industries because of their prior relationship. Even regulators who did not have backgrounds in regulated industries could not be trusted to act against the interests of powerful private interests. The best opportunities to cash in on their regulatory experience lay with regulated companies. Job opportunities would disappear if life were made difficult for regulated enterprises. The so-called revolving door problem became a major target for the regulatory reformers of the early 1970s.[15]

The Nader explanation seemed reasonable to the newspaper reporters and broadcast journalists, who received constant complaints from citizens about increases in electric, telephone and gas bills and auto insurance rates. Intense scrutiny of the nuclear power industry and growing public concern about the safety of nuclear power plants also helped to make the thesis of regulatory capture more plausible. Something had gone badly wrong with the regulatory process. The solution to the problem apparently involved placing a Chinese wall between regulators and regulated industries. Critics focused much of their criticism on the movement of individuals between regulated industries and regulatory agencies. Overnight, the revolving door became a national problem.[16]

The 1962 revision of the federal conflict-of-interest and bribery laws, as noted earlier, codified new restrictions on the lobbying activities of former executive branch officials. These restrictions established a new lifetime ban on officials' leaving federal agencies and immediately representing private clients in a federal proceeding if the former employee "had participated personally and substantially" in the matter during the employee's period of government service.[17] Most conflict-of-interest experts regarded the lifetime "switching sides" prohibition as a reasonable restriction on the employment options of former federal officials. Regulatory-capture advocates held very different views.

The 1962 postemployment lobbying restrictions did not stop quarterbacking by former officials. Quarterbacking involves the practice of former officials' giving a new employer behind the scenes advice on how to deal with the employee's former government agency. The 1962 law, in addition, did not prohibit former officials from working for clients on matters in which the former official did not have any involvement while working for the government. The Kennedy administration, in 1962, opposed broader revolving-door rules because it feared tighter restrictions would make it more difficult to recruit and retain essential managerial and technical personnel.

The Watergate scandal and the resignation of Richard Nixon gave revolving-door critics an opportunity to get congressional approval of much more sweeping new revolving-door restrictions. When Common Cause, in 1976, called for new revolving-door restrictions to deal with regulatory capture, Washington listened. When agencies "draw high percentages of their top policy makers" from regulated enterprises, stated a 1976 Common Cause report, these policy makers will certainly "inherit industry biases or accept industry's point of view on key policy issues."[18]

Running as a Washington outsider, Jimmy Carter endorsed the theory of regulatory capture during his 1976 presidential campaign. He urged passage of a law "to limit the movement of persons employed by federal regulatory agencies into heavily regulated industries."[19] The theory of regulatory capture fit well with Carter's strategy of portraying himself as a Washington outsider who would bring a new era of high ethical standards to Washington. In less than six years, the theory of regulatory capture went from being a counterculture explanation for pro-business regulatory policies to a theory receiving a warm endorsement from the top candidate of one of the nation's two major political parties.

When Congress passed the Ethics in Government Act of 1978, it included new revolving-door restrictions. The most important provision was a new one-year cooling-off period for former high-level executive branch officials similar to the one proposed by the Douglas subcommittee back in 1951. The new one-year cooling-off period applied to employees at grade level GS-17 and above and prohibited them from contacting their former employers on behalf of private clients.[20] It prohibited certain former high-level federal officials from lobbying their former agencies on any matter for one year after leaving the government.[21]

Throughout the 1970s, supporters of revolving-door restrictions crusaded for tighter restrictions to help return control of regulatory agencies to individuals willing to exercise regulatory power in the public interest. Few imagined that their intense criticism of regulatory agencies would help to build support for the deregulation of regulation.[22] Instead of merely changing the regulators, why not eliminate regulatory agencies entirely? Airline, trucking and finance deregulation followed. Indeed, the Whitewater scandal of the 1990s had its origins in the banking deregulation episode of the 1980s.

THE REIGN OF REGULATORY REACTIONARIES

The 1980 election of Ronald Reagan provided modern progressives with a whole new set of challenges. Reagan "came to Washington with a firm commitment to regulatory reform and relief."[23] To the Reagan White House, regulatory reform meant pushing forward with deregulation and getting the remaining government regulators off the backs of American business and industry. To implement this agenda, President Reagan appointed Vice President George Bush to chair a Presidential Task Force on Regulatory Relief. Shortly thereafter, Reagan issued Executive Order 12291, which required agencies to conduct a cost-benefit analysis with respect to any proposed rule and vastly increased the power of the Office of Management and Budget (OMB) to review regulations proposed by federal agencies and departments.[24]

Reagan critics viewed these actions as an effort by the White House to destroy the independence of the regulatory process. OMB and the White House also came under intense criticism for allowing representatives of business and industry to make their case against specific government regulations behind closed doors.[25] Congressional critics and pro-regulation interest groups used controversies involving EPA's Anne Gorsuch, Rita Lavelle, and Secretary of the Interior James Watt, during Reagan's first term, to derail the Reagan regulatory agenda. Much like the Dixon-Yates controversy of the 1950s, conflict-of-interest allegations proved crucial in weakening support for a major presidential policy initiative.[26]

In his 1984 book *Capital Corruption*, sociologist Amitai Etzioni wrote, "The country is overdue for another Progressive Era, an age when encompassing and thorough reforms will reverse plutocratic tendencies, curb interest groups, and overcome PACs."[27] Published in the middle of the Reagan revolution, Etzioni's book constituted a call to arms for citizens to demand that government protect the public from powerful special interests. "Once people inform themselves and evolve group consensus," stated Etzioni, "the time is ripe to alert others; to form more encompassing circles, associations, and organizations; to promote the needed reforms and institutional changes. Soon coalitions of such reforming groups, backed by an alerted public, will be able to overcome the resistance of special interests and open the way to the much overdue corrections."[28]

The country did not join Etzioni's call for a new progressive revolution. On the other hand, it also resisted conservative calls for accelerated deregulation of American business and industry. America apparently wanted clean air, water and safe drugs without any regulatory burden. The majority of Americans demonstrated scant interest in the ideological battle between sharply different views of the regulatory process.

George Bush, like Ronald Reagan before him, established as a high priority the reduction of the regulatory burden on American business and industry. To coordinate his regulatory reform initiatives, Bush established the President's Council on Competitiveness and appointed Vice-President Dan Quayle to chair it.[29] The council took an active role in attempting to block federal regulations that would make it more costly for small businesses to operate. To the anger of progressives, the council publicly supported weakening antitrust laws, limiting the tort liability of American business, narrowing the definition of wetlands and relaxing regulation of bioengineering firms.[30]

Congressional and interest groups, critics of the activities of the council, in late 1991 challenged the impartiality of the council's director, Allan Hubbard, on conflict-of-interest grounds. Democrat Henry Waxman reported that Hubbard owned stock in chemical and utility companies that would benefit him personally if Congress adopted the council's recommendations on amendments to the Clean Air Act.[31] Waxman used the disclosure to raise doubts in the public mind regarding the motivation behind the regulatory reform proposals of the Competitiveness Council.[32] Even though White House lawyers ruled that Hubbard had done nothing wrong, he agreed to place his assets in a blind trust and to give "1000 shares of PSI Resources, Inc., a utility holding company, to charity."[33]

A MANDATE FOR CHANGE

Throughout the 1992 presidential campaign, Bill Clinton and Ross Perot attacked the power of the special interests in Washington. Like Ronald Reagan and Jimmy Carter, they ran as outside-the-beltway reformers who understood the pain experienced by people across the country. Clinton promised to create millions of new jobs and provide affordable health care to every American family. Perot promised to stop the "sucking sound" made by jobs going overseas as a result of what he perceived as the "unfair trade practices conducted by our trading partners around the world."[34]

New progressives greeted the Clinton victory with wild enthusiasm. A progressive president and a Democratic Congress would take the handcuffs off federal regulators. Special interests would no longer have preferential access to regulatory decision makers. But the Clinton victory sent shivers down the spines of both small and big businesses alike: now nothing stood in the way of Clinton and his friends from significantly increasing the regulatory burden on the more productive segments of the American economy.

Early Clinton actions provided strong evidence that Clinton did not intend to be an enemy of government regulation.[35] To the contrary, high budget deficits and strong public resistance to new taxes meant that Congress had no ability to appropriate federal funds or grant tax relief to help defray the cost of federal regulation. Government regulation allowed the White House to pass the cost of government regulation on to the private sector or to other levels of government.[36]

To fulfill a campaign promise to take steps to check the power of special interests on the regulatory process, on September 30, 1993, the White House issued an executive order sharply limiting the role of the OMB in federal rule making. The White House designed the order to stop special interests from secretly lobbying the OMB to delay or stop agency regulations.[37] The White House clearly wished to distance itself from the regulatory practices of the Reagan and Bush administrations and directed "that communications of the White House and OMB staff with outside interests concerning regulations be made in writing and placed in a public file."[38]

An Opportunity Lost

Historians and political scientists will debate for decades the question of why the Clinton White House believed it could obtain congressional approval of its health-care reform package. The proposal called for extensive use of government regulation to slow the growth of national health-care costs and to establish regional health cooperatives.[39] Its opponents spent hundreds of millions of dollars to defeat the proposal, convincing the American people that the Clinton plan would place government bureaucrats in charge of the nation's health-care system.[40] In this case at least, the White House badly misjudged the nation's tolerance for more government regulation.

NEWT'S REVOLUTION

When the Republican Party took control of both the House and Senate after the 1994 midterm congressional elections, regulatory reform became a top legislative priority.[41] The Republicans' "Contract With America" included a provision imposing a ceiling on the cost of federal regulations.[42] Legislation submitted by Republicans in the House required all regulatory agencies to perform complex cost-benefit analyses before issuing any new rules. But like the Clinton administration with its health-care reform proposal, conservative Republicans greatly overestimated public support for their regulatory reform initiatives. By early 1995, defenders of aggressive federal regulation had regained their footing and began an all-out lobbying campaign to prevent passage of the conservative reforms.

Progressive-leaning newspapers across the country joined in the criticism of these proposals. A February 12, 1995, *New York Times* editorial warned the nation that Newt Gingrich's plan for regulatory reform would, if it became law, destroy twenty-five years of progress in cleaning up the environment.[43] The Clinton White House, to deal with the impact of federal regulations on small business, developed its own regulatory reform proposals.[44] Clinton also unleashed a campaign accusing House Republicans of allowing corporate lobbyists to write the regulatory reform legislation.[45] It was alleged that House Republicans had allowed powerful special interests to capture the legislative process. Citizens for Sensible Safeguards, a coalition of 203 interest groups, in May 1995 joined President Clinton in his attack against the Republican regulatory reform proposals and claimed that most of the regulatory horror stories used by Republicans simply never took place.[46] These opponents argued that Republican regulatory proposals threatened the health and safety of millions of Americans.[47]

The campaign had its desired results. Despite the fact that the House passed the regulatory reform contained in the Contract with America, Senate majority leader Bob Dole proved unable to obtain the sixty votes necessary to stop a Democratic filibuster of the regulatory reform bill in the Senate.[48] By the end of 1995, a growing number of moderate Republicans expressed strong reservations regarding the impact of regulatory reform on the environment.[49] Many had second thoughts about going into the fall 1996 elections tagged as members of the party wishing to allow big business to destroy the environment. In early March 1996, opposition from moderate House Republicans forced the House leadership to pull regulatory reform legislation off the floor.[50] Congressman Sherwood Boehert, a Republican from rural upstate New York, told the press: "[we] don't want to put our members out there one more time taking a vote that the environmental extremists can twist and turn into campaign ads."[51]

REGULATORY VISIONS

Through much of the twentieth century, new progressives and movement conservatives have fought over the role of regulatory agencies in American society. With the emergence of the regulatory-capture theory of the 1960s and 1970s, regulatory reform became an urgent public integrity problem. Robotic servants of regulated industries lurked behind the doors of every regulatory agency. At the other end of the political spectrum, movement conservatives cast federal regulators as heartless bureaucrats intent upon enforcing rules, even if enforcement resulted in putting millions of Americans out of work. The fierce contest over national regulatory policy had escalated the level of stridency in the public integrity war.

NOTES

1. *Roe* v. *Wade*, 410 U.S. 113 (1973).
2. Richard C. Leone, "Public Interest Advocacy and the Regulatory Process," *Annals of the American Academy of Political and Social Science* 400 (March 1972): 46.
3. *Ethical Standards in American Public Life* (Philadelphia: *Annals of The American Academy of Political and Social Science*, 1952).
4. Paul H. Douglas, "Improvement of Ethical Standards in the Federal Government: Problems and Prospects," *Ethical Standards in American Public Life* (Philadelphia: *Annals of the American Academy of Political and Social Science*, 1952).
5. Ibid., p. 149.
6. Ibid., pp. 149–50.
7. Ibid., p. 150.
8. Robert Roberts, "Regulatory Bias and Conflict of Interest Regulation." In *Handbook of Regulation and Administrative Law*, eds. David H. Rosenbloom and Richard D. Schwartz (New York: Marcel Dekker, 1994), p. 489.
9. Ibid.
10. Marc Allen Eisner, "Economic Regulatory Policies: Regulation and Deregulation in Historical Context." In *Handbook of Regulation and Administrative Law*, eds. David H. Rosenbloom and Richard D. Schwartz (New York: Marcel Dekker, 1994), pp. 100–103.
11. Ibid., p. 101.
12. See Mark Green, ed. *The Monopoly Makers: Ralph Nader's Study Group Report on Regulation and Competition* (New York: Grossman, 1973); Louis M. Kohlmeier, Jr., *The Regulators: Watchdog Agencies and the Public Interest* (New York: Harper and Row, 1969).
13. Ibid., p. 102, cited in Mark J. Green, "Uncle Sam the Monopoly Man." In *The Monopoly Makers: Ralph Nader's Study Group Report on Regulation and Competition*, ed. Mark J. Green (New York: Grossman, 1973), p. 27.
14. Professor Calvin MacKenzie of Bates College in Maine coined the phrase. See G. Calvin MacKenzie, *The Politics of Presidential Appointment* (New York: Free Press, 1980).
15. William J. Lanoutee, "The Revolving Door—It's Tricky to Stop It," *National Journal* 9 (November 1977): 1796–803.
16. James D. Carroll and Robert N. Roberts, "If Men Were Angels: Assessing the Ethics in Government Act of 1978," *Policy Studies* 17 (Winter 1988-89): 440–41.
17. Robert Roberts, *White House Ethics* (Westport, CT: Greenwood Press, 1988), p. 101.
18. Ibid., p. 141, citing Common Cause, *Serving Two Masters: A Common Cause Study of Conflicts of Interest in the Executive Branch* (Washington, DC: Common Cause, October 1976), p. 1.
19. Ibid. p. 147. See also Common Cause, *Employment Backgrounds of ERDA and NRC officials* (Washington, DC: Common Cause, 1976).
20. Wendy L. Gerlach, "Amendment of the Post-Employment Laws," *Arizona Law Review* 33 (1991): 407.

21. Roberts, *Ethics*, p. 162.

22. Paul Stephen Dempsey, "Deregulation and Reregulation: Policy, Politics, and Economics." In *Handbook of Regulation and Administrative Law,* eds. David H. Rosenbloom and Richard D. Schwartz (New York: Marcel Dekker, 1994): 178–79.

23. Eisner, p. 105.

24. Ibid., p. 106.

25. Ibid., p. 107.

26. Ibid.

27. Amitai Etzioni, *Capital Corruption: The New Attack on American Democracy* (New York: Harcourt Brace Jovanovich, 1984), p. 221.

28. Ibid., p. 284.

29. Richard Fly, "Introducing Dan Quayle, Competitiveness Czar," *Business Week,* February 27, 1989, p. 37.

30. Michael Duffy, "Need Friends in High Places," *Time,* November 4, 1991.

31. Paul Magnusson, "Quayle's Pet Project Is Looking More like a Liability," *Business Week,* December 23, 1991, p. 39.

32. "Quayle Council Repels Attack on Role of Regulatory Agencies," *Chemical Marketing Reporter,* December 16, 1991, p. 22.

33. Magnusson, p. 39.

34. John Dillon, "Perot Puts Spotlight on Free-Trade Issue," *Christian Science Monitor,* July 3, 1992, p. 1.

35. Kenneth T. Walsh, "Regulation Returns," *U.S. News & World Report,* December 28, 1992, p. 52.

36. Bob Davis and Bruce Ingersoll, "Clinton's Team Moves to Extend Regulation to a Variety of Industries," *Wall Street Journal,* April 13, 1993, p. A1.

37. Stephen Barr, "White House Shifts Role in Rule-Making." *Washington Post,* October 1, 1993, p. A1, 22.

38. Ibid.

39. *The President's Health Security Plan: The Clinton Blueprint* (New York: Random House, 1993).

40. For example, see Barry Asmus, *ClintonCare: Putting Government in Charge of Your Health* (Phoenix, AZ: Ameri Press, 1994).

41. Stan Carey Crock, "A GOP Jihad against Red Tape," *Business Week,* November 28, 1994, p. 48–49.

42. John H. Cushman, Jr. "Republicans Plan Sweeping Barriers to New U.S. Rules," *New York Times,* December 25, 1994, p. A1. Also see Linda Grant, "Shutting Down the Regulatory Machine," *U.S. News & World Report,* February 13, 1995, p. 70.

43. Editorial, "The Next Environmental Threat," *New York Times,* February 12, 1995, p. A14.

44. Bill Clinton, remarks on regulatory reform in Arlington, Virginia, *Weekly Compilation of Presidential Documents* 31 (March 20, 1995): 426.

45. "Clinton Raps Lobbies' Role in Regulatory Legislation," *Wall Street Journal,* April 24, 1995, p. B9.

46. Guy Gugliotta, "Are the Rules Awry, or Rhetoric just Wry?," *Washington Post,* May 16, 1995, p. A15.

47. "Opponents Say Proposed Regulatory Reforms Would Threaten Health & Safety," *Nation's Health* 25 (April, 1995): 1.

48. "Victory in Defeat," *Wall Street Journal*, July 24, 1995, p. A12.

49. Edmund L. Andrews, "GOP Falters on Pro-Business Laws," *New York Times*, December 23, 1995, p. A39.

50. N.Y. Times News Service, "House GOP Leaders Delay Deregulation Debate," *Harrisonburg Daily News Record*, March 6, 1996, p. 3.

51. Ibid.

Chapter 7

Return of the Robber Barons

One month after his landslide victory, President-elect Eisenhower nominated Charles E. Wilson, president of General Motors, as secretary of defense. Wilson joined a number of other prominent businessmen nominated to Eisenhower's cabinet.[1] Shortly thereafter, Wilson informed the Senate Armed Services Committee that he owned 39,470 shares of General Motors stock.[2]

Since the late 1940s, the Senate Armed Services Committee had required nominees to high-level Defense Department positions to sell all their stock worth more than $10,000 in defense-related companies. However, federal law did not require federal officials to sell any financial holdings to comply with conflict-of-interest rules. Despite the rule, Wilson informed the committee that he did not plan to sell the stock, but that he would disqualify himself from any decision involving General Motors. Wilson's offer did not sit well with some members of the committee. However, if Wilson sold the stock, he would have to pay substantial taxes on the gain that had occurred in the value of the stock since the time of purchase.

During confirmation hearings, a senator asked Wilson what he would do if he had to make a decision adversely affecting the interests of General Motors. Wilson "achieved a kind of immortality by his public statement that 'what's good for our country is good for General Motors, and vice versa.' "[3] Wilson's statement caused a national uproar. Critics used the statement to support their contention that big business felt it could get anything it wanted from Eisenhower's Republican administration. The

White House and Wilson had no choice but to back down: Wilson agreed to sell his shares of General Motors stock.

Even though Dwight Eisenhower entered the presidency with an electoral landslide, his administration found that Washington did not welcome his business-community nominees with open arms. Business executives who entered the federal government faced a wide range of problems. In the first place, public-sector compensation made government service financially unattractive. Moreover, conflict-of-interest rules often forced presidential nominees and appointees to adjust their financial affairs. Although general conflict-of-interest rules did not require federal officers and employees to sell off financial holdings,[4] many appointees simply sold financial holdings to avoid any controversy. If the sale resulted in any capital gains, the appointee or nominee was required to pay the associated taxes.

THE FOXES IN THE CHICKEN COOP

Throughout most of American history, a debate has raged over the relationship between government and business or industry. Anti-Federalists had attacked the close ties between Federalists and powerful financial interests in the large eastern cities. The years following the Civil War saw big business flex its strengthened muscle across the land. "Railroads bought and sold state legislatures; mining companies kept labor in its place; timber and cattle overlords despoiled the public domain," wrote historians Morison and Commager.[5] Business and politics entered into a corrupt alliance. Yet a major political movement motivated to challenge the power of big business did not take root until the 1880s, when the populist movement developed over the frustration of farmers with their treatment by the railroads.[6]

From the populist movement of the 1890s, the progressive movement of the first two decades of the twentieth century and the New and Fair Deals of the respective postwar decades, suspicion germinated over the activities of individuals with business backgrounds. New antitrust laws enacted during the progressive era led to the breakup of a number of industrial monopolies.

Yet the end of the First World War ushered in a new era of respect for business executives in national politics. Republican presidents worked closely with the leaders of business and industry. And American business and industry entered into an unprecedented partnership.[7] Republican presidents adopted pro-business policies that included supporting high protective tariffs to protect American business from foreign competition. "The new ideal, as elaborated during that twelve years, was to foster economic self-government and economic nationalism."[8]

But the Great Depression and the failure of Herbert Hoover's policies for reviving the nation's economy contributed to the 1932 election of

Franklin Delano Roosevelt. More important, the Great Depression severely damaged the reputation of big business. New Deal Democrats blamed greedy capitalists for the unregulated speculation that preceded the Depression. The growing labor movement attacked big business for violently resisting union efforts to organize its workers.

The 1952 election victory of Dwight Eisenhower gave business another chance to prove to the country that it deserved a seat at the table. "It cannot be said, of course, that past suspicions and past antagonisms toward business are entirely dormant," wrote University of Illinois Professor of Economics Howard Bowen in 1952. "The memories of past abuses and of the Great Depression have been engraved indelibly upon the mind of the American public."[9]

Fear that business executives in government would secretly use their public positions to further private interests played a major role in building support for stronger ethics rules. Mandatory disclosure of assets, income and dealings in securities and commodities, argued Senator Paul Douglas in 1952, "will tend to deter individuals from accepting any income, holding any assets, or making any transactions which they believe are questionable."[10] Prohibiting officials from "divulging valuable commercial or economic information of a confidential nature" or "discussing future employment outside the government with a person or organization with which there is pending official business" would also help to deter misuse of public positions for private gain.[11]

Progressives also struggled to find a way to prevent individuals from cashing in on prior government service. "There can be no doubt that public service can be and is a springboard to private profit," wrote Carl W. McCardle, chief of the Washington Bureau of the Philadelphia Bulletin in 1952, "and one that can carry a man into lush, green fields of pay dirt."[12] Cashing in typically meant going to work for private-sector organizations or becoming a lobbyist.[13]

Cleaning Up the Mess in Washington

Many Republican business executives who entered the federal government during the 1950s did not understand why so much suspicion continued to exist regarding their participation in government. Many saw government as terribly inefficient. Government had much to learn from business. Many of these individuals viewed the preoccupation with government ethics as a thinly veiled attempt by defenders of big government to make it impossible for them to bring the efficiencies of business to Washington. As the economic recovery of the 1950s continued, calls increased to bring more level-headed business executives into government.

A series of studies completed during the 1950s found that the combination of low pay and confusing ethics rules made it much more difficult to recruit business executives for government positions.[14] Federal agencies, including the Department of Defense, blamed low pay and ethics rules for problems they faced in recruiting and keeping scientific and technical personnel. The Kennedy White House, as noted, began its ethics reform program in large measure to deal with these problems. The space race and the cold war made it clear that the country could no longer afford to fight the ghosts of the New Deal.

The Kennedy ethics initiatives, and changes in federal law made to ease the burden of ethics laws on business executives and technical and scientific personnel during the early 1960s, did not stop critics from maintaining that ethics rules deprived the country of badly needed expertise. "There is no satisfactory way of measuring just how much of a deterrent to federal recruitment is generated by the present system of conflict of interest restraints," wrote Bayless Manning in 1964.[15]

ETHICAL INOCULATIONS

Political ideology had persuaded both the Kennedy and Johnson White Houses that the benefits of tighter ethics regulation outweighed any cost in terms of restrictions on recruitment. Both presidents saw a larger role for the federal government. Neither Kennedy nor Johnson relied heavily on the business community for individuals to manage the growing number of federal programs.[16]

By the mid-1960s, the panic over ethics barriers to recruitment subsided. Public administration programs provided a growing government with a steady stream of qualified managers. Better compensation packages helped to recruit a new generation of civic-minded men and women to work at all levels of government. Because vast differences existed between the cultures of business and government organizations, supporters of a professional civil service argued that government really did not need to recruit large number of political appointees to effectively run public programs.

Besides lacking experience in the management of public programs, many private executives, it was argued, experienced difficulty adjusting to public-sector ethics rules. Practices common in the private sector turned out to be totally unacceptable in the public sector. Few corporate executives would have agreed with the admonition of Senator Paul Douglas that "what starts out apparently as pure friendship concludes by being a purchase."[17] The wining and dining of potential customers constituted good business in the private sector. Providing potential customers tickets to a Broadway play or to a sporting event was good corporate hospitality.

Until the Second World War, the White House spent little time checking the backgrounds and reviewing the financial affairs of presidential nominees and appointees. National security concerns, not ethics issues, had led President Eisenhower to institute FBI background checks on presidential nominees. But by the 1960s, tighter financial conflict-of-interest rules and the fear of conflict-of-interest scandals led to much closer scrutiny of the financial affairs of private-sector nominees and appointees.

The new self-dealing prohibition, Section 208 of Title 18 of the United States Code, proved particularly troublesome.[18] The statute treated as a financial interest of the employee the financial interests of the employee's spouse, minor children, business partners, and any organizations in which the employee served as an officer.[19] It prohibited executive branch officials and employees from taking action with respect to any matter that might affect the value of one of their financial interests.

Faced with the scope of this law, future presidents had no choice but to begin screening the financial affairs of high-level officials. President Johnson, as noted, in 1965 began a confidential financial reporting system. In the aftermath of Watergate, political commentators, Congress and President Carter saw public financial disclosure as a way to restore public confidence in government. Public financial disclosure, however, had the greatest impact on individuals with substantial wealth entering government.

President Kennedy did succeed in persuading Congress to relax certain public ethics restrictions viewed as a deterrent to executive recruitment. The 1917 criminal supplementation of salary ban made it illegal for private employers to supplement the salaries of employees who accepted federal government assignments. The 1962 revision of federal bribery and conflict-of-interest laws amended the salary supplementation ban to permit those entering federal service to continue to "participate in bona fide pension or other welfare plans maintained by former employers."[20]

Sharp differences of opinions over the appropriate role of business executives in government during the 1950s and 1960s explain why presidents and Congress supported both a tightening and a relaxing of ethics rules. Both the Kennedy and Johnson administrations attempted to chart a pragmatic middle-of-the-road course. But events during the 1970s led to renewed apprehension over the impartiality of business executives who served in policy-making positions in government.

RESTORING CORPORATE RESPONSIBILITY

The 1970s did little to restore the image of business executives and corporate America. Environmental, public-interest and consumer groups blamed American business for everything from dirty air to dangerous products and long gasoline lines. Big business and other special interests continued to pour more and more money into political campaigns to protect their privileged positions.[21] The economic boom of the 1950s and 1960s gave way to the economic stagnation of the 1970s.

In the early 1970s, Congress sought to control the flow of private-interest money into federal elections by prohibiting direct contributions to political campaigns by corporations, labor unions, "entities in certain regulated in-dustries—for example, banks, savings and loans" and other private organ-izations.[22] Federal law, however, did permit special interests to funnel money through political action committees (PACs) to campaigns and po-litical parties. The cost of running for office continued to spiral out of control.

Besides destroying the Nixon presidency, disclosures that large corpo-rations illegally funneled millions of dollars into the 1972 Nixon reelection campaign gave big business another black eye.[23] Public financing of elec-tions became the latest solution for restoring public trust in government. Indeed, public financing of presidential campaigns became the feature of the 1974 amendments to the Federal Election Act of 1971.

A congressional investigation in 1975 concluded that the Executive In-terchange Program had spent little time checking the backgrounds of loan executives before approving their assignments to federal agencies and de-partments.[24] The Ford White House withdrew the nomination of Andrew Gibson as head of the Federal Energy Administration after a storm of con-troversy erupted over a *New York Times* report that Gibson had a ten-year separation agreement with his former employer, Interstate Oil Transport Company of Philadelphia. The agreement paid Gibson $1 million over a ten-year period.[25] Critics argued that the agreement might violate the fed-eral salary supplementation prohibition.[26]

In 1976, a much more serious controversy erupted with the disclosure that a number of major defense contractors routinely provided civilian and military Pentagon officials free entertainment and lodging at corporate-owned facilities. The disclosures reinforced widely held perceptions that contractors did anything in their power to curry favor with government officials who played a role in making multibillion dollar procurement de-cisions.[27]

Watergate and strong pressure from new progressives led the Carter tran-sition team and White House to accept the claim that a crisis existed in public service ethics that required drastic action.[28] New ethics guidelines issued by the Carter White House required nominees to provide a detailed accounting of their finances. The guidelines also required covered officials, including cabinet officers, to sell off financial assets if continued possession of assets required frequent disqualification from matters within the scope of their official responsibility.[29] Carter, finally, made appointees agree not to lobby their former agencies for two years after leaving the government.

The Ethics in Government Act of 1978 added to the existing ethics rules and public financial disclosure requirements new rules governing the es-tablishment of blind trusts and new revolving-door restrictions.[30] The Ethics Act placed a 15 percent earned income limitation on all presiden-tial nominees. This restriction effectively prevented nominees from hold-ing a second job to supplement their public salaries. The Carter ethics reform initiatives and the Ethics Act did little to make individuals with business backgrounds `feel welcome in the federal government.[31]

The Burt Lance affair, during the Carter administration, revealed the limits of any ethics clearance program and the scrutiny individuals with business backgrounds had to face when accepting high positions in government. Jimmy Carter, after his 1976 election victory, appointed old Georgia friend Burt Lance to head the Office of Management and Budget (OMB).[32] Because OMB exercised such an important role in the budgetary and regulatory processes, Lance agreed to place his National Bank of Georgia stock in a blind trust. The blind trust agreement required his trustee to sell the stock by the end of 1977.[33] Lance's problems began when the value of his bank stock dropped sharply during the first half of 1977. If the trustee of his blind trust had proceeded with the sale, Lance would have suffered huge financial losses. President Carter formally asked the Senate Committee on Governmental Affairs to allow modification of the provisions of Lance's blind trust to permit the trustee to hold on the stock for a longer period of time.[34] Subsequent hearings brought to the surface numerous allegations regarding Lance's banking and personal finances, and the ensuing controversy forced Lance to resign his post on September 21, 1977.[35] Throughout the controversy, Jimmy Carter stood behind his close friend. The scandal helped to take the glow off of the squeaky clean image of the Carter administration.

A FRIEND IN THE WHITE HOUSE

The extent of Ronald Reagan's 1980 election victory caught national political experts entirely off-guard. Most had given Ronald Reagan the edge, but they did not anticipate either his winning almost every state or the Republican Party's taking control of the Senate. Intent upon dismantling the administrative state, Reagan sent out a call for business executives to help him with his revolution. The Reagan transition, however, greatly underestimated how complex ethics clearance had become over the years since Watergate forced Richard Nixon's resignation.

Pendleton James, who ran the White House personnel operation from 1981 through 1983, in 1988 looked back at the experience of the Reagan transition with conflict-of-interest clearances. "One of the things that takes a lot of the time in the transition is filling out the financial disclosure forms," commented James. "They are so confusing and intimidating."[36] Besides the problems of completing financial disclosure statements, James stressed the time-consuming process of conducting FBI background checks on some 600 presidential nominee appointments and many of the 2,000 other presidential appointments to various boards and commissions.[37] Ronald Reagan's transition team found the recruitment of experienced business executives much more difficult than anticipated.[38] Presidential transition scholar G. Calvin MacKenzie, in 1988, completed a much more objective assessment of the impact of the Ethics Act upon the presidential recruitment process:

There can be no doubt, in logic or in fact, that the Ethics in Government Act has impeded the recruitment of presidential appointees, has added a new disincentive to public service. Certainly there is nothing about the requirements imposed by the act that would make public service more desirable. It invades privacy, it restricts income and investment flexibility, and it constrains employment options after government service is concluded. None of these are attractions to public service.[29]

A mid-1980s National Academy of Public Administration survey of presidential appointees revealed that many Reagan appointees were forced to take corrective action to resolve ethics problems. Remedies included the creation of blind trusts, the sale of stocks or other assets, resignation from positions in corporations or other organizations and agreements to disqualify themselves from participating in matters in which they or a family member had a financial interest.[40] Other reports issued during the mid-1980s criticized the impact of public ethics rules on the recruitment of presidential appointees and nominees.[41] Professor MacKenzie, summing up the realities of modern ethics management, wrote: "the law is the law. Regrettably, but inevitably, some people will have to pay if they want to play."[42] Throughout much of the 1980s, articles continued to appear in popular publications reporting on the problems faced by business executives who accepted positions in government.[43] Other authors provided business executives expert advice on what to expect if they accepted positions in Washington.[44]

The 1988 election of George Bush as president and a series of congressional ethics scandals brightened the outlook for the enactment of measures designed to reduce the burden of ethics rules on presidential appointees and nominees. When enacting the Ethics Reform Act of 1989, Congress included a number of key provisions designed to ease the transition of presidential nominees and appointees from the private to the public sector.

VILLAINS OR VICTIMS?

By the end of the Reagan administration, two views of the role of businessmen in the Reagan administration emerged. One view focused on the ethical conduct of Reagan appointees with business backgrounds. Looking back at the Reagan era in 1995, Howard Kurtz of the *Washington Post* wrote:

Reagan's avowed philosophy was to get government off the backs of business. Wealth was celebrated. Many of Reagan's regulators were drawn from the industries they were expected to oversee. In short, much of the administration seemed to be staffed by businessmen trying to cash in on government service or do favors for their corporate pals.[45]

Other commentators, however, saw post-Watergate Washington as increasingly hostile to individuals with successful private-sector backgrounds. Ideology, not the lack of personal integrity, explained the hostility toward business executives in government. New progressives simply did not trust individuals with business backgrounds to advocate policies against their own interests or against the interests of their business associates outside the government.

The growth of the administrative state vested vast power in the hands of unelected public officials. Like appointments to the Supreme Court, public policy experts understood that unelected public officials had acquired the ability to implement major shifts in administrative policy without receiving legislative approval. The battle over who occupies key policy-making positions simply constitutes another front of the public integrity war.

NOTES

1. Samuel Eliot Morison and Henry Steele Commager, *The Growth of the American Republic*, 2 vols. (New York: Oxford University Press, 1962), p. 2:954.

2. Robert Roberts, *White House Ethics* (Westport, CT: Greenwood Press, 1988), p. 59.

3. Morison and Commager, p. 2:954.

4. Specific statutes prohibited employees and officials working for certain federal organizations from owning certain types of financial instruments.

5. Morison and Commager, p. 2:163.

6. Ibid., p. 2:213.

7. *Business-government Cooperation 1917–1932: The Rise of Corporalist Policies* (New York: Garland, 1994, 1973) contains a collection of articles regarding the role of business in national politics.

8. Morison and Commager, p. 2:633.

9. Howard R. Bowen, "How Public Spirited Is American Business?" *Annals of the American Academy of Political and Social Science* 280 (March 1952): 85.

10. Paul Douglas, "Improvement of Ethical Standards in Federal Government," *Annals of the American Academy of Political and Social Science* 280 (March 1952): 156–57.

11. Ibid.

12. Carl W. McCardle, "The Public Service as a Springboard for Private Profit," *Annals of the Academy of Political and Social Science* 280 (March 1952): 77.

13. Ibid., pp. 80–81.

14. Roberts, *Ethics*, pp. 66–68.

15. Bayless Manning, "The Purity Potlatch: An Essay on Conflict of Interests, American Government, and Moral Escalation." *Federal Bar Journal* 24 (Summer 1964): 243–49.

16. For the names of individuals with business backgrounds nominated for high-level positions in the Kennedy and Johnson administrations, see Philip H. Burch, Jr., *Elites in American History: The New Deal to the Carter Administration* (New York: Holmes & Meier, 1990); for Kennedy, see pp. 451–62; for Johnson, see pp. 463–77.

17. Paul Douglas, *Ethics in Government* (Cambridge, MA: Harvard University Press, 1952), p. 48.

18. Robert N. Roberts, *Report to the Administrative Conference of the United States, A Federal Guide to Federal Ethics Laws for Presidential Appointees.* In *Sourcebook on Governmental Ethics for Presidential Appointees* (Washington, DC: Office of the Chairman, Administrative Conference of the United States, December 1988), pp. 18–21.

19. Roswell B. Perkins, "The Federal Conflict of Interest Law," *Harvard Law Review* 76 (April 1963): 1132.

20. Ibid., p. 2.

21. For a discussion of early 1970s regulation of corporate contributions to political campaigns, see William French Smith, *Corporate Political Contributions: The Law and the Practice* (Washington, DC: National Association of Manufacturers, 1973).

22. Robert F. Sittig, "Campaign Reform: Interest Groups, Parties, and Candidates," *Annals of the American Academy of Political and Social Science* 537 (January 1995): 86.

23. See Lester A. Sobel, *Money & Politics: Contributions, Campaign Abuses and the Law* (New York: Facts on File, 1974).

24. U.S. House, Committee on Small Business, Subcommittee on Energy and Environment, *Conflict of Interest Problems within the Presidential Executive Interchange Program*: Hearing before Subcommittee, 94th Cong., 1st Sess., December 3, 5, 1975.

25. Roberts, *Ethics*, p. 139.

26. Ibid., p. 139.

27. U.S. Congress, Joint Committee on Defense Production and the Department of Defense, *Industry Relations: Conflict of Interest and Standards of Conduct*, Hearing, 94th Cong., 2d Sess., February 2 and 3, 1976 (Washington: U.S. Government Printing Office, 1976).

28. Bruce Adams and Kathryn Kavanagh-Baran, *Promise and Performance: Carter Builds a New Administration* (Lexington, MA: Lexington Books 1979), p. 88.

29. Ibid., p. 89.

30. "Revolving Door Proposal Strikes a Nerve," *Broadcasting* 20 (February 1978): 44.

31. G. Calvin MacKenzie, *Presidential Transitions and the Ethics in Government Act of 1978.* Issues and opinion paper prepared for the Working Conference on Ethics in Government (Washington, DC: Administrative Conference of the United States, March 1988), pp. 6–13. In *Sourcebook on Governmental Ethics for Presidential Appointees* (Washington, DC: Office of the Chairman, Administrative Conference of the United States, December 1988).

32. Adams and Kavanagh-Baran, p. 92.

33. Ibid.

34. Ibid.

35. Ibid.

36. Administrative Conference of the United States, *Ethics in Government: Proceedings of a Working Conference* (Washington, DC: The Conference, 1988), p. 9.

37. Ibid.

38. "Reagan's headhunting woes," *Nation's Business* 69 (August 1981): 28–29.

39. MacKenzie, *Presidential Transitions*, p. 10.

40. Ibid., p. 14.

41. Presidential Appointee Project, National Academy of Public Administration, *Leadership in Jeopardy: The Fraying of the Presidential Appointments System* (Washington, DC: 1985); Marshall J. Breger, "Can Corporate masters afford to become public servants?" *Business and Society Review* 71 (Fall 1989): 42–46; National Commission on the Public Service, *Committing to excellence: recruiting and retaining a quality public service* (Washington, DC: National Commission on the Public Service, 1989); Twentieth Century Fund, *Obstacle Course: The Report of the Twentieth Century Fund Task Force on the Presidential Appointment Process* (New York: Twentieth Century Fund, 1996).

42. MacKenzie, *Presidential Transitions*, p. 15.

43. See Robert H. Norton, "Who Wants to Work in Washington," *Fortune* 120 (August 14, 1989): 77–80; Breger, pp. 42–46.

44. See Lee Fritschler, *How Washington Works: The Executive's Guide to Government* (New York: Harper Business, 1987).

45. Howard Kurtz, "The Big Sleazy: Is Clinton's Low-Rent as Reagan's?" *Washington Post*, March 26, 1995, pp. C1–2.

Chapter 8

The Public Integrity Shock Troops

On June 18, 1996, the Senate Whitewater committee released the findings of its two-year investigation. "Tuesday was basically a day of competing political briefs, representing a form of party proxy campaign warfare in a Presidential election year," commented a *New York Times* editorial.[1] Majority committee Republicans and minority committee Democrats reached totally different conclusions with respect to whether Hillary Rodham Clinton and other administration officials had engaged in any improper conduct. Recognizing the fact that partisan warfare had tainted the Whitewater findings, the *New York Times* stressed that Whitewater independent counsel Kenneth Starr "must eventually report to a court and the public on whether the Clintons and their allies have engaged in illegality or regrettable but noncriminal lapses of judgment and duty."[2] The independent counsel, in less than two decades, had evolved into a position of untold power.

Throughout American history, political ethics scandals have come and gone.[3] And throughout this period, ethics investigations have attempted to determine the guilt or innocence of those implicated.[4] Since Watergate, however, the growth of a vast and powerful public integrity bureaucracy has transformed the nature of public ethics investigations.[5] Federal law enforcement agencies have acquired the ability to unravel even the most complex public corruption schemes.[6]

Watergate constituted the single most important factor in building support for a new public integrity bureaucracy. Public confidence in government, some argued, could be restored only with much greater vigilance regarding the conduct of public officials. Not everyone has found the trend a positive one. "Success in Washington," wrote Washington lawyer and criminal defense attorney Peter W. Morgan, "more and more is gauged not by how many substantive accomplishments one can point to, but rather whether and how well one has avoided any charges of misconduct or ill-chosen words."[7]

THE NEW PUBLIC INTEGRITY BUREAUCRACY

No accurate figures exist on the number of local, state and federal officials who spend significant time enforcing criminal and administrative ethics laws and rules. Some thirty-six states, however, "have boards, commissions, or offices dedicated to overseeing ethics regulations."[8] These boards and commissions typically conduct public ethics investigations, issue advisory opinions and collect and review financial disclosure statements.[9] State attorney general offices and local prosecutors routinely enforce state public corruption statutes. Federal law enforcement agencies, however, have borne the brunt of carrying out the most serious public corruption investigations.

More than fifty major federal law enforcement agencies have some responsibility for enforcing federal criminal laws.[10] The Federal Bureau of Investigation (FBI), the Public Integrity Section of the Criminal Division of the Department of Justice, United States attorneys, independent counsels appointed under the Ethics in Government Act and various inspectors' general offices—all have major roles in uncovering, investigating and prosecuting corrupt public officials at the local, state and federal levels.

Between the 1980s and 1992, "the number of criminal cases filed in the federal courts grew by 70 percent, from 27,968 to 47,472."[11] During this same period, federal prosecutors obtained 12,897 public corruption indictments against local, state, and federal officials and others involved in public corruption activities.[12] Federal prosecutors obtained 11,256 public corruption convictions over this period.[13]

Criminal Public Corruption Units

After Watergate, federal law enforcement agencies gradually assumed greater and greater responsibility for public corruption investigations and prosecutions of local, state and federal officials. The Public Integrity Section of the Department of Justice, United States attorneys and the Federal Bureau of Investigation have led federal efforts to identify and prosecute public officials for violations of criminal law. Independent counsels have handled a limited number of cases involving prominent Washington political figures.

The Public Integrity Section of the Department of Justice

In 1976, the Justice Department established the Public Integrity Section of the Criminal Division. The attorney general gave the section primary responsibility to oversee "the federal effort to combat corruption through the prosecution of elected and appointed officials at all levels of government and supervising the investigation and prosecution of election crime."[14]

The establishment of the Public Integrity Section within the Criminal Division of the Department of Justice did not mean, however, that the new unit assumed all responsibility for public corruption investigations and prosecutions.[15] U.S. attorneys across the country continued to have primary responsibility for bringing public corruption charges against local, state and federal officials.[16] But over time, the Public Integrity Section developed a high degree of expertise in how to conduct successful public integrity investigations and prosecutions.

The Public Integrity Section works closely with U.S. attorneys across the country.[17] The section does not, however, have the authority to order U.S. attorneys to pursue or not pursue public integrity investigations.[18] This situation permits the U.S. attorneys to exercise a great deal of discretion in deciding what public integrity cases to pursue.[19]

A 1988 study commissioned by the Administrative Conference of the United States provides an excellent description of the working relationship between U.S. attorneys and the Public Integrity Section.

With determinations made on a somewhat *ad hoc* basis, any given investigation or prosecution may be handled solely by the United States Attorney with little or no coordination with Public Integrity Section, jointly by both the United States Attorney and Public Integrity Section, or exclusively by Public Integrity Section, with the United States Attorney having no role at all or only an administrative or logistical support role.[20]

Whoever receives the referral of the allegation of possible criminal conduct, according to the report, normally controls the investigation and prosecution.[21] The Public Integrity Section receives referrals from inspectors general, private citizens, congressional committees, the OGE, the IRS, the FBI, and the Department of Justice Office of Professional Responsibility (OPR).[22] The Public Integrity Section also begins investigations on the basis of newspaper and media reports on information from "an anonymous caller, or a criminal investigation by another law enforcement agency or another part of the Department of Justice into other types of criminal conduct."[23] Unlike the FBI, the Public Integrity Section does not conduct stings.[24]

U.S. Attorneys and the War Against Grassroots Corruption

The late 1960s, as noted, saw the Nixon Justice Department urge U.S. attorneys to devote more of their resources to the pursuit of corrupt federal, state and local officials. The Kennedy and Johnson Justice Departments laid the groundwork for a new federal public corruption initiative. The Department of Justice, under the leadership of Attorney General Robert F. Kennedy, "shifted its focus from bank robbery to corruption, labor racketeering, organized crime and white-collar criminals."[25] During the 1960s, Congress passed a series of statutes giving federal law enforcement agencies the authority to pursue organized crime figures.[26]

It did not take much experience to establish a direct link between organized crime and public corruption, particularly in large cities. "Prohibition and later organized gambling," wrote political scientist James Q. Wilson, "extend the rewards of municipal corruption beyond the time when rapid capital formation was at an end."[27] To control organized crime ultimately meant going after corrupt urban officials who permitted organized crime to operate freely.

Then U.S. attorney for the Northern District of Illinois, James R. Thompson, who subsequently served as governor of Illinois for twelve years, led the way in expanding federal prosecutions of state and local officials during the early 1970s. Thompson, for example, prosecuted Otto Kerner, former Democratic governor of Illinois, on public corruption charges related to conduct that occurred when Kerner was governor. Speaking to the *Washington Post* in 1975 concerning the wave of federal prosecutions of state and local officials, then-governor James Thompson explained, "The current wave of prosecution of official corruption can be trace—irony of ironies— to the Nixon-Mitchell Justice Department. No administration ever did more to upgrade, professionalize and staff U.S. Attorneys' offices in the field, and then leave them unfettered on their choices of prosecution."[28]

Federal courts across the country played a major role in helping U.S. attorneys pursue corrupt state and local government officials. Many federal courts accepted broad interpretations of the Hobbs Act, the Mail and Wire Fraud Statutes, the Travel Act, and RICO (Racketeer Influenced and Corrupt Organizations) to prohibit corrupt acts by local, state and federal officials.[29] These statutes provided federal prosecutors with the jurisdiction to prosecute state and local government officials on public corruption charges.

The success of the federal public corruption initiative led to increased criticism of the trend during the mid-1980s. Arthur Maass, Frank G. Thompson professor emeritus of government at Harvard University, wrote: "If federal legislation had intended that the acts be used for a purpose as politically sensitive as prosecuting elected state and local officials, it seems that they would have mentioned it in the legislative history, if not in the language of the statute."[30] Maass painted an "Orwellian" picture of the activities of federal law enforcement agencies in their pursuit of corrupt public officials:

In the prosecutorial mode, U.S. attorneys or FBI agents sense that a public official or city administration may be corrupt based on political gossip and other circumstantial evidence. They open an investigation to collect evidence to confirm the hunch. They have a vast array of resources, including grand juries and agents, examiners and auditors of the FBI, Drug Enforcement Administration, Internal Revenue, Bureau of Alcohol, Tobacco and Firearms, Customs Service, bank examining agencies, Marshals' Service, Postal Inspection Service and Secret Service. With information from the investigation, the U.S. attorney pages through statute books to discover provisions under which similar conduct has been found criminal. If there are no clear provisions, the prosecutor may interpret a statute creatively so that it fits the facts.[31]

The early 1990s saw U.S. attorneys and the FBI conduct a number of high-profile state public corruption investigations.[32] Major political corruption scandals swept the states of Arizona, California, New York, Tennessee, Texas, Rhode Island and West Virginia. "Operation Lost Trust," a sting conducted by the FBI in 1990, netted five members of the South Carolina legislature who agreed to sell their votes to support a bill authorizing parimutuel horse and dog racing.[33] Operation Boptrot resulted in fifteen top Kentucky legislators, lobbyists and other public figures being convicted on various federal public corruption charges. This FBI sting uncovered significant corruption related to the state's large horse racing industry.[34]

Between 1974 and the end of 1993, federal prosecutors convicted 6,824 federal officials, 1,195 state officials, 3,706 local officials and 4,186 other individuals on federal public corruption charges.[35] These investigations and convictions provided strong evidence that state law enforcement agencies continued to have considerable difficulty uncovering public corruption at the state level and local level.[36] The states needed federal assistance to bring corrupt state and local officials to justice.

Independent Counsels: On the Firing Line

Efforts by the Nixon White House to block the Watergate investigation led directly to the enactment of the independent counsel provisions of the 1978 Ethics in Government Act.[37] Congress enacted the independent counsel provisions to guarantee that the executive branch could not interfere in any future investigation of alleged criminal conduct by high-level executive branch officials. But constitutional separation of powers problems forced Congress to establish a cumbersome process for the appointment and supervision of independent counsels.

Allegations leveled against high-level executive branch officials first go to the attorney general. Then the attorney general conducts a preliminary investigation to establish whether credible evidence exists to believe that further investigation is warranted.[38] If the attorney general finds that credible evidence exists, the law then requires the attorney general to ask the Special Division of the U.S. Court of Appeals for the District of Columbia to appoint an independent counsel. The Special Division establishes the scope of the independent counsel investigation.

Independent counsels have powers identical to those of U.S. attorneys and the attorneys working for the Public Integrity Section of the Department of Justice to investigate corruption by public officials. The act places no limits on how much money independent counsels can spend on investigations. Like the Public Integrity Section or U.S. attorneys' public corruption investigations, an independent counsel may request assistance from the FBI and other federal agencies. To mitigate the financial impact on the independent counsel law on officials placed under investigation, the Independent Counsel Act gave the special judicial panel the authority to order the federal government to pay the legal expenses of officials not prosecuted by independent counsels.[39] Ronald Reagan, for example, received $562,111 for Iran-*Contra* legal costs.[40] Former Bush administration officials Janet G. Mullins and Elizabeth M. Tamposi, who were investigated for allegedly searching the passport records of presidential candidate Bill Clinton, received $240,000 to pay legal bills.[41]

The first five years of the independent counsel law produced few fireworks. Independent counsels investigated allegations of illegal drug use by Carter White House Chief of Staff Hamilton Jordan and Timothy Kraft, Carter national campign manager, but found no evidence to support the allegations.[42] In 1982, Congress extended the law for another five years without substantial opposition from the Reagan White House.[43] In the years between 1983 and 1989, however, the Special Judicial Panel appointed eight separate independent counsels to investigate allegations of illegal conduct by members of the Reagan administration.[44]

The large number of independent counsel investigations led to a backlash against the independent counsel law. After 1985, the Reagan Justice Department launched a constitutional challenge to the constitutionality of the law on the grounds that it violated the Constitution's separation of powers doctrine to permit the Special Panel to appoint independent counsel.[45] Only the attorney general, according to this line of reasoning, had the authority to appoint an independent counsel. A federal appeals court decision striking down the constitutionality of the independent counsel law put in doubt the legality of the Iran-*Contra* investigation then being conducted by independent counsel Lawrence Walsh.[46]

The attack against the independent counsel law did not prevent President Reagan in 1987 from signing a reauthorization of the independent counsel law. A veto of the bill a year before a presidential election would have brought back memories of President Nixon's firing of Watergate special prosecutor Archibald Cox. The Supreme Court, to the surprise of many court observers, by a vote of seven to one in June 1988, upheld the constitutionality of the independent counsel law.

The decision did not end Republican efforts to kill the independent counsel law. The $40 million plus cost of the Iran-*Contra* investigation made Washington wonder whether the independent counsel law had outlived its usefulness.[47] In 1992, the Democratic leadership of Congress failed to round up enough votes to overcome Republican opposition to the law. The law died a quiet death.[48]

President George Bush, in a decision demonstrating contempt for the Iran-*Contra* independent counsel Lawrence Walsh and his lengthy investigation, pardoned Casper Weinberger, secretary of defense during the Reagan administration, and other Iran-*Contra* figures just before leaving office.[49]

It appeared that official Washington had little stomach for the continuation of the independent counsel law until the August 1993 suicide of Associate White House Counsel Vince Foster. By early 1994, public pressure forced the Clinton White House to ask the attorney general to appoint an independent counsel to investigate the Clinton's Whitewater investment and the death of Vincent Foster. Because the independent counsel law had lapsed, Attorney General Janet Reno appointed New York lawyer Robert Fiske to conduct the investigation. Congress reauthorized the independent counsel law in late spring 1994. The Special Judicial panel, in a very controversial decision, replaced Robert Fiske with Washington lawyer Kenneth Starr in early August 1994.

Honesty Testing and the Federal Bureau of Investigation

In the years following Watergate, the Federal Bureau of Investigation made public corruption investigations a high priority. The FBI gathered evidence in almost every public corruption case brought before the Public Integrity Section or U.S. attorneys. By the early 1980s, the FBI moved from collecting evidence to setting up elaborate stings to test the honesty of public officials. The use of stings marked a major escalation of the federal war against public corruption.

The 1980 ABSCAM investigation constituted the most publicized early use of the public corruption sting. FBI agents posed as individuals with Middle Eastern backgrounds who needed help with a number of personal matters. The operation taped a number of Congressmen accepting large amounts of cash in return for their assistance.[50] The operation stood official Washington on its head. Few questioned the right of the FBI to investigate allegations of illegal conduct by members of Congress. Some questioned the propriety of the FBI's setting up stings to test the honesty of members of Congress or other public officials.

After ABSCAM, the FBI accelerated its use of stings in a wide range of criminal investigations.[51] FBI stings targeted corrupt local police officers,[52] state legislators[53] and even employees and contractors of the National Aeronautics and Space Administration.[54]

By the early 1990s, federal law enforcement agencies had acquired the expertise to unravel the most complex public corruption scheme.

NONCRIMINAL PUBLIC INTEGRITY AGENCIES

The post-Watergate period also saw the proliferation of federal agencies with noncriminal public integrity responsibilities. These organizations have primary responsibility for reviewing the financial affairs of federal employees and officials for conflicts of interest, for interpreting criminal and administrative public integrity rules, and for making sure federal employees and officials understand criminal and administrative restrictions.

Experience and the Office of Legal Counsel

Long before Watergate became a household word, the Office of Legal Counsel (OLC) of the Department of Justice had primary responsibility for issuing interpretations of federal criminal public corruption laws for the White House, and federal agencies and departments.[55] The OLC, over time, established itself as the primary source of expert advice on the scope of federal public corruption and conflict of interest laws.

The OLC, for example, ruled in the 1960s that the new salary supplementation prohibition, Section 209, Title 18 of the United States Code, prohibited nonpublic sources from making lump-sum payments to individuals entering the federal government before or after the individual entered the federal government, if the nonfederal source made the payment to make it easier for the individual to serve in government.[56] For almost three decades, no one inside or outside the federal government challenged this interpretation.[57] Yet in 1990, the Supreme Court found that Boeing Corporation had done nothing improper when it provided a number of its executives who accepted positions with the Reagan administration substantial lump-sum payments before they became federal employees to help them make the transition from Boeing to the federal government.[58] The total of these payments ran into hundreds of thousands of dollars.[59]

The OLC continues to exercise primary responsibility for interpreting the scope of federal criminal laws for federal agencies and departments.

The Office of Government Ethics[60]

In 1978, the Ethics in Government Act established the Office of Government Ethics (OGE) to provide "overall direction of executive branch policies related to preventing conflicts of interest on the part of officers and employees of any executive branch agency."[61] Congress, in fact, established the OGE to take over the Civil Service Commission's responsibility for overseeing the executive branch ethics program established during the Kennedy and Johnson administrations. Congress also delegated to the OGE responsibility for enforcing the public financial disclosure requirement of the Ethics Act.[62]

The Office of Government Ethics oversees agency ethics programs that, in 1993, covered "more than 4 million people, including civilian, uniformed and special government employees."[63] In 1993, federal agencies employed 144 designated agency ethics officials (DAEOs) who, in turn, employed "14,399 individuals in full-time and part-time capacities."[64] Ethics education, enforcement of government-wide administrative standard of conduct regulations and management of the public and confidential financial disclosure programs all fall within the scope of the noncriminal federal ethics program coordinated by the OGE.[65]

Through the late 1970s and into the first half of the 1980s, the OGE kept a low profile. The office spent most of its time reviewing the public financial disclosure statements of presidential nominees, approving blind trusts and issuing and interpreting regulations interpreting the revolving-door restrictions included in the act.[66] "OGE was to coordinate policy through designated agency ethics officials (DAEOs), who would be appointed within every department and agency in government."[67] No one expected the OGE to function as an investigatory unit of government. But the OGE, by the mid-1980s, found itself being pushed to expand its role in ethics management.

The 1978 Ethics Act gave the director of the OGE the authority to "order corrective action."[68] The OGE had primary responsibility for interpreting the standard of conduct provisions of President Johnson's Executive Order 11222. The order, as discussed earlier, directed all federal employees to avoid the appearance of impropriety. The OGE, in theory, had jurisdiction to determine whether federal employees violated the appearance of impropriety standard.

Early in 1984, President Reagan nominated Edwin Meese, III, for the position of attorney general. Reports soon surfaced that California friends of Edwin Meese provided Meese with financial help in making the move from California to Washington. The disclosure led to the appointment of an independent counsel to determine whether the assistance violated any criminal laws. In September 1984, the independent counsel found insufficient evidence to seek a criminal indictment.[69]

After the independent counsel issued its report, the Senate Judiciary Committee requested that the OGE rule on whether Meese had violated any of the standards of conduct rules found in Executive Order 11222. A firestorm erupted when David Martin, director of the OGE, seemed to indicate to the committee, in January 1985, that the standards of conduct in the executive order were "aspirational" in nature.[70] Martin also ruled that Meese had not violated any of the standards of conduct. The decision angered critics of Meese and disturbed agency ethics officials, who feared it would make it more difficult for agencies to discipline employees for misconduct.[71]

Meese, after being confirmed attorney general, found himself the subject of another conflict-of-interest controversy. Meese had reported a partnership as a "limited blind partnership." However, federal law did not permit such a financial arrangement to qualify as a blind trust.[72] Meese argued that he had made an honest mistake and criticized the OGE for not catching the inadvertent mistake. In short, pressure increased for the appointment of another independent counsel. A second independent counsel investigation turned up insufficient evidence of criminal wrongdoing to support a criminal indictment.[73] A short time after the independent counsel issued his report, Attorney General Meese then resigned from office. Frank Nebeker, the new director of the OGE, reversed the position of the OGE on the issue of the enforceability of the appearance of impropriety standard of Executive Order 11222. On September 12, 1988, after the resignation of Edwin Meese, Judge Nebeker issued a report highly critical of Meese's conduct. The report accused Meese of "violating all six of the general provisions of the standards of conduct."[74] Meese rejected all of the OGE findings.

The events of the mid-1980s led Congress to make the OGE an independent agency, instead of a unit within the Office of Personnel Management. The provision went into effect on October 1, 1989.[75]

Suddenly Being Taken Seriously

The 1988 election of George Bush turned out to be a turning point for the OGE.[76] President Bush's new standards of conduct executive order and the Ethics Reform Act of 1989 significantly expanded the responsibilities of the OGE.[77] Stephen D. Potts became the head of the Office of Government Ethics. Potts moved quickly to restructure the operations of the OGE and to seek increased funding and staff. Potts' efforts paid off handsomely. The *Washington Post*, on January 15, 1992, noted that the office was suddenly "being taken seriously" and that "for a low-key agency, overseeing standards is a field of growth."[74] Responsibilities of the office now included operating the public and confidential financial reporting systems, monitoring the effectiveness of agency ethics programs, issuing new executive branch standard of conduct regulations, reviewing the financial disclosure statements of presidential nominees for conflicts of interest and issuing certificates of divestiture to permit executive branch employees to roll over capital gains from financial assets sold to comply with ethics rules. The Office of Government Ethics, in brief, evolved from an obscure federal office into a major player in federal public integrity management.

Inspector General Offices

In the same year Congress enacted the Ethics in Government Act, it also passed the Inspector General Act, which established independent units within a number of federal agencies and departments to investigate allegations of waste, fraud and abuse in federal programs.[79] By the early 1990s, some twenty-seven cabinet departments and large federal agencies had inspector general offices headed by presidential appointees.[80]

Congress established inspector general offices in order to focus more attention on waste, fraud and abuse in federal programs, but these offices do not have the authority to bring criminal charges against anyone. They must refer alleged criminal conduct to the Department of Justice.

SCANDAL MANAGEMENT AND THE PRESIDENCY

The growth of the new public integrity management has contributed to a major improvement in the ethics management practices of federal agencies and departments. Since the resignation of Richard Nixon, presidents have found it exceptionally difficult to accept the power of the new public integrity bureaucracy. The public integrity war has destroyed the ability of the White House to investigate allegations of impropriety by members of its own administration. Instead, the political opposition and the media have come to expect independent investigations of almost any allegation of improper activity. Indeed, an independent investigation is required to prove that administration or White House officials did *not* do anything improper.

The Rise and Fall of the Office of White House Counsel

In the early 1940s, Franklin Roosevelt created the staff position of White House counsel.[81] Over time, presidents assigned the office more and more responsibilities. Reviewing legislation, drafting legislation, writing speeches and handling pardons became common duties of the office.[82] Not until Richard Nixon's White House Counsel John Dean became a key figure in Watergate scandal did anyone outside the White House pay much attention to the operation of the office.[83]

Beginning in the early 1960s, the White House counsel's office assumed more responsibility for reviewing the backgrounds of presidential appoint-

ees for conflicts of interest and other problems that might disqualify them
from serving in high-profile positions. White House Counsel John Dean,
for instance, found his office swamped with work related to ethics questions
and issues.[84] After the passage of the Ethics in Government Act of 1978,
the White House counsel's office, the Office of Legal Counsel of the Department of Justice and the Office of Government Ethics worked together
closely to resolve financial conflict-of-interest problems.[85]

Besides using personal information collected directly from the nominee,
the White House counsel's office came to rely heavily on background
checks conducted by the FBI to uncover detrimental information. The background checks, however, had a major limitation. "An FBI investigation,"
according to one analysis of the White House clearance process, "takes six
weeks. . . . The bureau merely collects statements from friends, neighbors,
relatives, employers, and others who know the nominee; it makes no attempt to synthesize its findings or draw factual conclusions."[86] Addition-
ally, the FBI background check provides no guarantee that other negative
information about a nominee will not surface after the president sends a
nomination to the Senate. In brief, the White House counsel's office has its
hands full just dealing with routine ethics clearance responsibilities.

The Watergate experience, however, forced presidents to face the problem of how to deal with allegations of impropriety made against the president, other members of the administration and family members and
associates of the president. The White House counsel's office became the
logical place for such internal investigations.

President Reagan assigned Attorney General Edwin Meese responsibility
for investigating possible violations of federal law when stories of arms for
hostages appeared.[87] C. Boyden Gray, President Bush's White House counsel, in 1991 faced the task of investigating the travel practices of President
Bush's chief of staff, John Sununu.[88] After Gray's investigation, the White
House counsel's office tightened rules regarding White House personnel use
of military transportation and acceptance of free trips and lodging from
corporations.[89] Yet the investigation clearly embarrassed President Bush.

The August 1993 suicide of Vince Foster, associate White House counsel, brought scandal into the White House counsel's office itself. The re-
moval of President Bill and Hillary Clinton's personal files from Vince
Foster's office became one of the central issues surrounding Whitewater. In
late June 1996, the White House found itself faced with another major
controversy over alleged misuse of FBI background files by the White
House Office of Personnel Security. Because no one would accept the findings of an internal White House investigation, the White House asked Attorney General Janet Reno and the FBI to conduct an investigation of the
FBI file controversy.

Instead of ordering a Justice Department investigation, Attorney General
Reno asked the Special Judicial Panel to direct Whitewater independent

counsel Kenneth Starr to investigate the possible misuse of FBI background files by White House personnel.[90]

THE NEW GUARDIANS OF THE PUBLIC TRUST

The new public integrity bureaucracy has become the final arbitrator for many public integrity disputes. The growth of the new public integrity bureaucracy began before Watergate. But the increased intensity of public integrity disputes after Watergate would provide the new public integrity bureaucracy with an influx of resources that would permit the public integrity bureaucracy to expand the scope of its operations and to gain an unprecedented level of independence.

NOTES

1. "Commentary: Sparring Over Whitewater," *TimesFax*, June 19, 1996, p. A8.

2. Ibid.

3. Hubert G. Locke, "Ethics in American Government: A Look backward," *Annals of the American Academy of Political and Social Science* 537 (January 1995): 14–24.

4. See also C. Van Woodward, ed., *Responses of the President to Charges of Misconduct* (New York: Delacorte Press, 1974).

5. See the entire volume of "Ethics Investigations," *Journal of Law & Politics* 11 (Summer 1995).

6. John W. Moore, "Grass-roots Graft," *National Journal* (August 19, 1987): 1962–67.

7. Peter Morgan, "Broader Costs of the New Prosecutorial Ethics," *Journal of Law and Politics* 11 (Summer 1995): 546.

8. Mark W. Huddleston and Joseph C. Sands, "Enforcing Administrative Ethics," *Annals of the American Academy of Political and Social Science* 537 (January 1995): 145.

9. For a state-by-state review of the responsibilities of state ethics boards and commissions, see Council of State Governmental Ethics Laws, *COGEL Blue Book, 9th Ed.: Campaign Finance, Ethics, Lobby Law & Judicial Conduct* (Lexington, KY: The Council of State Governments, 1993). Also see Carol W. Lewis, "Ethics Codes and Ethics Agencies: Current Practices and Emerging Trends." In *Ethics and Public Administration*, ed. H. George Frederickson (Armonk, NY: M.E. Sharpe, 1993), pp. 136–57.

10. Sara Sun Beale, "Federalizing Crime: Assessing the Impact on the Federal Courts," *Annals of the American Academy of Political and Social Science* 543 (January 1996): 44.

11. Ibid., p. 45.

12. U.S. Department of Justice, Public Integrity Section, Criminal Division, *Report to Congress on the Operations of the Public Integrity Section for 1992* (Washington, DC: U.S. Department of Justice, 1992), pp. 36–37.

13. Ibid.

14. Deanne C. Siemer, "Enforcement of the Federal Ethics Laws as Applied to Executive Branch Personnel," Issues and options paper prepared for the Working Conference on Ethics in Government, March 1, 1988. In *Sourcebook on Government Ethics for Presidential Appointees* (Washington, DC: Administrative Conference of the United States, December 1988), p. 28.

15. *Report to Congress on the Operations of the Public Integrity Section for 1992* (Washington, DC.: Public Integrity Section, Criminal Division, U.S. Department of Justice, 1992), Introduction.

16. Ibid.

17. Ibid.

18. U.S. Department of Justice, Criminal Division. *Prosecution of Public Corruption Cases*, 1988.

19. Alan Ehrenhalt. "Justice and Ambition: U.S. Attorneys Can Do What They Want in Prosecuting Public Corruption. Is that Wise?" *Governing* 2 (September 1989): 38

20. Siemer, p. 29.

21. Ibid., p. 30.

22. Ibid.

23. Ibid., p. 32.

24. Ibid.

25. Beale, p. 42.

26. Ibid.

27. James Q. Wilson, "Corruption: The Shame of the States." In *Political Corruption*, ed. Arnold J. Heidenheimer (New Brunswick, NJ: Transaction Books, 1970), p. 302.

28. George C. S. Benson, Steven A. Maaranen and Alan Heslop, *Political Corruption in America* (Lexington, MA: Lexington Books, 1978), p. 250. The quotation was originally taken from Neil Pierce, *Washington Post*, April 19, 1975, p. A18.

29. Robert N. Roberts and Marion T. Doss Jr., "The Federalization of 'Grass Roots' Corruption," *Spectrum*, 66 (Winter 1993), pp. 9–12.

30. Arthur Maass, "Bad Federal Policy," *Spectrum* 66 (Winter 1993): 20; Also see Arthur Maass, "U.S. Prosecution of State and Local Officials for Political Corruption," *Publius: The Journal of Federalism* 17 (Summer 1987).

31. Ibid., p. 21.

32. Gwen Ifill, "Scandals Cast New Light on Statehouse," *Washington Post*, February 24, 1991, p. A3.

33. Ronald Smothers, "5 South Carolina State Officials Indicted in Corruption Inquiry," *New York Times*, August 25, 1990, p. A1.

34. Martin Booe, "Kentuckians Amazed that $400 Can Buy a Lawmaker," *Los Angeles Times*, April 13, 1990, p. 5.

35. U.S. Department of Justice, Public Integrity Section, Criminal Division, *Report to Congress on the Activities and Operations of the Public Integrity Section for 1993* (Washington, DC: U.S. Department of Justice, 1993), p. 35.

36. See Kenneth J. Meier and Thomas M. Holbrook, " 'I Seen My Opportunities and I Took 'Em': Political Corruption in the American States," *Journal of Politics* 54 (February 1992): 135–55.

37. See Stanley I. Kutler, *The Wars of Watergate: The Last Crisis of Richard Nixon* (New York: Knopf, 1990).

38. James D. Carroll and Robert N. Roberts, "If Men Were Angels: Assessing the Ethics in Government Act of 1978," *Policy Studies* 17 (Winter 1988-89), p. 437.

39. David E. Rosenbaum, "Clinton May Gain as Counsel Bill Clears Congress," *New York Times*, June 22, 1994, p. A1.

40. Toni Locy, "Reagan to Receive $562,111 for Iran-Contra Legal Costs," *Washington Post*, September 4, 1996, p. A24.

41. Toni Locy, "Fees Paid in Passport Inquiry," *Washington Post*, June 1, 1996, p. A6.

42. CQ Researcher, "Political Scandals," *Congressional Quarterly*, May 27, 1994, p. 475; "Tripping Down Special-Prosecutor Memory Lane," *Time*, August 22, 1994, p. 16.

43. Nadine Cohodas, "Congress Weighing Revisions in Special Prosecutor Law," *Congressional Quarterly Weekly Report* 40 (April 24, 1982), p. 907.

44. CQ Researcher, "Political Scandals," p. 475. Labor Secretary Ray Donovan, 1981 (no indictment); Presidential Counsellor Ed Meese, 1984 (no indictment); White House Aid Michael Deaver, 1986 (convicted of perjury); White House aide Lyn Nofziger, 1987 (conviction on improper lobbying after leaving office overturned on appeal); in "Tripping Down Special-Prosecutor Memory Lane," p. 16.

45. David Beckwith, "Picking on the Prosecutor," *Time*, March 9, 1987, p. 31.

46. Jefferson Morley, "Reagan vs. Walsh," *Nation*, April 23, 1988, pp. 556–57.

47. The Iran-*Contra* investigation resulted in "14 indictments: 7 guilty pleas; four convictions after trials; 2 overturned on appeal (Oliver North, John Poindexter); 1 dismissal; 2 withdrawn after pardons." See CQ Researcher, "Political Scandals," pp. 475–76.

48. "Special Prosecutors, Down but not Out," *U.S. News & World Report*, December 21, 1992, p. 26.

49. Holly Idelson, "Bush Leaves Partisan Mark with Surprise Pardons." *Congressional Quarterly Weekly Report*, January 2, 1993, pp. 31–32.

50. James Q. Wilson, "The Changing FBI—the road to Abscam," *Public Interest* (Spring 1990): 3–14.

51. Robert I. Blecker, "Beyond 1984: Undercover in America: Serpico to Abscam," *New York Law School Review* 28 (1989): 823–1024.

52. See Michael Parlstein and Walt Philbin, "Nine Cops Charged in Drug Sting," *New Orleans Times-Picayune*, December 8, 1994, p. A1; Toni Locy, "Ex-officer Says Greed Guided Him into Net of Drug Sting," *Washington Post*, October 20, 1994, p. C1; Dan Terry, "30 in Cleveland Police Held in Federal Gambling Inquiry," *New York Times*, May 31, 1991, p. A21.

53. "Carolina Inquiry Indicts 18th Lawmaker," *New York Times*, August 22, 1991, A24.

54. Deborah Tedford, "Justice Department Scrutinizes NASA Sting," *Houston Chronicle*, September 15, 1994, p. A21.

55. For a discussion of the history of the OLC, see James Michael Strine, "The Office of Legal Counsel: Legal Professionals in a Political System." Ph.D thesis, Johns Hopkins University, 1992, U.M.I. no. 92-29411.

56. Robert Roberts, *White House Ethics* (Westport, CT: Greenwood Press, 1988), p. 176.

57. See Robert Roberts, *Report to the Administrative Conference of the United States. A Guide to Federal Ethics Laws for Presidential Appointees.* In *Sourcebook on Governmental Ethics for Presidential Appointees* (Washington, DC: Administrative Conference of the United States, 1988), pp. 12–13; See also Linda Greenhouse, "Boeing Wins Plea on Severance Pay," *New York Times*, February 28, 1990, p. A21.

58. *Crandon v. United States*, 494 U.S. 152 (1990).

59. Roberts, *Ethics*, pp. 175–76.

60. For Detailed Information on the Operation of the Office of Government Ethics see the OGE Home Page. January 3, 1997. URL: http://www.access.gpo.gov/usoge/index.html

61. Roberts, *Ethics*, pp. 175–76.

62. J. Jackson Walter, "The Ethics in Government Act: Conflict of Interest Laws and Presidential Recruitment," *Public Administration Review* 41 (November–December 1981): 659–65.

63. Stuart C. Gilman, "Presidential Ethics and the Ethics of the Presidency," *Annals of the American Academy of Political and Social Science* 537 (January 1995): 74.

64. Ibid.

65. For an overview of standard of conduct rules applicable to federal executive branch employees, see U.S. Office of Government Ethics, *Take the High Road: An Ethics Booklet for Executive Branch Employees* (Washington, DC: Government Printing Office, 1992).

66. Walter, pp. 659–65.

67. Gilman, p. 72.

68. Roberts, *Ethics*, p. 162.

69. Mary Thorton, "Inquiry Ends Into Loan, Federal Hirings: Probe Rules Out Prosecution of Meese," *Washington Post*, September 21, 1984, p. A1. See also *Report of Independent Counsel Concerning Edwin Meese III*, before Senior Circuit Judge Robb, Washington, DC, Division for the Purpose of Appointing Independent Counsels, U.S. Court of Appeals for the District of Columbia Circuit.

70. See Ronald Brownstein, "Agency Ethics Officers Fear Meese Ruling Could Weaken Conflict Laws," *National Journal*, March 23, 1985, p. 642.

71. Ibid.

72. Ibid.

73. Ed Magnuson, "A Mixed Verdict for Meese," *Time*, August 1, 1988, p. 24.

74. Gilman, p. 73.

75. The decision to make the OGE an independent agency was included in the 1988 reauthorization of the Ethics in Government Act of 1978.

76. Gilman, p. 73.

77. Ibid.

78. Dana Priest, "Suddenly Being Taken Seriously At Office of Government Ethics: For Low-Key Agency, Overseeing Standards Is Field With Growth," *Washington Post*, January 15, 1992, p. A21.

79. Huddleston and Sands, p. 144.

80. Ibid.

81. Jennifer Wang, "Raising the Stakes at the White House: Legal and Ethical Duties of the White House," *Georgetown Journal of Legal Ethics* 8 (1994): 118.

82. Ibid., p. 119.

83. For John Dean's view of Watergate, see John Dean, *Blind Ambition* (New York: Simon & Schuster, 1976).

84. Jeremy Rabkin, "White House Lawyering: Law, Ethics, And Political Judgements." In *Government Lawyers: The Federal Legal Bureaucracy and Presidential Politics* (Lawrence, KS: University Press of Kansas, 1995), p. 115.

85. Ibid., p. 116.

86. Bruce Adams and Kathryn Kavanagh-Baran, *Promise and Performance: Carter Builds a New Administration* (Lexington, MA: Lexington Books, 1979), p. 91.

87. Ibid., p. 123.

88. Dan Goodgame, "Fly Free or Die," *Time*, May 13, 1991, pp. 16–18.

89. Ann Devoy and Charles Babcock, "Sununu Travel Rules Tightened," *Washington Post*, June 22, 1991, p. A1.

90. John F. Harris and George Lardner Jr., "Reno Seeks Probe of FBI Files," *Washington Post*, June 21, 1996, p. A1.

Chapter 9

War Reporting

Historians have given the *Washington Post* much of the credit for uncovering the Watergate scandal. Watergate helped to ignite a new era of investigatory journalism. By the 1990s, however, many members of the public and a multitude of media experts blamed the media for the crisis in public service ethics. From one perspective, the media spend too much time reporting on the personal lives of public officials and too little time investigating scandals involving serious mismanagement of public programs.[1] Other critics blame the constant stream of stories bashing government for the tremendous erosion in public trust and confidence in government.[2]

Watergate lulled many journalists into a false sense of security. Journalists, like the muckrakers of the early twentiethth century, expected the public to embrace them with open arms. To the astonishment of many, however, the extensive coverage of the private lives of public officials and of other public figures caused a backlash against both print and broadcast journalists. By the late 1970s and early 1980s, the country seemed to be trapped in a great moral and ethical morass. Americans searched for new heroes to restore the nation's faith in itself. Yet the media seemed much more interested in destroying public figures than in helping the nation deal with serious fundamental problems.

Between 1976 and 1994, the Gallup Poll surveyed the American public to determine perceptions of ethical standards regarding various professionals. Thirty-three percent of those surveyed in 1976 gave journalists a very high–high combined rating, but only 20 percent of those surveyed in 1994 gave journalists the very high–high combined rating.[3]

Journalists ranked below druggists, clergy, dentists, college teachers, engineers, medical doctors and even bankers.[4] However, they consistently ranked higher than car salesmen, congressmen, insurance salesmen, senators, advertising practioners, state officeholders, labor union leaders, real estate agents, stockbrokers and lawyers.[5] The Watergate-inspired respect for journalists turned out to be short-lived. Seventy percent of those surveyed in a January 1992 poll conducted for *Time* by Yankelovich Shulman said that the media should not inform the public about the private lives of presidential candidates, including about their extramarital affairs. Eighty-two percent responded that the press pays too much attention to the presidential candidates' personal lives.[6] "Generally," according to media scholar Warren Francke, "Americans believe that news coverage is too negative and, particularly, that watchdogs bark too loud and too long about petty wrongdoing by public officials, namely, private misbehavior."[7]

Despite public unhappiness over media coverage of the private lives of public officials, the public appears to have few reservations about media investigations of illegal conduct by public officials. A 1992 NBC-*Wall Street Journal* poll, for example, found that 50 percent of those questioned believed tax problems should disqualify a person from becoming president of the United States.[8] The public clearly has a love-hate relationship with the media: the public wants the media to hold public officials and public agencies accountable, but gets angry when the media shatter widely held perceptions of public figures.

Besides being held responsible for turning saints into sinners, the media is routinely blamed by new progressives and movement conservatives for being biased in their coverage of political scandals. From the perspective of movement conservatives, liberals control the establishment media. If given the opportunity, conservatives fear the media will use their power to destroy any conservative who appears ready to develop a large following or who criticizes programs dear to liberal hearts. New progressives, on the other hand, blame the media for spending too much time criticizing government and not enough time investigating efforts by powerful special interests to influence the formulation and implementation of public policy.[9]

FROM LAPDOG TO WATCHDOG

Throughout much of the late eighteenth and most of the nineteenth century, newspapers and journalists made little effort to hide their loyalty to a particular party or political figure. Well-established Federalist and Anti-Federalist publications fought it out over ratification of the Constitution and subsequently over the role of the new national government.[10] Rumors regarding members of the opposition routinely appeared "in pamphlets and newspapers owned by fierce ideological activists."[11] Throughout the first half of the nineteenth century, many newspapers made no attempt to maintain the façade of political neutrality. "Partisan advocacy was the central content of these newspapers, and what we would call editorials today constituted the form of newspaper writing."[12] Many editors, in addition, "worked to organize party activities in their town or area."[13]

The relationship between newspapers and politics did not stop with political endorsements by newspaper editors. Political machines provided direct financial support to newspapers. Newspapers received lucrative printing contracts from political parties and governments agencies.[14] Indeed, because income from circulation fell far short of meeting circulation costs, political financial support proved vital to the survival of many newspapers.

In the second half of the nineteenth century, the press gradually lost its need for patronage. As cities grew, newspapers learned that the public wanted news, not just opinion. A demand for reporters surged.[15] The Civil War, in particular, gave newspapers the opportunity to prove that they could cover extremely difficult stories with reasonable objectivity. Moreover, the industrial revolution provided many newspapers with adequate revenue to cut their ties with political machines.[16] "American businesses needed to market their goods on a mass scale."[17] Newspapers constituted the only method of mass distribution of product information available to American business.

By 1900, many metropolitan newspapers had turned into large businesses employing hundreds of employees, including large numbers of professional reporters.[18] Instead of having to go begging to politicians for favors, the large papers forced politicians to seek endorsements from editors and publishers. To multiply circulation and advertising revenue, large urban newspapers increased the number of stories concerning "the everyday lives of Americans."[19] Stories dealing with "tragic suicides, scandalous divorces, sordid crimes" appeared in newspapers regularly. Freed of reliance upon revenue from political sources, some newspapers even aggressively began to report about corruption in government. Newspaper editors and publishers learned that political scandals sold newspapers.

When newspapers began to print large numbers of stories dealing with corruption and mismanagement in government, their prior political activities created a credibility problem. Political figures portrayed in a negative light often tried to deflect public attention by accusing the newspapers of running the stories for partisan political reasons. The defense seemed plausible, particularly to those still loyal to the political figures who came under attack.[20] "Just as Nixon and Agnew blamed media bias for negative accounts of their conduct in Washington and Baltimore, earlier targets of investigations challenged the source."[21]

The Muckrakers and the Purification of Political Reporting

The difference was vast between reporting on the corrupt conduct of public officials and leading a campaign for political reform or for the expansion of government in American society. The progressive era and the rise of muckraker journalists permanently changed the political landscape of the country. Instead of reporting only on problems in American society, muckraker journalists joined with progressives to put pressure on elected officials to deal with the damage caused to society by the industrial revolution.[22] Journalists, more than at any previous time in American history, constituted the driving force for national political reform.[23]

With the end of the progressive era, however, newspapers stopped publishing the stories of muckraker journalists. Urban newspapers still devoted considerable effort to attacking the evils of political machines, but few attempted to investigate the conduct of public business in state capitals or in Washington. Instead of being outside the establishment, many large newspapers had become part of the establishment. Few wanted to rock the boat that sent advertising dollars into their pages. Yet during the first half of the twentieth century, powerful publishers often made it difficult for politicians who did not hold their views of government and American society.[24] In sharp contrast to their practices in the progressive era, publishers and editors put their reporters on a tight leash.

Other trends helped to limit the extent of investigatory journalism. The establishment of nationwide wire services and national radio networks during the 1920s forced the new entries into the mass communication market to tailor their stories to a national audience. Reports that might not offend New Yorkers might offend those living in Middle America. Radio networks, unlike newspapers, needed federal licenses to operate. The corporations that controlled the new electronic media could not afford to offend listeners or anger public officials, who might bring pressure to take their licenses away or deny them new licenses.

Between the First and Second World Wars, public outrage over the content of motion pictures saw a number of states establish "state boards of censors for moving pictures."[25] The motion picture industry realized that if such a trend continued, the industry would lose the ability to distribute pictures on a nationwide basis. To stem further state regulation, during the early 1930s the motion picture industry established the Hays Commission. Before a picture could be distributed, it had to receive a seal of approval from the commission.

The growth of large media corporations, a backlash against changing moral standards and fear over revocation of licenses led print and broadcast journalists to adopt an unwritten code of conduct for dealing with information involving alleged misconduct by public officials. Most publishers and editors had few problems printing stories of public corruption involving urban political machines. Urban newspapers, prior to the Second World War, had led crusades against corrupt urban political machines. According to James Q. Wilson, writing in 1966, "the most important fact about American municipal government over the last twenty years has been the dramatic improvement in the standards and honesty of public service. In no large city today is it likely that a known thief could be elected mayor (how many unknown thieves are elected must be a matter of speculation); a few decades ago, it would have been surprising if the mayor were not a boodler."[26]

Wilson did not have the same view of reform at the state level. State government corruption flourished because of the lack of scrutiny of the conduct of state officials. "Big cities have big newspapers, big civic associations, and big blocs of newspaper reading, civic-minded voters," wrote Wilson.[27] The location of the vast majority of state capitals in largely rural areas meant that small newspapers typically covered state government. Few local citizens were interested in confronting state officials regarding their conduct. The same view prevailed with respect to individuals holding positions of power at the federal level.

The purification of political reporting included not printing or broadcasting stories regarding the private lives of public officials. The fact that President Warren Harding's mistress Nan Britton had a child by Harding did not become widely known until after Harding died in San Francisco on August 2, 1923. After the end of the Teapot Dome scandal in 1927, Nan Britton published *The President's Daughter* in an effort to obtain part of Harding's estate. She received nothing.[28] "Call it cronyism, sweetheart reporting, or proper cultivation of sources," wrote journalistic historian Warren Francke, "relationships between news gatherers and news sources influence journalistic treatment of ethics."[29] The lack of women publishers, editors and reporters also played a role in journalists' not reporting on the private indiscretions of public officials. Many reporters did not find anything wrong with a male public figure having a good time.[30]

The purification of political reporting permitted public officials to lead separate public and private lives. A number of Washington reporters, for example, knew of John Kennedy's sexual exploits while he served as president. It took years after the death of President Kennedy for the details of his activities to work their way into the record of his presidency.[31] Much as American television portrayed American life in suburbia, the media presented the American public with a sanitized view of American government.

But the 1960s ended the practice of journalists' not reporting on the private lives of public officials and of giving government the benefit of the doubt. A new generation of journalists viewed government and public officials much more skeptically. These journalists no longer accepted as truthful information provided by government officials. Instead of criticizing journalists for their new frankness, a growing segment of the population now applauded aggressive coverage of government. The public integrity war had begun decades before the new journalism of the 1960s; the media simply stopped ignoring the deep fissures between American society and politics. This no-holds-barred nature of media coverage shocked the nation and shattered a generation of myths that had grown up around the administrative state since the early 1930s. Government *could* make mistakes. Corrupt public officials *could* be found outside large cities.

Watergate and the New Watchdog Journalists

The 1960s saw a revolution in moral standards. Stories regarding the indiscretions of public officials gradually became less shocking. Broadcast and print outlets no longer faced public condemnation for publishing material that might offend significant segments of the nation's population. Many journalists who entered the profession during the 1960s saw serious problems within American society. Children went without food and clothing; race and sex discrimination made it difficult for millions of Americans to make a decent living; states seemed to be willing to let their urban centers rot from within; and rural poverty was ignored. Much like the muckrakers of the first two decades of the century, younger journalists blamed government and public officials for letting these conditions exist. Some journalists may have supported radical solutions for the problems facing America, but the vast majority just wanted government to work better.

By the end of the 1960s, a larger percentage of the American public believed that the country was headed in the wrong direction. One segment of the population saw law and order and a return to the values of an earlier era as the solution. Another segment saw radical political, social and economic reform as the only solution. Both these perspectives wanted the media to report the decay of society as a means of persuading citizens to join their respective movements.

Growing suspicion of government and of public officials led to enactment of new laws giving the public and journalists unprecedented access to information and public meetings. The 1971 Pentagon Papers case emboldened the press to more agressively report on the non-public conduct of public agencies. In that case the Supreme Court refused to block the *Washington Post* from publishing papers highly critical of U.S. involvement in Vietnam taken from the Pentagon by Daniel Elsberg.[32] Freedom of information and open-meeting laws made it much more difficult for public agencies and public officials to keep information secret. Journalists found an increase in the number of individuals in public agencies willing to blow the whistle on misconduct. Journalists made much more effective use of interviews to pin down public figures on their involvement in particular events.[33] Prosecutors responsible for conducting public corruption investigations leaked information to journalists regarding the status of their investigations. A growing number of interest groups, such as Common Cause, worked hard to persuade journalists to distribute the findings of their studies—studies often highly critical of government and public officials.[34]

The packaging of political candidates by media experts and sophisticated public relations operations by public agencies also made publishers, editors and reporters more willing to spend time and resources to verify discrepancies between the public and private lives of officials and to confirm the accuracy of government information. As journalist Shelly Ross explained in his history of American political scandals, *Fall from Grace*, "Americans can be a very forgiving people. But while we accept apologies and embrace candor, we loathe denials and cover-ups."[35] Few politicians and their advisors believed that the American public would forgive them for their private indiscretions. Many more believed that their political enemies would use any hint of political scandal to destroy them. More effective management of the media became the preferred solution to the media problem. Richard Nixon, for example, placed Spiro Agnew on the ticket as vice-president in 1968 largely to hammer at the liberal media in the East.

Besides the trends discussed above, dramatic expansion of the First Amendment rights of media outlets and their reporters and journalists made it possible for post-Watergate newspapers and broadcast outlets to print stories that, during an earlier time, might have resulted in judgments for libel or slander. The Supreme Court, in the 1964 landmark decision case of *New York Times* v. *Sullivan*,[36] found that a public official seeking to collect damages for libel from a newspaper must prove actual malice by the newspaper, not simply the falsehood of information.[37] Justice Brennan, writing for the majority, based the decision on the "profound national commitment to the principle that debate on public issues should be uninhibited, robust, and wide-open, and that it may well include vehement, caustic, and sometimes unpleasantly sharp attacks on government public officials."[38] The establishment of the public-figure libel exception made it possible for a much larger cross-section of the media to search out and publish information critical of public officials.[39]

The proliferation of media outlets made it impossible to reinstate the earlier form of self-censorship that limited coverage of the indiscretions of public officials.[40] Communication satellites expanded the number of available channels. Conservative newspapers and magazines began to flourish as movement conservatives gained converts. Talk radio, tabloid television and a new generation of ideological magazines and newsletters provided a forum for almost any conspiracy theory, as well as for those angry with government and the perceived lack of accountability by public officials. The 1990s saw the information highway, with the Internet and the World Wide Web, further weaken control of the established media as the primary method of distributing information about government and public officials. A brave new world of journalism evolved. Public officials quickly learned that they could pay a heavy price for attempting to keep skeletons in their closets.

DEMYSTIFICATION AND ATTACK JOURNALISM

Blaming the media for the public integrity war has become a growth industry. The public integrity war, it must be remembered, started long before the 1960s or the Watergate scandal. However, media coverage of political ethics has played a major role in making it next to impossible for public officials to lead public and private lives. Much of the unhappiness over the selection of leaders comes from the impression that few political figures of our day have the same personal qualities of earlier leaders. The problem may be that we simply know much more about the lives of our prospective leaders before we decide to entrust them with tremendous responsibilities.

No practical way exists to get the genie back inside the bottle. Even if the traditional media outlets agreed to implement a code of conduct for reporting allegations of impropriety, the proliferation of other media forms means that any allegation will ultimately make its way to the public. New progressives and movement conservatives show little inclination to stop trying to portray one another as leading the nation to ruin.

Therefore, media coverage of the public integrity war has played into the hands of both the new progressives and the movement conservatives. New progressives believe that if the media focus on the power of special interests, the electorate will eventually see the light and place new progressives in positions of authority. Movement conservatives, on the other hand, believe extensive media coverage of waste, fraud and abuse in public programs will inevitably convince the public that too much government actually makes things worse.

Print and broadcast journalists have done a remarkable job covering the battles of the public integrity war. One can only estimate the number of words written and spoken on the subject of ethics since the resignation of Richard Nixon in August 1973. Many journalists believe that by focusing on ethics in government, public confidence in government will ultimately be restored. Unfortunately, this has not happened and is unlikely to happen.

After years of struggling with allegations, investigations and reports, the public appears ready to put such stories in perspective. The 1992 election of Bill Clinton and the subsequent Whitewater investigation provide strong evidence that ethics allegations have lost their potency as political weapons. Because mudslinging has become such a common feature of American politics, the public pays little attention to new allegations of improper conduct by public figures.

NOTES

1. For two highly critical views of the post-Watergate performance of the media, see Larry J. Sabato, *Feeding Frenzy: How Attack Journalism Has Transformed American Politics* (New York: Free Press, 1991); Suzanne Garment, *Scandal: The Crisis of Mistrust in American Politics* (New York: Random House, 1991).

2. For an excellent discussion of the arguments for and against the coverage of the personal lives of public officials see CQ Researcher, "Politicians and Privacy," April 17, 1992, pp. 338–59.

3. *Gallup Poll Monthly*, October 1994, p. 4.

Honesty & Ethics Trend
(very high/high combined)

1976	1977	1981	1983	1985	1988	1990	1991	1992	1993	1994
33	33	32	28	31	23	30	26	27	26	20

4. Ibid.

5. Ibid.

6. CQ Reseacher, "Politicians and Privacy," p. 341.

7. Warren Francke, "The Evolving Watchdog: The Media's Role in Government Ethics," *Annals of the American Academy of Political and Social Science* 537 (January 1995): 111.

8. CQ Researcher, "Politicians and Privacy," p. 342.

9. For a vocal defense of government, see Charles T. Goodsell, *The Case for Bureaucracy: A Public Administration Polemic*, 3d ed. (Chatham, NJ: Chatham House, 1994).

10. Francke, p. 113.

11. CQ Researcher, "Politicians and Privacy," p. 345.

12. David Paul Nord "The Nineteenth-Century Origins of Modern American Journalism." In *Three Hundred Years of the American Newspaper*, ed. John B. Hench (Worcester, MA: American Antiquarian Society, 1991), p. 408.

13. Ibid., p. 409.

14. Francke, p. 115.

15. Ibid., p. 114.

16. "Nineteenth-Century Origins," p. 409.

17. Ibid.

18. Ibid., p 411.

19. Ibid., p. 414.

20. Francke, p. 114.

21. Ibid.

22. See Richard Hofstadter, *Age of Reform* (New York: Vintage Books, 1955).

23. Arthur Weinberg, *The Muckrakers: The Era in Journalism that Moved America to Reform, 1902–1912* (New York: Simon and Schuster, 1961).

24. Francke, p. 114.

25. Samuel Eliot Morison and Henry Steele Commager, *The Growth of the American Republic*, 2 vols. (New York: Oxford University Press, 1962), p. 2:661.

26. James Q. Wilson, "Corruption: The Shame of the States." In *Political Cor-*

ruption: Readings in Comparative Analysis, ed. Arnold J. Heidenheimer (New Brunswick, NJ: Transaction Books, 1970), p. 301.

27. Ibid.

28. *American Heritage Pictorial History of the Presidents* (New York: American Heritage, 1968), p. 730.

29. Francke, p. 119.

30. For a summary of rumors regarding presidential indiscretions see CQ Researcher "Politicians and Privacy," pp. 343–53.

31. Ibid., p. 349.

32. Dorothy Giobbe, "Pentagon Papers' Strategist," *Editor & Publisher,* January 27, 1996, p. 9.

33. Francke, pp. 116–17.

34. Common Cause, state public interest research groups, Public Citizen, and the Center for Public Integrity have issued numerous reports highly critical of government between the mid-1970s and the mid-1990s. For example, see Common Cause, *Serving Two Masters: A Common Cause Study of Conflicts of Interest in the Executive Branch* (Washington, DC: Common Cause, 1976); Carla B. Reinganum, *Toxic Wastelands: Environmental and Public Health Implications of Six New York City Municipal Landfills* (New York: Public Interest Research Group, 1987); John Claybrook, *Retreat from Safety: Reagan's Attack on America's Health* (New York: Pantheon Books, 1989); Jean Cobb, *Short-Changed: How Congress and Special Interests Benefit at the Expense of the American People* (Washington, DC: Center for Public Integrity, 1991).

35. Shelly Ross, *Fall From Grace* (New York, Ballantine Books, 1988), p. xx.

36. 376 U.S. 254 (1964).

37. Craig R. Ducat and Harold W. Chase, *Constitutional Interpretation: Rights of the Individual,* 5th ed. (St. Paul: West Publishing, 1992) p. 1165.

38. Ibid., p. 1164.

39. Francke, p. 120.

40. See Henry A. Williams, "How to Report the Lewd and Unproven," *Time,* May 16, 1994, p. 46; Todd Gitlin, "Media Lemmings Run Amok!" *Washington Journalism Review,* April 1, 1992, p. 28; Lee Wilkins, "Journalists and the Character of Public Officials/Figures," *Journal of Mass Media Ethics* 9 (1994): 157.

PART III

THE PUBLIC ETHICS FIRESTORM

The preceding chapters have detailed the origins of the public integrity war that began long before Watergate became symbolic of political corruption. Watergate, however, ignited a major escalation of the public integrity war. In the aftermath of Watergate, new progressives and movement conservatives used the perceived decline of ethics in government to further their respective causes.

The ensuing firestorm over ethics failed to win many converts for either side. In fact, the public integrity war quickly evolved from a crusade into a war of attrition. And print and broadcast journalists found that they had little choice but to cover each new allegation. The new public integrity bureaucracy found itself with more business than it could handle.

Public figures found that ethics controversies simply did not go away without intense media scrutiny and some type of official investigation. The public integrity war had entered a new phase where ethics disputes went hand-in-hand with being a public servant.

Chapter 10

The Great Ethics Crusade

Scholars, journalists and political commentators have written countless books and articles examining the impact of the Watergate scandal on the nation's political system.[1] Richard Nixon, of all the major political figures of his era, entered the White House most prepared to withstand the brutality of the public integrity wars. In his later writings, Nixon characterized his political career as a series of victories, defeats and renewals.[2] It is said that Nixon viewed the world as filled with enemies intent upon destroying him, politically and personally. According to this vision, if he didn't get them, his enemies would surely find a way to get him. Nixon's preoccupation with these real or imagined enemies ultimately led to his downfall: the Nixon White House lost the ability to distinguish between political hardball and criminal conduct.[3] Nixon provided his critics with the evidence they needed to drive him from office in disgrace.

Critics of Richard Nixon seriously misjudged the long-term political significance of Watergate, however. Badly disillusioned by his 1968 election victory, new progressives saw Watergate as an opportunity to reshape the American political system and restore the administrative state to its rightful place overarching American society. Movement conservatives came to see Watergate as further evidence that the defenders of the administrative state would do anything to prevent the dismantling of big government.

Political commentator Kevin Phillips, in his 1994 book *Arrogant Capital*, described a Washington unchanged by the Watergate scandal. If anything, Washington had moved even further from understanding the hopes and concerns of the majority of Americans:

Most Washington influence wielders, policy shapers, and molders **bridle** [emphasis in the original] at being referred to as parasites. They are, in their own minds, notable contributors to the commonweal. But the question whether the capital needs forty thousand to fifty thousand lawyers and a total of ninety thousand persons involved with lobbying, whether lobbyists for foreign interests should thrive along the Potomac as in no other major country, and whether the U.S. Congress requires a staff of twenty thousand, four or five times as large as any other national legislative body, is simply not something that most Washingtonians let themselves think about.[4]

Apparently, plowing Washington under constitutes the only real solution to this level of institutional rot. Yet Watergate gave new progressives a brief opportunity to implement their reform agenda and save big government. New progressives lobbied Congress and state legislatures to enact sweeping political reform legislation. Campaign finance reform and other good-government legislation flooded Congress and state capitals. Progressives succeeded beyond their wildest imagination. "An enduring myth of American politics," according to Professors Harold Seidman and Robert Gilmour, "is that we can solve deep-seated problems of government by structural changes."[5] Watergate progressives based their entire reform initiative on the validity of this myth.

New progressives looked longingly back to the first two decades of the century and saw how political reform had changed the country. Civil service reform, the city manager form of government, nonpartisan elections, the line-item budget and competitive bidding for public contracts[6] all helped to increase the professionalism of public service.

Watergate-inspired reformers badly misjudged the mood of the nation, however. Even before Watergate, a grassroots revolt against higher taxes had taken hold in a number of states. Average Americans did not understand why they had to pay more taxes to feed big government bureaucracies for poorer services. Despite the chaotic nature of the 1960s, the decade saw the national economy boom. The early 1970s did not look nearly so promising. Continued tension in the Middle East threatened the nation's supply of cheap oil. Inflation combined with a slow growth rate made future economic growth highly uncertain. Public service ethics no longer constituted the most serious problem facing the United States.

THE NEW PROGRESSIVE BATTLE PLAN

After Watergate, new progressives faced the serious problem of finding structural reforms that would restore public trust in government and control the influence exercised on government by special interests. The decade prior to Watergate, as noted, had seen a significant tightening of federal corruption statutes and of the administrative rules governing the conduct of federal officials and employees. Federal law enforcement agencies had already begun expanding their role in pursuit of corrupt state and local officials.

Because the Watergate investigation revealed how President Nixon's re-election campaign had collected millions of dollars of unreported and illegal campaign contributions, campaign finance reform might have become the top objective of the good government reformers after Watergate. The 1976 Supreme Court decision in *Buckley* v. *Valeo*,[7] however, made it next to impossible for Congress to control the role of money in national politics. The High Court did uphold the authority of Congress to limit individual contributions to political candidates, to require candidates to disclose campaign and personal finances and to provide for public financing of presidential elections. However, the court struck down the constitutionality of mandatory limits on independent political expenditures by individuals and groups. That decision constituted a major setback for supporters of political reform.

Left with few workable reforms designed to prevent another Watergate, post-Watergate progressives turned to bureaucratic solutions to solve the perceived ethics crisis. The restructuring plan put forward after Watergate included: (1) provisions for the appointment of independent special prosecutors to investigate allegations of criminal acts by high-level executive branch officials, (2) public financial disclosure for high-level federal officials, (3) earned income limitations, (4) statutory blind trust requirements, (5) new revolving-door restrictions and (6) establishment of an independent Office of Government Ethics.[8] Nothing guaranteed that either political party would endorse this reform agenda, however. Beginning in the early 1970s, the Democratic Party began to move further left on the political spectrum. The core constituency of the Democratic Party believed that the money and power of special interests blocked the party's ability to regain control of the White House and to build broad-based public support for aggressive government regulation of the nation's economy.

If the pardon of Richard Nixon had not created enough problems for Gerald Ford, Ronald Reagan and the extreme right of the Republican Party made clear that they intended to fight Gerald Ford and the moderate wing for party control. Grassroots conservative Republicans felt that Ford and other moderate Republicans simply wanted to maintain the status quo and not make the drastic cuts in government programs necessary to end oppression by big government.

Jimmy Carter's ability to gain the Democratic nomination for president should have put the Democratic Party on notice that the nation's view of Washington had undergone a radical transformation. Carter ran as an outsider willing to take on the Washington bureaucracy. Yet many Americans believed that a left-leaning Democratic Party had no intention of either reining in government or lessening the tax burden. By election day, Jimmy

Carter's huge lead had almost entirely disappeared.[9] To the amazement of new progressives, Watergate had not caused a massive realignment of voters from the Republican to the Democratic Party. And Ford came very close to duplicating the 1948 come-from-behind victory of Harry S. Truman.

First as candidate and then as president-elect, Jimmy Carter had ample opportunity to distance himself from the rhetoric of new progressives. Nothing in Carter's background indicated that he accepted the theory of regulatory capture or wanted to broaden the role of government in American society. While Carter had served as a one-term governor of the very conservative state of Georgia, he adopted the party line of the progressive wing of the Democratic Party, which blamed the nation's problems on greedy special interests who used various forms of "honest graft" to persuade government decision makers to do their bidding.[10] Throughout the 1976 campaign, Carter "spoke out against the 'revolving door' and the 'sweetheart relationship' between industry and government."[11]

On January 4, 1977, President-elect Carter announced that "it [will] be the policy of the Carter-Mondale Administration to appoint and nominate for appointment only persons of high ability who will carry out their official duties without fear or favor and with an equal hand, unfettered by any actual or apparent conflicts of interest."[12] The Carter guidelines "required top officials to sign a letter of agreement pledging": (1) "to file net worth and income statements for themselves and members of their immediate household"; (2) not to take any action with respect to any matter "involving a person or organization with which they had been associated with for financial gain in the year previous to taking office or with which they have or are negotiating an arrangement for future employment"; (3) "not to appear for compensation before their former agency for one year after leaving government service" and (4) "to serve a full term."[13]

The Carter transition apparently believed that such requirements would not prevent the administration from finding qualified individuals to serve in key positions. Critics of the new ethics guidelines received little attention in the media.[14] But Proposition 13, not Watergate, turned out to be a much better gauge of the mood of the American people by the time Jimmy Carter became president. In November 1976, an angry California electorate voted overwhelmingly for Proposition 13, which "slashed property taxes by 60 percent and imposed strict limitations on the ability of local governments to raise property taxes in the future."[15] State after state followed the lead of California and enacted state limitations on new taxation and public expenditures.[16] While the tax revolt did not advocate dismantling the administrative state, it did constitute a statement by millions of Americans that they believed government could operate much more efficiently and effectively.

Great Expectations and the Ethics in Government Act of 1978

On October 26, 1978, more than four years after the resignation of Richard Nixon, Congress passed the Ethics in Government Act.[17] To its supporters, the act promised to usher in a golden age of ethics in government.[18] In the end, the act included only a handful of new federal crimes—specifically new restrictions on former high-level federal official lobbying their former agencies. Despite this little-recognized fact, pundits and commentators routinely described the passage of the act as a milestone in the evolution of modern public ethics management.[19]

The act did expand the system for federal ethics management by creating new federal public ethics units. But it was the provision for the appointment of independent special prosecutors to investigate allegations of criminal conduct by high-level executive branch officials that received the greatest amount of attention in the press.[20]

New revolving-door restrictions expanded existing restrictions put in place as part of the 1962 conflict-of-interest and bribery statute. The most significant restriction prohibited former "senior executive branch officials for one year after leaving government service from attempting to influence anyone in his or her former agency with respect to a particular matter in which the former agency has an interest."[21] Senator Paul Douglas had proposed an almost identical measure in 1951.[22]

Finally, the act required public financial disclosure for thousands of high-level officials in all three branches of the federal government.[23] Supporters of public financial disclosure for decades had argued that such disclosure would help to restore public confidence in government because it would give the media and the public the opportunity to review the financial holdings of high-level officials. Moreover, public disclosure might deter some officials from purchasing or retaining financial interests that might conflict with the performance of their official duties.

The Ethics in Government Act did force the White House and federal agencies and departments to devote much more time and energy to public ethics management. Although the act had nothing to do with increased funding of federal corruption investigations, it did help the Justice Department and U.S. attorneys to make a stronger case for funding such corruption investigations.

The Ethics in Government Act constituted a bureaucratic solution to declining public confidence in the ethics of public officials. Provisions for the appointment of independent counsels, a new Office of Government Ethics and public financial disclosure all reflected progressive beliefs that improved ethics management would have a positive impact on public trust in government. But new progressives had made the same mistake progressives had made during the early twentieth century. The progressives assumed that, if political reforms succeeded in cleaning up government, Americans would support a larger role for government in American society. Little relationship existed, in fact, between political reform and increased public support for more government regulation or for larger public programs.

The Public Confidence Meltdown

Movement conservatives did a much better job of measuring the mood of the American public than did the new progressives. Surveys conducted in 1978 and 1979 found that the American public believed that federal agencies wasted 48 cents out of every tax dollar spent.[24] Equally disturbing to the Carter administration and to the Democratic majority in Congress, polls indicated that a large percentage of Americans believed that federal employees just did not work very hard. Sixty-seven percent of those polled by the Gallup organization in May of 1977 agreed that the federal government employed too many people. The same number believed that private-sector employees worked harder than federal employees.[25]

The shift in national attention from the evils of special interests to the inefficiency of government changed the political landscape of the nation.[26] By 1980, the Carter White House and Democratic Congress found opponents blaming them for a large number of domestic and international failures. The nomination of Ronald Reagan as presidental candidate breathed new life into the sagging presidency of Jimmy Carter. Few political observers believed that Ronald Reagan had any chance of winning his bid for the presidency.

The fact that the Carter White House experienced its own ethics problems made it difficult for Jimmy Carter to run on a public integrity platform. After beating back the primary challenges of Ted Kennedy and Jesse Jackson, the Carter campaign tried to portray Ronald Reagan and his supporters as extremists who planned to turn the clock back on fifty years of progressive reforms. Despite public concerns over Republican extremism, the Iran hostage crisis, high interest rates and distrust of Washington led the general public to question Jimmy Carter's ability to handle the presidency. The public would overcome its apprehension that a Ronald Reagan presidency might ruin the country. Up until the last week of the campaign, Ronald Reagan held only a small lead over President Carter. On election day, however, American voters repudiated the leadership of Jimmy Carter by handing Ronald Reagan a clear landslide victory.

Whether the voters merely rejected Jimmy Carter or voted affirmatively for Ronald Reagan remains open to debate.[27] The fact remains that Reagan painted a hopeful vision for the future of America. Through bureaucrat bashing, criticizing Carter for destroying the U.S. military and promising large tax cuts, Reagan assured the American people that the country would reemerge as an economic and world power.

The years following Watergate saw new progressives succeed in putting into place an extensive system for public integrity management. However, the reforms did little to end the growing debate over the appropriate role of government in American society. New progressives believed that, in the aftermath of Watergate, there was ample opportunity to restructure the nation's political system. The Ethics in Government Act was a first step toward freeing government from control by powerful special interests.

TRENCH WARFARE AND THE REAGAN REVOLUTION

Much like the incoming Eisenhower administration in 1953, the Reagan administration took over the presidency with high hopes of dismantling institutionalized big government. The Reagan transition team beat the bushes for hard-headed business executives who could begin shrinking the administrative state. Many of these recruits came to Washington intent on doing what Reagan had promised during his campaign—they refused to let anything stand in their way. Unfortunately, the judgment of some was clouded by their zealous commitment to the Reagan revolution.

And much like the Eisenhower administration three decades earlier, the Reagan administration recruited large numbers of individuals from the private sector to implement the Reagan agenda. Just as the Eisenhower administration had done, the Reagan White House underestimated the problems members of its administration would have in complying with the wide spectrum of administrative and criminal ethics restrictions.[28] By the time Reagan left the White House in January 1989, hundreds of Reagan officials faced allegations of improper on- or off-the-job conduct.[29]

Reagan appointees and nominees entered a world of public financial disclosure forms, blind trusts, appearances of impropriety, gift acceptance restrictions, earned income limitations and disqualification or divestiture requirements.[30] Anyone coming to Washington intent on dismantling big government could easily have seen the maze of ethics rules and regulations as a plot to make it difficult for Reagan appointees to function. Although the Ethics in Government Act added few new substantive restrictions, the White House incorrectly perceived the act as the source of many of its ethics-related problems.[31]

It is beyond the scope of this volume to chronicle each of the allegations made against Reagan administration officials. One publication—*All Four Feet and a Snout in the Trough*—provides a somewhat partisan review of some two hundred alleged ethics violations by Reagan appointees.[32] Suzanne Garment's *Scandal: The Crisis of Mistrust in American Politics* portrayed many Reagan appointees who became embroiled in ethics controversies as the victims of an overzealous press.[33]

Table 10–1
Honesty and Behavior Standards[34]

	Satisfied	Dissatisfied	No Opinion
1986	33%	63%	4%
1973	22	72	6
1963	34	58	8

To the amazement of most political observers, the scandals had little impact on public support for President Reagan or for the Republican Party. Throughout the 1980s, voters expressed concern over the decline of ethics in government. As described in Table 10–1, a 1986 Gallup poll reported "amid widespread reports of unethical conduct and illegal activities in many areas of public life, almost two-thirds of Americans [expressed] dissatisfaction with the honesty and standards of behavior of their compatriots."[35] The country had made little progress in raising public trust in government between 1973 and 1986.

Another Gallup poll in the same year revealed great pessimism in how Americans viewed the honesty of their politicians. When asked whether "the overall level of ethics and honesty in politics has risen, fallen or stayed the same during the past 10 years," 42 percent responded that it had fallen.[36] Yet a similar poll conducted in 1983 found 59 percent of those surveyed as seeing a decline in the ethics of politicians.[37] Despite the almost daily reports of official misconduct by local, state and federal officials between 1983 and 1986, public cynicism over the honesty of politicians actually had declined.

Seventy-nine percent of those responding to a Gallup poll in March 1988 said "the issue of honesty in government [would] weigh more heavily in their choice of a president this year than it had in previous elections."[38] Republicans, however, continued to hold a highly favorable opinion of the Reagan administration and Democrats a very negative view.[39] Forty-three percent of independents surveyed agreed that the Reagan administration's record for honesty and ethical standards was worse than those of other administrations.[40]

Neither new progressives nor movement conservatives made much progress during the 1980s in persuading the American people to blame the ethics crisis on the opposition. Even the $40 million Iran-*Contra* investigation did little to shake Republican support. Vice-President George Bush successfully painted Michael Dukakis as someone who loved big government, who wanted to let criminals out of jail and who would destroy the United States military.

During the 1980s, political scandals fell into a predictable routine. First, some allegation of impropriety by a public official appeared in print. Second, the official denied the allegation and publicly defended his or her integrity. The accused official blamed political opponents for pursuing the allegation. Third, other news operations rushed to confirm or discredit the story. Fourth, pressure mounted for a formal investigation of the charges. Fifth, the official hired a lawyer and waited for the results of the formal investigation. Sixth, the subsequent investigation normally cleared the official of criminal charges, but sometimes found violations of administrative standards of conduct. Some cases, however, stretched out for years because of their complexity.

Observing a predictable life cycle of public integrity scandals convinced Americans that the majority of public servants put their interests ahead of the public's interests. Despite the small number of public servants implicated in wrongdoing during the 1980s, the public tended "to lump together all public officials—the politically appointed and the merit-based civil servant."[41] Yet the public failed to find anyone or any party to blame for this predicament.

The fact that public corruption scandals had little impact on support for established political parties did not deter various actors from pursuing their reform agendas. New progressives pushed for even more comprehensive political reform. Movement conservatives intensified their attacks on the evils of big government. Apparently, corruption in government went hand-in-hand with big government.

Common Cause, for example, continued to argue that special-interest money corrupted all parts of the nation's political system. "The 1980s brought an anything-goes attitude," stated a 1990 Common Cause publication, "that dominated a decade when basic values were under attack and self-interest reigned supreme. The major reforms of the 1970s were undermined by the practices of the 1980s, generating widespread public cynicism toward government officials."[42]

PRISONERS OF WAR AND POLITICAL CRIMES

The illegal lobbying prosecutions of former White House officials Michael Deaver and Lyn Nofziger came to symbolize both the lowering of ethical standards in government and the increasing brutality of the public integrity war. Despite the intense media scrutiny of both scandals, the scandals did little to alter the political leanings of the vast majority of American voters.

Michael Deaver, who served as a key White House aide to Ronald Reagan between 1981 and 1985, came to the White House with little money and left to become a highly paid Washington lobbyist. Allegations surfaced in mid-1986 that Deaver might have violated federal revolving-door prohibitions—specifically, the one-year ban on former high-level executive branch officials lobbying anyone in their former agency. A ten-month investigation by independent counsel Whitney North Seymour resulted in

Deaver's being indicted on "five counts of perjury involving his testimony before a House subcommittee and a grand jury."[43] The indictment did not allege, however, that Deaver had violated any of the criminal postemployment lobbying prohibitions. On December 17, 1987, a federal jury convicted Deaver on three counts of perjury.[44] Whitney North Seymour subsequently issued a scathing attack on the ethical climate in Washington.[45] Within a relatively short time of his conviction, Washington welcomed Deaver back as an expert on Washington politics and the public integrity war.[46]

Following closely on the heels of the Deaver investigation were allegations that former Reagan White House aide and political operative Lyn Nofziger might have violated the one-year no-contact rule. Nofziger allegedly violated the provision of the Ethics in Government Act of 1978 that prohibited senior executive branch officials from contacting anyone in their former agency on behalf of private parties for one year after leaving government.[47] On February 3, 1987, at the request of the attorney general, a three-judge federal court panel appointed Washington attorney James C. McKay to investigate these illegal lobbying allegations. McKay subsequently obtained an indictment, and in February 1988 a Washington federal district court convicted Nofziger of violating the ethics rule.[48] Nofziger's conviction constituted the first conviction of a former high-level federal official for violating the one-year waiting period. To the surprise of many ethics observers, the U.S. Court of Appeals for the District of Columbia reversed Nofziger's conviction on the grounds that the trial court had improperly instructed the jury with respect to key elements of the one-year restriction. A *New York Times* editorial subsequently sharply criticized the decision.[49] Nofziger quickly returned to the Washington scene.

Toward the end of Ronald Reagan's second term, the Iran-*Contra* investigation, the Department of Defense Ill-Wind investigation and the Housing and Urban Development influence-peddling scandal resulted in numerous prosecutions and a flood of criminal convictions. For reasons difficult to understand, neither the media nor the public seemed to care much about the outcome of these investigations.

Lawrence E. Walsh, independent counsel for the Iran-*Contra* investigation, conducted the most extensive federal integrity inquiry since Watergate. Walsh spent over $40 million looking into the conduct of executive branch officials in the White House and other federal agencies for illegal conduct related to the arms-for-hostages deal and subsequent efforts to prevent Congress from learning about the transactions. Walsh obtained fourteen indictments, seven guilty pleas, and four convictions.[50]

Despite his massive investigation, Walsh failed to develop enough evidence to implicate Ronald Reagan or George Bush in any criminal wrongdoing. Oliver North, the most famous of the Iran-*Contra* figures, found himself cleared of all charges when the U.S. Court of Appeals for the District of Columbia overturned his convictions on the grounds that Walsh had used information gained from testimony before Congress made under a grant of immunity.[57]

On Christmas Eve 1992, President Bush pardoned former Secretary of Defense Casper Weinberger, who was then under indictment, and eighteen other Iran-*Contra* figures.[52] To the surprise of many, key Democrats in Congress backed Weinberger's pardon.[53] The majority of the public, however, disapproved of the pardon.[54] Lawrence Walsh reacted angrily to the Bush pardons, claiming that they made it impossible for his investigation to undercover the truth regarding Iran-*Contra*.[55]

Many of those caught up in the post-Watergate public integrity disputes came to regard themselves as political prisoners. The Bush Iran-*Contra* pardons disturbed the public, but they did not ignite a major backlash against Republicans. Washington found it easy to accept back into its fold individuals cleared of allegations—and even those found guilty of violating the public trust. The ordeal of the investigation, to many, seemed sufficient punishment.

STALEMATE AND THE PUBLIC INTEGRITY BATTLEFIELD

For all the sound and fury associated with the Reagan-era political scandals, they had little measurable impact on the balance of political power. Democrats continued to control Congress, and the country elected another Republican president, even though independent counsel Walsh maintained that Vice President George Bush knew much more about Iran-*Contra* than he was willing to admit. Instead of building support for reauthorizing the independent counsel law, Iran-*Contra* had convinced congressional conservatives to oppose it. Even more important to the future of the public integrity war, media attention began to shift away from the executive branch and toward Congress. Critics asked why federal law imposed much stricter ethics rules on executive branch employees and officials than it did on members of Congress and congressional staffs.

In October 1988, Congress passed a new ethics reform bill that expanded the scope of revolving-door restrictions on former federal officials. President Reagan vetoed the bill on the grounds that these new revolving-door rules would make it more difficult to recruit and retain badly needed personnel.

Watergate had raised expectations that political reform could restore public trust in government and redistribute political power from special interests to civic-minded individuals committed to exercising power in the public interest. But ethics reform fell far short of its goal because new progressives underestimated the depth of public disdain for big government. Movement conservatives, on the other hand, failed to understand that public anger with government did not mean that the public wanted an end to government programs designed to provide citizens with a social safety net, protect the environment, make it easier for students to attend college or guarantee poor children health care.

The 1980s provided dramatic evidence of the futility of the public integrity war. The constant drumming of stories regarding corrupt public officials and waste, fraud and abuse in public programs simply made it more difficult for anyone to govern. The warring parties, however, gave little indication of a willingness to accept a truce. New progressives continued to believe that movement conservatives planned to destroy the administrative state and ignore the less fortunate. Movement conservatives blamed new progressives for exacerbating the problems confronting the country. And so the stalemate continued as the casualties mounted. Both sides suffered mightily from battle fatigue.

NOTES

1. See Frederick C. Mosher, *Watergate: Implications for Responsible Government: A Special Report at the Request of the Senate Select Committee on Presidential Campaign Activities* (New York: Basic Books, 1974); "Watergate: chronology of a crisis," *Congressional Quarterly*, 1975; Fred Emery, *Watergate: The Corruption of American Politics and the Fall of Richard Nixon* (New York: Times Books, 1994).

2. Richard M. Nixon, *In the Arena: A Memoir of Victory, Defeat, and Renewal* (New York: Simon and Schuster, 1990).

3. See American Civil Liberties Union, *Why President Nixon should be impeached* (Washington: Public Affairs Press, 1973).

4. Kevin Phillips, *Arrogant Capital* (Boston: Little, Brown, 1994), p. 38.

5. Harold Seidman and Robert Gilmour, *Politics, Position and Power*, 4th ed. (New York: Oxford University Press, 1986), p. 51, cited in Thomas M. Holbrook and Kenneth J. Meier, "Politic, Bureaucracy, and Political Corruption: A Comparative Analysis." In *Ethics and Public Administration*, ed. George Frederickson (Armonk, NY: M.E. Sharpe, 1993).

6. Joseph F. Zimmerman, *State and Local Government Review* 14 (September 1982): 98.

7. *Buckley* v. *Valeo*, 424 U.S. 1 (1976).

8. Robert Roberts, *White House Ethics* (Westport, CT: Greenwood Press, 1988), pp. 152–61.

9. For a history of the 1976 Ford campaign, see Malcolm D. MacDougall, *We Almost Made it* (New York: Crown, 1977).

10. Bruce Adams and Kathryn Kavanagh-Baran, *Promise and Performance: Carter Builds a New Administration* (Lexington, MA: Lexington Books, 1979), pp. 87–98.

11. Ibid., p. 99.

12. Ibid.

13. Ibid., pp. 88–89.

14. Irving Kristol, "Post-Watergate Morality: Too Good for our Good?" *New York Times Magazine*, November 14, 1976, pp. 35, 50–51, 53, 55.

15. Ann Bowman and Richard C. Kearney, *State & Local Government* (Boston: Houghton Mifflin, 1990), p. 365.

16. Ibid.

17. Public Law 95–521.

18. Stuart Gilman, "Presidential Ethics and the Ethics of the Presidency," *Annals of the American Academy of Political and Social Science* 537 (January 1995): 73.

19. Ibid., p. 72.

20. Ann Cooper, "Carter Signs Government-Wide Ethics Bill," *Congressional Quarterly Weekly Report* October 28, 1978, pp. 3126–27.

21. Robert Roberts, *Report to the Administrative Conference of the United States: A Guide to Federal Ethics Laws for Presidential Appointees.* In *Sourcebook on Governmental Ethics for Presidential Appointees* (Washington, DC: Administrative Conference of the United States, 1988), pp. 42–43.

22. For a discussion of the entire spectrum of regulations proposed by Senator Paul Douglas, see Paul Douglas, *Ethics in Government* (Cambridge, MA: Harvard University Press, 1952).

23. James D. Carroll and Robert N. Roberts, "If Men Were Angels: Assessing the Ethics in Government Act of 1978," *Policy Studies* 17 (Winter 1988–89): 439.

24. "Public Says 48 cents of each Federal Tax Dollar is Wasted," *Gallup Opinion Index*, December 1979, pp. 15–16.

25. "Most See Federal Bureaucrats as Overpaid, Lazy, Pampered," *Gallup Opinion Poll, Report No. 146*, September 1977, pp. 20–24.

26. Richard Cohen, "Will the 96th Become the 'Oversight Congress?' " *National Journal*, January 13, 1979, p. 44.

27. For two excellent histories of the 1980 presidential election, see Jack Germond, *Blue Smoke and Mirrors: How Reagan Won and Why Carter Lost the Election of 1980* (New York: Viking, 1981); Elizabeth Drew, *Portrait of an Election: The 1980 Presidential Campaign* (London, Routledge & Paul, 1981).

28. Gilman, p. 73.

29. Howard Kurtz, "Reagan's People: Issues of Propriety: Deaver Case Revives Questions About Senior Officials' Conduct," *Washington Post*, April 27, 1986, pp. A1, A11–13.

30. For an excellent discussion of the problem faced by the Reagan administration in complying with the Ethics in Government Act of 1978, see Administrative Conference of the United States, *Ethics in Government: Proceedings of a Working Conference*, Washington, DC, March 1, 1988. In Office of the Chairman, Administrative Conference of the United States, *Sourcebook on Government Ethics for Presidential Appointees* (Washington, DC: Administrative Conference of the United States, December 1988).

31. Gilman, p. 73.

32. *All Four Feet and a Snout in the Trough: 200 Alleged Ethics Violations by Reagan Administration Appointees* (Upland, PA: Diane Publishing, 1987).

33. Suzanne Garment, *Scandal: The Crisis of Mistrust in American Politics* (New York: Random House, 1991).

34. "Honesty and Behavior Standards: Americans Chide Counterparts for Dishonesty, Unethical Behavior," *The Gallup Report*, May 1986, pp. 12–13.

35. Ibid.

36. "Americans Still Perceive Politicians as Dishonest," *The Gallup Report*, November 1986, p. 28.

37. Ibid.

38. "Honesty in Government Stirs Great Concern in Huge Majority of Voters," *The Gallup Report*, 270 (March 1988), p. 26.

39. Ibid.

40. Ibid.

41. H. George Frederickson and David G. Frederickson, "Public Perceptions of Ethics in Government," *Annals of the American Academy of Political and Social Science* 537 (January 1995): 170.

42. Fred Wertheimer "20 Years: Common Cause: Advancing Honesty and Fairness in our Political System," *Common Cause Magazine*, Fall 1992, p. 3.

43. Roberts, *Ethics*, p. 186.

44. Bill McAllister, "Deaver Found Guilty of Lying About Lobbying: Former Reagan Aide Acquitted on 2 Counts," *Washington Post*, 18 December 1987, p. A1.

45. Bill McAllister, "Seymour 'Loose Money,' Law Ethics Plague Capital," *Washington Post*, December 18, 1987, p. A1.

46. Gilman, p. 73, n. 58.

47. "Pen Pal," *Time*, November 17, 1986, p. 34.

48. "Nofziger's Turn," *Time*, February 22, 1988, p. 31.

49. Martin Tolchin, "Nofziger Wins Court Reversal of Conviction," *New York Times*, June 28, 1989, p. A1.

50. CQ Researcher, "Political Scandals," *Congressional Quarterly*, May 27, 1994, p. 475.

51. Ibid.

52. Bob Cohen, "Anatomy of a Pardon: Why Weinberger Walked," *Newsweek*, January 11, 1993, pp. 22–23.

53. Robert L. Jackson and Ronald J. Ostrow. "Key Democrats Backed Pardon of Weinberger," *Los Angeles Times*, December 26, 1992, p. A1.

54. Richard Benedetto, "Most Disapprove of Iran-Contra Pardon," *USA Today*, December 30, 1992, p. A4.

55. Michael Hedges, "Walsh Says Pardon Hid Truth," *Washington Times*, February 9, 1993, pp. A1,4.

Chapter 11

Returning Fire

Fred Wertheimer, president of Common Cause, at the beginning of the 1988 presidential campaign told *The National Journal* that the Iran-*Contra* incident would have the same type of impact on the 1988 presidential election as the Watergate scandal had on the 1976 presidential election. The ethics issue, according to Wertheimer, would be "reflected" in the campaign to the disadvantage of Republicans.[1] Presidential candidate Al Gore, senator from Tennessee, warned Democrats, however, not "to assume that the Iran-contra affair is going to produce victory in the upcoming election. They will have to outline a vision for the American people."[2] Gore's prediction proved accurate and Wertheimer's was badly off the mark. Iran-*Contra* failed to catch on as a major campaign issue.[3]

Throughout the 1988 campaign, George Bush put considerable distance between himself and the Reagan administration's poor ethics record. Early in March 1988, he stressed that members of his administration would comply with strict ethics rules.[4] In a May campaign speech, Bush announced his support for legislation tightening conflict-of-interest laws.[5] He pledged that members of his administration would comply with a tough new staff code of conduct.[6]

The Dukakis campaign tried to make the ethical record of the Reagan administration a major campaign issue.[7] The Dukakis campaign attacked the Reagan-Bush administration for its record of "sleaze."[8] Despite the fact that the Dukakis campaign kept raising the character issue, swing voters simply did not care or believe that Bush had anything to do with Iran-*Contra* or the ethics problems of the previous administration.

THE BUSH ETHICS CAMPAIGN

The Bush transition team took immediate steps to make sure that ethics problems would not hamper its operations. On November 15, 1988, the transition team presented a new code of conduct for transition employees and volunteers.[9]

Patterned after recommendations of the Administrative Conference of the United States,[10] the Bush transition required workers

to sign a five part pledge as a condition of employment agreeing (1) to hold in confidence and use exclusively for purposes of the transition any non-public information provided in the course of the transition; (2) not to permit any use of such information for any private gain for anyone at any time; (3) not to participate in any transition matter that creates so much as an appearance of a conflict with any financial interest of the worker or his or her close family or business associates; (4) to conserve and safeguard any federal property, using it solely for transition activities; and (5) to waive personal privacy in regard to this commitment and to seek clarification of these standards as necessary.[11]

The Bush transition believed the new code of conduct would prevent the recurrence of the type of criticism that had followed the Carter-Reagan transition. The Reagan transition had placed some six hundred individuals, mostly volunteers, in federal agencies all over Washington. Many of those assigned to an agency had worked in private-sector organizations that had a direct interest in the policies formulated or enforced by that agency. Because many of these transition volunteers were not classified as federal employees, federal law did not require that they comply with many key conflict-of-interest laws and regulations. Critics argued that nothing prevented these volunteers from using their positions to lobby for policies favorable to their private interests.

Because many Reagan administration officials continued to work in the Bush administration, the Bush transition did not have nearly the number of problems associated with a transition from a Republican to a Democratic president. The transition code of conduct, however, did help the Bush administration get off on the right foot.

Potholes on the Road to Reform

The Bush transition did face a small number of well-publicized personnel problems. Secretary of State James A. Baker III, for example, reluctantly sold substantial stock holdings in a bank with large numbers of Third World loans.[12] White House Counsel C. Boydon Gray, the chief ethics officer of the Bush White House, gave up his $50,000-a-year salary as chairman of his family's communication firm and placed his large financial holdings into a blind trust to avoid any appearance of impropriety.[13] Many other high-level Bush appointees, as required by federal law, agreed not to participate in matters that might affect the value of their financial holdings.[14]

The most damaging transition controversy involved the nomination of former Texas Senator John Tower for the position of secretary of defense. The *Dallas Morning News*, shortly after the announcement of the nomination, reported that John Tower had received some $1.65 million from major defense contractors for consulting and lobbying services.[15] Although Tower clearly had not violated any ethics laws, critics accused Tower of leaving government and cashing in on his contacts in government. The nomination, according to this line of reasoning, sent a bad message to the American people.

Concern over Tower's drinking habits, not the payments, ended up sinking the nomination. Washington social circles knew that Senator Tower enjoyed a good drink. Throughout his years in the Senate, however, no one had questioned Tower's ability to perform his duties. A pledge by Tower to refrain from drinking while serving as defense secretary did little to reduce concern over his qualifications. A March 1989 Gallup Poll found 53 percent of the American public opposed to his confirmation.[16] The poll also found that 72 percent of those questioned and large majorities of all political persuasions supported Senate inquiries into the personal lives of cabinet nominees.[17]

Taking everything into consideration, the Bush transition operated as smoothly as any since the end of the Second World War.[18] The White House counsel's office, headed by C. Boyden Gray, did an outstanding job handling transition ethics issues.

LEVELING THE PLAYING FIELD

The Tower affair did not stop the Bush White House from pushing ahead with an ambitious ethics reform agenda. Taking a page directly out of President Kennedy's ethics reform handbook, on January 25, 1989, President Bush established the President's Commission on Federal Ethics Law Reform.[19] President Bush appointed distinguished jurist and public ethics expert Malcolm Richard Wilkey to chair the panel and Carter administration attorney general Griffin B. Bell to the position of vice-chairman. The panel of well-respected Washington veterans turned out to have serious reservations about the direction of federal ethics reform and great concern about the condition of congressional ethics.[20]

President Bush directed the panel to consider four key guiding principles:

First, "ethical standards for public servants must be exacting enough to ensure that the officials act with the utmost integrity and live up to the public trust in them." Second, "standards must be fair, they must be objective and consistent with common sense." Third, "the standards must be equitable all across the three branches of the federal government." Fourth, the country "cannot afford to have unreasonably restrictive requirements that discourage able citizens from entering public service."[21]

Tony Eastland, resident scholar at the National Legal Center in Washington and a Justice Department official from 1985 to 1988, urged President Bush to push forward with his ethics initiatives. He suggested the president challenge "Congress to abide by the same ethics laws it has legislated for the executive branch," and praised the president for his intention to throw down the ethics gauntlet at the feet of Congress.[22] Eastland reasoned that a "Congress forced to abide by executive-branch ethics rules just might realize the excesses of those rules and conform them to reason and common sense, another stated goal of the President."[23] A vocal opponent of the independent counsel law, Eastland did not intend to forgive progressive critics in Congress for beating up on high-level Reagan officials.

On March 9, 1989, the President's ethics commission issued a sweeping report that bore striking similarities to the report issued early in 1961 by President Kennedy's ethics commission.[24] The commission found few problems with the executive branch ethics program but many problems with congressional ethics management. It strongly backed the concept of a level playing field for ethics regulation.

To move toward a level playing field, the commission recommended extending the federal criminal self-dealing prohibition, Section 208, to "non-Member officers and employees of the judiciary and Congress"[25] and their staff. The commission proposed to prohibit federal employees in all three branches from accepting honoraria and salary supplements from private sources. Senior officials from all three branches of the government also would be subject to the 15 percent earned income limitation established by the 1978 Ethics Act. Only Congress, at the time of the report, permitted its employees and members to accept significant honoraria and outside earned income.

The commission proposed to extend revolving-door rules to high-level legislative and judicial staff. To expedite investigations of wrongdoing by members of Congress and by congressional employees, the commission proposed that Congress appoint an independent ethics official to head a permanent congressional ethics office and extend the independent counsel provisions of the 1978 Ethics Act to members of Congress. The proposed congressional ethics officials would have broad authority to investigate misconduct and to make recommendations to congressional ethics committees on possible disciplinary actions. Independent counsels would have the authority to pursue criminal investigations and prosecutions.

Putting Back the Welcome Mat

Besides supporting extending ethics rules to all three branches of government, the commission proposed changes in federal law designed to make it easier for individuals to move between the private sector and the federal government.

Since the early 1960s, federal agencies had complained that financial conflict-of-interest rules deterred some experts from accepting positions on federal advisory committees. The commission proposed to give agencies the authority to waive financial self-dealing rules "for advisory committee members where the appointing authority determines, after review of financial disclosure forms, that the need for a member's expertise outweighs the potential conflict of interest."[26]

The commission also proposed raising the categories of value for reporting income and assets on public financial disclosure statements in order to provide officials with greater privacy and to reduce inadvertent violations of disclosure requirements.[27]

The certificate-of-divestiture proposal of the commission's report constituted the most important of the reform proposals. To ease the financial burden on those individuals directed to sell financial assets in order to comply with conflict-of-interest rules, the commission proposed allowing federal employees and officials to roll over any capital gains into "neutral holdings such as Treasury bills, municipal bonds, or bank certificates of deposit,"[28] thus avoiding capital gains taxes.

Federal agencies also had complained that limited travel budgets often made it difficult for employees to do their jobs. To deal with this problem, the commission proposed giving all federal agencies gift acceptance authority.[29] At the time of the report, federal law permitted only agencies and departments with individual gift acceptance authority to solicit help from nonpublic sources. Such a change in the law would permit all federal agencies to seek private funds to supplement their budgets.

Not unexpectedly, the commission expressed its strong opposition to enactment of new revolving-door lobbying restrictions. From the perspective of the commission, tighter restrictions would only complicate the recruitment process. Instead, the commission proposed prohibiting former federal officials, for two years after leaving the government, from either using or disclosing "certain specifically defined non-public information" in association with representing private parties before the government.[30]

On April 12, 1989, the Bush White House issued a new standards of conduct executive order replacing the one issued by President Johnson in 1965. Executive Order 12674 made few substantive changes in conduct rules established by the Kennedy and Johnson ethics directives.[31] Issuing the order, however, gave President Bush the opportunity to demonstrate his commitment to high standards of conduct in government. The Office of Government Ethics subsequently issued over sixty pages of regulations implementing the order.[32] The Bush order expanded existing prohibitions by prohibiting any employee "appointed by the President to a full-time noncareer position in the executive branch" from accepting any earned income from outside employment.[33]

The Congressional Ethics Mess

A December 1988 Gallup Poll found that only 19 percent of those questioned rated the ethical standards of senators as very high or high.[34] Members of the House did not fare any better. Only 16 percent of those polled rated the ethical standards of House members as either very high or high.[35] Various public-interest groups pounded Congress for its lax ethics standards. Common Cause, in particular, mounted an aggressive lobbying campaign, focusing its criticism on members of Congress who were accepting tens of thousands of dollars in honoraria for giving speeches or attending conferences.[36]

On April 12, 1989, President Bush sent legislation to Congress to "toughen some federal ethics standards, loosen some others, make the laws more uniform across the three branches and give federal judges a 25 percent pay raise."[37] In a speech before the American Society of Newspaper Editors Convention, President Bush made clear that he wanted Congress to reform its ethical standards;[38] "The same standard that applies to a staff person at HUD should also apply to housing subcommittee staff on Capitol Hill. . . . And if Washington is to be a level playing field, then every player should be treated the same."[39]

The Bush administration's Government-wide Ethics Act included: (1) uniform financial reporting for officials in the three branches, (2) extension of current federal conflict-of-interest laws to officers and senior employees in Congress, (3) uniform gift and travel reimbursement rules for the three branches, (4) new postgovernment lobbying restrictions, (5) extension of the independent counsel statute to Congress and (6) extension of the executive branch's 15 percent outside earned income limitation to members of Congress.[40]

The Government-wide Ethics Act did not go as far as some congressional critics wanted, however.[41] The act did not include a ban on members of Congress' accepting honoraria for giving speeches or attending conferences. Fred Wertheimer, president of Common Cause, accused President Bush of "walking away from the issue" of stopping members of Congress from accepting honoraria.[42] The *Washington Post* argued that President Bush could not afford to ignore the congressional honoraria issue:

We are not advocating an impossibly high standard here. We do not believe in Sani-Gov, in trying somehow—contradiction in terms—to insulate a democratic government from interest groups, its legislative branch especially. But somewhere out there in the littered, muddy farm yard is a line or zone between right and wrong, and the honoraria system is on the wrong side of it. Mr. Bush needs to say so and to see that something is done about it.[43]

Nothing guaranteed the passage of President Bush's ethics reform legislation. Progressive members of Congress wanted much tighter revolving-door rules. A new round of congressional ethics scandals, however, made it increasingly difficult for Congress to resist reform. On April 17, 1989, the House Ethics Committee charged Speaker of the House Jim Wright (Dem., Texas) with accepting improper gifts from Texas developer George Mallick. Mallick paid Wright's wife, Betty, an "$18,000-a-year salary and gave her use of a company car and condominium—benefits the committee valued at a total of $145,000 over ten years."[44] The committee also alleged that Wright arranged bulk sales of his book, *Reflections of a Public Man*, to avoid House earned income limitations.[45]

On May 31, 1989, in an emotion-packed speech before the House, Wright announced his intention to resign. Wright portrayed himself as a "victim of a partisan vendetta and denounced the mindless cannibalism of attacks on politicians' personal ethics."[46] He resigned from the House on June 30.

Allegations of ethics violations made by Newt Gingrich and other conservative Republican members of the House led to the investigation that ultimately forced Wright from the House.[47] A week before Wright resigned, House Majority Whip Tony Coelho announced his intention to resign after revealing that he had failed to report a $50,000 loan to buy junk bonds.[48] "Suddenly a lot of Democrats are not having any fun anymore," explained columnist George Will.[49] "Won't some referees blow the whistle, call time out, reset the clock, do something? The best thing about Wright's travail is that it may cause a few hundred Democrats to decide that ethics is not such a good dodge after all."[50]

Through the summer, pressure increased on the Congress to act. The new Speaker of the House, Thomas S. Foley, faced a difficult task of reconciling White House demands with strong congressional resistance to doing away with honoraria.[51] Gradually a compromise took shape by November of 1989.[52] The House, in return for a substantial pay increase, would accept sharp limits on its members' accepting honoraria, tighter gift-acceptance rules and some restrictions on lobbying by former members of Congress and congressional staff. The White House, however, wanted more.

The White House demanded that "congressional staff members be included under the same conflict-of-interest laws that govern executive branch officials."[53] Although the White House House and Senate negotiators refused to accept this demand, they did agree to relax a number of executive branch ethics restrictions. A few days before Thanksgiving, Congress passed the ethics package and sent it to President Bush for his signature.[54]

The Ethics Reform Act of 1989: More than Meets the Eye

With considerable fanfare, President Bush signed into law the Ethics Reform Act in November 1989. Members of Congress received a large pay increase in return for agreeing to strict limits on the acceptance of honoraria. The Ethics Reform Act also turned out to be a vehicle for relaxing a number of executive branch ethics restrictions.[55]

To the surprise of rank-and-file executive branch employees, the honoraria ban prohibited them from accepting any honorarium, regardless of the purpose of the talk or the nature of the event. This provision outraged federal employees. The Supreme Court, in a 1995 decision in *National Treasury Employees Union* v. *United States*,[56] held that this provision violated the First Amendment rights of rank-and-file executive branch employees because it had a chilling effect on their willingness to give talks and write articles. But the High Court left intact the congressional honorarium ban and restrictions on high-level executive branch officials' accepting honorarium.

Gifts and Gratuities for All

The Ethics Reform Act rolled back executive branch ethics rules in a number of important ways. The act included a uniform gift acceptance statute that prohibited all federal officers and employees in all three branches of government "from soliciting or accepting anything of value from a person (1) seeking official action from, doing business with or (in the case of executive branch officers and employees) conducting activities regulated by the individual's employing agency; or (2) whose interests may be substantially affected by the performance or nonperformance of the individual's official duties (5 USC 7353[a], Supp. I 1989)."[57]

The uniform gift acceptance statute, however, included a major loophole.[58] The act gave the supervising ethics unit for each branch of the federal government authority "to issue rules or regulations implementing the [gift acceptance provisions] and providing for such reasonable exceptions as may be appropriate."[59] Rules subsequently issued by the House did tighten gift-acceptance rules but permitted members to accept an unlimited number of gifts of "minimal value."[60] The act also clarified a possible conflict between the illegal gratuity statute and gift-acceptance rules.

Since the 1962 revision of federal bribery and conflict-of-interest statutes, federal prosecutors increasingly used the illegal gratuity statute to convict officials in all three branches of the federal government on public corruption charges. To convict an official for accepting a bribe, prosecutors had to show an agreement.[61] Prosecutors could obtain an illegal gratuity conviction merely by showing that the official accepted something of value from a nonfederal source because of past performance of official duties or in anticipation of future performance.[62] The Ethics Reform Act made clear that gifts accepted under gift-acceptance rules could not be classified as an illegal gratuity.[63]

The travel-reimbursement acceptance provisions of the Ethics Reform Act (31 USC 135[3], Supp. I 1989) gave all executive branch agencies authority to accept such reimbursements from nonpublic sources. For decades, House and Senate ethics rules had allowed members to accept free travel and lodging from nonfederal sources.[64] A January 9, 1990, column by Jack Anderson and Dale Van Atta reported that the Bush White House had demanded enactment of the travel-reimbursement provision in return for signing on to the pay increase for members of Congress and congressional employees.[65] "The judgment underlying the Ethics Reform Act must be that increased executive branch participation with the private sector no longer endangers the appearance of the integrity of the employee," stated a 1990 commentary on the Ethics Reform Act.[66] Regulations subsequently issued by the GSA implementing the travel reimbursement provisions even permitted federal agencies to accept travel reimbursements from conflicting nonfederal sources if the agency made a ruling that the benefits in accepting the travel reimbursements outweighed any conflicts created by "the nature and sensitivity of any pending matter affecting the interests of the conflicting non-Federal source."[67]

Certificates of Divestiture and Presidential Recruitment

The certificate of divestiture provisions of the Ethics Reform Act constituted an even larger victory for the Bush White House. The act added Section 1043(a) to Title 26 (federal tax laws) of the United States Code. Entitled "Sale of property to comply with conflict-of-interest requirements,"[68] the new tax provision "permit[ed] an officer or employee of the executive branch of the federal government to roll over any gain on property sold in order to comply with any conflict of interest requirements."[69] The capital gains rollover provision provided executive branch ethics officers a valuable new tool to resolve the financial conflict of interest problems of presidential appointees and other federal employees. During the years 1990 through 1993, the director of OGE issued 461 certificates of divestiture. Three hundred and fifty-three family units received more than one certificate of divestiture during the four-year period reviewed.[70]

The Revolving Door Spins Again

Surprisingly, the Ethics Reform Act made only minor adjustments to existing revolving-door provisions.[71] The mid-1980s prosecutions of Reagan aides Mike Deaver and Lyn Nofziger had led to demands for tighter revolving-door rules. Ronald Reagan, in late 1988, vetoed revolving-door legislation. Specifically, the act established a new one-year no-contact ban for former very senior executive branch officials.[72] For the first time, Congress passed legislation restricting former members of Congress and former congressional employees from lobbying Congress.[73] Despite the publicity surrounding these changes in revolving-door rules, Washington lobbyists did not find it necessary to put their homes up for sale.

FROM BAD TO WORSE

The ethics reform program succeeded beyond the expectations of the Bush White House. Congressional ethics had become a national preoccupation. Congress hoped the Ethics Reform Act and the ban on honoraria would take the heat off. The Bush White House hoped it could avoid major ethics problems. But both Congress and the White House badly underestimated the power of forces driving the public integrity war. New congressional ethics scandals and the travel practices of Bush's chief of staff, former New Hampshire governor John Sununu, made clear that the time had not yet arrived for public officials to take off their body armor.

The Best Help Money Can Buy

The 1980s collapse of the savings and loan industry cost the taxpayers of the country hundreds of billions of dollars. Many critics blamed both the Reagan administration and Congress for supporting the deregulation of the savings and loan industry during the early 1980s. The Keating-Five scandal became symbolic of the collapse of congressional ethics.

Charles Keating, a Phoenix, Arizona, land developer, took advantage of savings and loan deregulation to move aggressively into the business. In 1984, a Keating company purchased Lincoln Savings and Loan of California. In short time, Keating transformed Lincoln from a small savings and loan into a "high-flying institution that boomed on the strength of relatively risky investments."[74] By 1985, the risky investments of Lincoln Savings and Loan had aroused concern among state and federal regulators.

Keating had no intention of cooperating with state or federal regulators. He looked for help anywhere he could, and that included the U.S. Senate. It took until April 1989 for federal regulators to shut down Lincoln, and the collapse cost federal taxpayers an estimated $2 billion.[75]

In September 1989, a number of Ohio Republicans filed an ethics com-

plaint against Senator John Glenn, alleging that he had improperly intervened with regulators on behalf of Keating. It soon became known that
four other Senators also had intervened on behalf of Keating. Five Senators
twice in 1987 had participated in meetings with federal regulators "who
were closing in on Keating's thrift."[76] Senators Alan Cranston, John Glenn,
Dennis Deconcini, John McCain, and Donald W. Riegle, Jr., had received
substantial campaign contributions from Keating.[77] All denied that they
had done anything improper in attending the meetings, and they maintained that their intervention had absolutely nothing to do with the political
contributions they received from Keating. Common Cause called for an
investigation of all five senators supposedly involved with Keating.[78] During
the 1980s, Keating "gave a total of $1.5 million to the campaigns and
political causes" of Senators.[79]

The Senate Ethics Committee hired Washington attorney Robert S. Bennett to conduct the inquiry into the conduct of the five senators. Bennett
took the position that the Ethics Committee had the authority to seek punishment of the senators for violating an unwritten appearance-of-
impropriety standard. A senator, according to Bennett, "should not engage
in conduct which would appear to be improper to a reasonable, nonpartisan, fully informed person."[80] The five Senators argued that the Senate
Ethics Committee had jurisdiction only to determine whether they had violated written Senate ethics rules.

The two-year Keating-Five investigation ended with four of the five senators escaping punishment.[81] However, the committee criticized the conduct of senators Dennis Deconcini, John Glenn, John McCain, and Donald
Riegle for exercising poor judgment and engaging in activities that gave the
appearance of being improper. In contrast, the committee strongly admonished Alan Cranston for the relationship he had developed with Charles
Keating.[82] Cranston subsequently announced his intention not to run for
reelection in 1992.[83]

Live Free or Fly

If George Bush had hoped to go into the 1992 presidential election as
the president who restored trust in government, the travel problems of
White House chief of staff John Sununu shattered that dream. Much like
Eisenhower's chief of staff Sherman Adams, Sununu came from New
Hampshire and had served as governor of that state. As chief of staff,
Sununu maintained a tight ship. He made a great many enemies in Wash-
ington, however.

The *Washington Post*, in late April 1991, reported that Sununu had used
military aircraft for some sixty trips during the preceding two years.[84] In
itself these disclosures raised eyebrows. In addition, the article claimed that
Sununu had used military aircraft for personal business and partisan travel.

The ensuing months saw a constant flow of reports detailing Sununu's travel activities. The White House reported that Sununu had taken seventy-seven trips on military aircraft, many involving trips to New Hampshire and four to ski resorts.[85] Sununu maintained that the trips involved official business and he reimbursed the government for some of the trips that might raise questions. Meanwhile, the Office of Government Ethics began an investigation of whether Sununu had violated standards-of-conduct regulations.[86]

Things quickly went from bad to worse. Sununu used his official car to attend a New York City stamp auction. He began to use corporate aircraft for free travel.[87] Since the passage of the Ethics Reform Act of 1989, federal law did not prohibit agencies from accepting such free travel. It did, however, not permit individuals to solicit free travel. Sununu had solicited at least one trip.[88] C. Boyden Gray, the Bush White House counsel, took immediate steps to prevent this from happening again. But these steps did not stop the *New York Times* from condemning the practice.[89] In early December 1991, Sununu resigned as chief of staff to return to CNN's Cross Fire.

Following the Bouncing Checks

On September 18, 1991, the General Accounting Office disclosed that members of the House had written 8,331 bad checks against their House Bank accounts during a 12-month period ending on June 30, 1990. The October 1991 House vote to close the bank did little to end that controversy.[90] Every American understood that banks do not permit them to bounce checks without facing heavy fees, cancellation of bank accounts or even criminal prosecution. House rules, however, did not prohibit the practice.[91] The House leadership maintained that the bank only used the deposits of other members to cover overdrafts.

The House Committee on Standards of Official Conduct, facing strong pressure from the Republican minority, on April 1, 1992 "listed 22 current and former members who, it concluded, had abused their privileges at the House bank."[92] Other members voluntarily disclosed the number and amount of bounced checks as part of their apologies to their constituents.[93] On April 16, 1992, the House ethics committee released the names of "252 sitting and 51 former lawmakers who overdrew their checking accounts."[94] President Bush unleashed a series of strong attacks against Congress, portraying it as "a privileged class of rulers who stand above the law."[95]

Presidential politics turned the House banking scandal into a political football. The attorney general appointed Judge Malcolm Richard Wilkey to determine whether any violations of federal criminal law had occurred in the operations of the bank. Wilkey demanded that the House leadership turn over the records of the bank, while the House leadership argued that it had to resist the subpoena to protect the doctrine of separation of powers.

Opposition to the subpoena fell apart when presidential candidate Bill Clinton told reporters that he believed Congress should comply with the subpoena.[96] Shortly thereafter, the House leadership handed over the records.[97]

By mid-October 1992, the Justice Department had sent "all but about two dozen of the 325 current and former lawmakers who overdrew their House bank accounts" letters clearing them of criminal wrongdoing.[98] Judge Wilkey completed his nearly nine-month investigation in December 1992. Approximately twenty former and current members of the House had not received clearance letters.[99] Wilkey left it to the Public Integrity Section of the Department of Justice to complete the criminal investigation of these members.

The House Post Office scandal provided critics of Congress additional ammunition that Congress had lost touch with the American people. The event contributed directly to the downfall of Illinois Democratic Representative Dan Rostenkowski, chairman of the powerful House Ways and Means Committee.

The criminal probe of the House Post Office began with an investigation by the U.S. attorney for the District of Columbia, Jay B. Stevens, of some "stamp clerks suspected of embezzlement and drug dealing."[100] The matter grew to include an investigation of whether House members avoided franking restrictions by using campaign funds to purchase stamps and turn stamps into cash.[101] A subsequent Justice Department investigation of Rostenkowski led to his indictment on numerous charges related to misuse of his office, a loss of his seat in Congress and a subsequent guilty plea and a sixteen-month jail sentence.

FREE-FIRE ZONE

By early 1992, the public integrity war had returned with a vengeance. Republicans believed that they could take over Congress and keep the presidency by running *against* Congress and big government. The Democratic party fought to define itself. And Ross Perot put himself forward as an alternative to politics as usual. At the beginning of 1992, few political pundits gave the Democrats any chance of winning back the White House. Suddenly, out of nowhere, came Bill Clinton, a former governor of the small southern state of Arkansas. Clinton put himself forward as a new Democrat with new ideas.

The primary campaign would put to a test the theory that voters cared much more about character than about issues. Clinton would run an issues-driven campaign. The media would focus on a wide range of character issues that would make many observers wonder how he could make a run for the presidency with so many skeletons in his closet. Clinton turned out to understand the public much better than the pundits did.

NOTES

1. Don Bonafede, "Ethics and the 88 Race," *National Journal*, August 8, 1987, p. 1971.

2. Ibid.

3. Dan Morgan and Walter Pincus, "Regan says President Knew of Cover Story: Account of Arms Sale Differs from Reagan's," *Washington Post*, July 31, 1988, p. A1.

4. David Hoffman, "Bush Calls for 'Strict' Ethics Code for White House," *Washington Post*, March 8, 1988, p. A4.

5. Paul Taylor, "Bush Endorses Widened Ethics Bill," *Washington Post*, May 3, 1988, p. A4.

6. David Hoffman, "Bush Pledges Staff 'Code of Conduct': Congress Again Pressed to Adopt Comparable Ethics Standards," *Washington Post*, July 27, 1988, p. A4.

7. "Dukakis Vows Strict Rules on Lobbying: Democrats Slam Bush over 'Sleaze' Factor," *Washington Post*, September 29, 1988, p. A18.

8. Ibid.

9. Judith Haverman, "Ethics Pledge to Be Transition Hallmark: Bush to Impose Strict Conflict-of-Interest, Financial Disclosure Rules on Staff," *Washington Post*, November 16, 1988, p. A17.

10. Administrative Conference of the United States, *Presidential Transition Worker's Code of Ethical Conduct* (Washington, DC: The Conference, 1988); also see Philip J. Harder, *Standards of Conduct for Presidential Transition Workers. Report to the Administrative Conference of the United States* (Washington, DC: The Conference, 1988).

11. Haverman, "Ethics Pledge," *Washington Post*, November 16, 1988, p. A17.

12. Burt Solomon, "The Lingering Ethical Quandaries of Nice People with Old Money," *National Journal*, February 25, 1989, p. 483.

13. Ibid.

14. W. John Moore, "Hands Off: To Avoid Conflict-of-Interest Questions, Many of President Bush's Appointees Are Holding on to Corporate Stocks but Disqualifying Themselves from Issues Involving Specific Firms," *National Journal*, July 1, 1989, pp. 1678–83.

15. Solomon, p. 483.

16. "Tower Nomination: Majority Opposes Tower Confirmation," *Gallup Report*, March/April 1989, p. 17.

17. Ibid, p. 20.

18. Moore, p. 1678–83.

19. *Congressional Quarterly Weekly Report* 47, January 28, 1989, p. 199.

20. Other members included Jan Witold Brown, Judith Hippler Bello, Lloyd N. Cutler, Fred Fisher Fielding, Harrison H. Schmit and R. James Woolsey.

21. President's Commission on Ethics Law Reform, (Fact sheet) *To Serve with Honor: Report of the President's Commission on Federal Ethics Law Reform*, Pres-

ident's Commission on Federal Ethics Law Reform, Washington, DC: The Commission, March 10, 1989, p. 1.

22. Terry Eastland, "An Aggressive Approach to Ethics," *Washington Post,* February 1, 1989, p. A23.

23. Ibid.

24. Robert Roberts, *White House Ethics* (Westport, CT: Greenwood Press, 1988), pp. 79–80.

25. *To Serve with Honor: Report of the President's Commission on Federal Ethics Law Reform*, 1, p. 12 (Washington, DC: Government Printing Office, March 1989).

26. Ibid., 5, p. 28.

27. Ibid., 16, p. 79.

28. Ibid., 4, p. 25.

29. Ibid., 8, p. 43.

30. Ibid., 11, p. 61.

31. Stuart Gilman, "Presidential Ethics and the Ethics of the Presidency," *Annals of the American Academy of Political and Social Science* 537 (January 1995): 73.

32. 5 CFR 2635.

33. Sec. 102, Limitation on Outside Earned Income, Executive Order 12674.

34. "Professional: Pharmacists, Clergy Rated Highest for 'Honesty' and 'Ethical Standards,' " *Gallup Report*, No. 279, December 1988, p. 3 (Very High, 3 percent; High, 16 percent; Average, 52 percent; Low, 19 percent; Very Low, 5 percent; and No Opinion, 5 percent).

35. Ibid. (Very High, 2 percent; High, 14 percent; Average, 52 percent; Low, 20 percent; Very Low, 7 percent; and No opinion, 5 percent).

36. Chuck Alston, "Common Cause: A Watchdog that Barks at Its Friends," *Congressional Quarterly Weekly Report* (August 26, 1989): 2204.

37. David S. Cloud, "Bush's Package on Ethics, Pay Seeks Uniform Standards," *Congressional Quarterly Weekly Report* (April 15, 1989): 817.

38. Ann Devoy, "Bush Offers Proposal on Ethics, Pay," *Washington Post*, April 13, 1989, p. A1.

39. George Bush, "Remarks by the President To American Society of Newspaper Editors," White House Office of the Press Secretary, April 12, 1989.

40. Devoy, p. A8.

41. George Bush, "The Government-Wide Ethics Act of 1989—President Bush's Ethics Reform Proposals." White House Office of the Press Secretary, April 12, 1989.

42. David Hoffman, "Bush Retreats on Hill Honoraria Ban: Ethics Commission's Proposal to Be Left out of Legislative Package," *Washington Post*, April 11, 1989, p. A6.

43. "An Ethics Test for Mr. Bush," *Washington Post* April 12, 1989, p. A22.

44. Tom Kenworthy, "House Committee Charges Wright with 69 Ethics-Rule Violations: Improper Gifts, 'Scheme' to Evade Income Limit by Book Sales Cited," *Washington Post*, April 18, 1989, pp. A1, A10.

45. Charles R. Babcock, "Behind Charges: 279 Pages of Detail: New Disclosures Include Oil Well Investment; Further Probe Planned," *Washington Post*, April 18, 1989, p. A12.

46. Janet Hook, "Passion, Defiance, Tears. Jim Wright Bows Out," *Congressional Quarterly Weekly Report* 47 (June 3, 1989): 1289.

47. Don Phillips, "Stepping Into the Ethics Thicket: Reluctant Congress Moves Toward Possible Revision of Laws," *Washington Post*, April 27, 1989, p. A21.

48. Ibid.

49. "Personal Ethics," *Washington Post*, April 18, 1989, p. A29.

50. Ibid.

51. Christopher Madison, "Ethics as Usual?" *National Journal*, July 8, 1989, pp. 1743–44.

52. Don Phillips, "Congress Aims to Pass Pay and Ethics Bill Before Thanksgiving," *Washington Post*, November 14, 1989, p. A9.

53. Don Philips and Tom Kenworthy, "Pay-Ethics Plan Delayed by Demands from Bush," *Washington Post*, November 15, 1989, p. A7.

54. Don Phillips, "Pay and Ethics Legislation," *Washington Post*, November 21, 1989, p. A23.

55. For a discussion of the new revolving-door rules applicable to executive branch and legislative personnel, see Roger Darley, "Personal Conflict of Interest Digest," *Public Contract Law Journal* 20 (1991): 302; Wendy Gerlach, "Amendment of the Post-Employment Laws," *Arizona Law Review* 33 (1991): 401.

56. 115 S.Ct. 1003 (1995).

57. Robert Roberts and Marion T. Doss, Jr., "Public Service and Private Hospitality," *Public Administration Review* 52 (May/June 1992): 265.

58. Ibid.

59. Roberts and Doss, "Public Service," p. 265.

60. The House Ethics Committee set the initial limit at $180.

61. Ibid.

62. Roberts and Doss, "Public Service," p. 267.

63. See *United States* v. *Brewster*, 506 F.2d 62 (D.C. Cir. 1974). Also see Susan M. Kuzma, "Bribery and Gratuities," Appendix A. In U.S. Department of Justice, *Prosecution of Public Corruption Cases*. Washington, D.C. U.S. Department of Justice. February 1988, pp. 299–300.

64. For an excellent discussion of the impact of the Ethics Reform Act on the gift acceptance and travel reimbursement acceptance authority of federal agencies and members of Congress, see June E. Edmondson, "And Gifts And Travel for All: A Summary and Explanation of the Ethics Reform Act of 1989," *Federal Bar News & Journal* 37 (September 1990): 402–406.

65. Jack Anderson and Dale Van Atta, "For 'Parity,' Some Ethics Rules Relaxed," *Washington Post*, January 9, 1990, p. B8.

66. Edmondson, p. 405.

67. Roberts and Doss, "Public Service," p. 266.

68. "Tax Notes: Executive Officials May Be Entitled to Deferral of Gain," *The Army Lawyer* (July 1990): 52.

69. "Qualified Rollover Can Also Avoid Conflict of Interest," *Journal of Taxation* 73 (September 1990): 138.

70. The Ethics Reform Act, as noted, treats assets of spouses and minor children as the assets of the official. Section 208 of title 18 and other conflict-of-interest regulations require remedial steps be taken by spouses and dependent children. The OGE, consequently, has issued a significant number of certificates of divestiture to

spouses and dependent children of federal officials. Robert Roberts and Marion T. Doss, "Recruitment of American Presidential Nominees: Divestiture and Deferred Taxation of Gain." *Journal of Social, Political and Economic Studies* 21 (Spring 1996), pp. 49–53.

71. Robert Roberts, "Regulatory Bias and Conflict of Interest Regulation." In *Handbook of Regulation and Administrative Law*, eds. David H. Rosenbloom and Richard D. Schwartz (New York: Marcel Dekker, 1994), pp. 495–96.

72. 72. Section 207(d) of Title 18, United States Code.

73. Wendy Gerlach, "Amendment of the Post-Employment Laws," *Arizona Law Review* 33 (1991): 401.

74. "Panel Probes Senators' Aid to Keating," *Congressional Quarterly Almanac*, 1990, p. 519.

75. Ibid.

76. Ibid.

77. "Key Players in the Keating Five Case," *Congressional Quarterly Almanac*, 1990, p. 79.

78. Ibid., p. 80.

79. Ibid.

80. Ibid., p. 87.

81. "Four of 'Keating Five' Escape Punishment," *Congressional Quarterly Almanac*, 1991, p. 37E.

82. Ibid., p. 38E.

83. For an overview of the Keating-five scandal, see Michael Binstein, *Greed, Keating, Congress and the S & L debate* (New York: Putnam's 1991); Michael Binstein, *Trust Me: Charles Keating and the missing billions* (New York: Random House, 1993).

84. Charles Babcock, Ann Devoy and Lucy Shackelford, "Sununu: Frequent Flier on Military Aircraft," *Washington Post*, April 21, 1991, p. A1.

85. Julia Malone, "Sununu's Travel Data Released," *Atlanta Constitution*, April 24, 1991, p. 1.

86. "Ethics Office Is Reviewing Sununu's Travel," *New York Times*, May 23, 1991, p. A22.

87. David Lauter, "Sununu Using Corporate Jets for Free Travel," *Los Angeles Times*, June 18, 1991, p. A1.

88. Ann Devoy and Charles Babcock, "Sununu Travel Rules Tightened," *Washington Post*, June 22, 1991, p. A1.

89. "Legal Travel? Then It's a Rotten Law," Editorial *New York Times*, July 1, 1991, p. A12.

90. Ibid.

91. "Voters Enraged Over House Bank Abuses," *Congressional Quarterly Almanac*, 1992, p. 24.

92. Ibid., p. 29.

93. Ibid., p. 30.

94. Ibid.

95. Martin Tolchin, "Bush Lambastes House and Senate," *New York Times*, October 25, 1991, p. A1.

96. "Voters Enraged Over House Bank Abuses," *Congressional Quarterly Almanac*, 1992, p. 35.

97. Ibid., pp. 36–37.

98. Ibid., p. 38.

99. Ibid., p. 41.

100. "Post Office Probe Hints at Larger Scandal," *Congressional Quarterly Almanac*, 1992, p. 47.

101. Ibid., p. 49.

Chapter 12

The Clinton Scandals

The Clinton presidency will go down as one of the more unusual in American history. Few observers in 1991 gave William Jefferson Clinton, governor of a poor southern state, any chance of winning the 1992 Democratic nomination, let alone the presidency. Few pundits, following the mid-term congressional election in 1994, gave him any chance of winning reelection. But by the beginning of May 1996, Clinton held a twenty-point lead over Republican challenger Bob Dole.

Political observers search to explain why Bill Clinton has faced such strong criticism throughout his presidency.[1] It has become clear that Clinton failed to understand how the public integrity war has ended any hope of privacy for a president or his family. For reasons impossible to understand, Clinton and his closest associates apparently believed that, once the campaign ended, the character issues that almost destroyed his candidacy would be forgotten. However, the new rules of public integrity warfare require full investigation of even the smallest allegation of wrongdoing. It may take historians and political scientists decades to determine why the Clinton camp believed that he was above the rules. This miscalculation has cost them dearly.

In the end, House Speaker Newt Gingrich and his contingent of movement conservatives saved Clinton from political oblivion. Gingrich had misread the 1994 election results as a mandate to dismantle the administrative state. But many Americans had second thoughts about his "revolution" when it became clear that he honestly intended to codify his reform agenda. As Americans compared Clinton with Gingrich, Clinton's standing rose.

But in retrospect, Clinton had taken a tremendous risk when he first decided to run for president. Since Watergate, experienced pols inside the Washington beltway understood that public figures no longer were permitted any personal secrets. If there were any skeletons in the Clinton closet, they surely would be uncovered during a national election.[2] Either Clinton's staff underestimated the difficulty of keeping embarrassing stories out of the mainstream media, or they believed swing voters cared much more about the economy than about any possible flaws in his character.

Clinton survived, in large measure, because public integrity allegations had lost much of their impact on the electorate. The public has come to expect character attacks on public officials. No practical way exists for the electorate to distinguish between legitimate criticism and attacks motivated by partisan politics or ideology.

TRIAL BY COMBAT

By June 1991, following a strong surge in President Bush's popularity as a result of the Gulf War, several potential Democratic candidates had announced decisions not to run against him. However, during the summer, Bill Clinton had sent a clear message that he intended to enter the 1992 race.[3]

Throughout the 1980s, Bill Clinton had established himself as one of a new generation of southern governors who put together a coalition of moderate whites and African Americans. These "New Democrats" preached fiscal conservatism, law and order, civil rights, education and welfare reform, abortion rights and environmental protection.[4] They argued that, unless Democrats moved toward the political center, key blocks of voters would continue to migrate to Republican ranks. The Democratic Leadership Council became the forum for New Democrats such as Robb of Virginia, Nunn of Georgia, Gore of Tennessee, and Clinton of Arkansas.[5] In sharp contrast, liberal Democrats argued that the long-term hope of the party rested on assembling a new coalition of women, minorities and progressive white males. Jesse Jackson saw his Rainbow Coalition as the answer to the new Republican coalition of angry white males and Christian conservatives.

Much as Jimmy Carter after Watergate, Clinton was a new face espousing new ideas.[6] However, progressive Democrats had serious reservations about both Clinton and Arkansas, which no one seriously regarded as progressive because its politics and wealth were controlled by a small group of powerful elites. Many Arkansans still lived below or just barely above the poverty line. And even before he announced his candidacy, Clinton and his advisors had recognized that rumors regarding his personal life could damage his bid.

In early August 1991, *Newsweek* published an article by Howard Fineman critical of how the media covered the private lives of public officials. The article mentioned rumors regarding extramarital affairs involving Clinton.[7] The Clinton camp moved quickly to end the rumors.[8]

A few weeks before the New Hampshire primary, a New York tabloid ran Gennifer Flowers's story of her alleged twelve-year affair with Clinton. The Clinton campaign responded by putting both Clintons on CBS's *60 Minutes* following the January 1992 Super Bowl game to answer questions regarding his alleged infidelity. During the broadcast, Bill Clinton conceded his involvement in marital "wrongdoing."[9]

This appearance on national television did not end Clinton's character problems. Rather, it triggered tremendous soul searching by the mainstream media over how the story should have been handled.[10] A debate over whether media outlets should have ignored the reports of infidelity helped Clinton survive the New Hampshire primary by generating strong support from political commentators outraged by the inability of public figures to enjoy private lives.[11]

Following the marital infidelity allegation, Clinton was soon beset by questions involving his Vietnam War draft status, and he found it extremely difficult to put forward a consistent story of how he had avoided the draft in 1969.[12] But he finished second in New Hampshire and survived.[13]

Jerry Brown, in a desperate attempt to prevent Clinton from capturing the nomination, attacked Clinton's record as governor. On March 15, 1992, Brown accused Bill and Hillary Clinton of unethical behavior. Brown alleged that, as governor, Clinton had funneled state business to the Rose law firm in which Hillary was a partner.[14] While these attacks did little to slow Clinton's drive for the nomination, many political commentators questioned his electability largely as the result of the character issues raised during the battles of the primaries.[15]

Throughout the 1992 presidential race, political experts waited for the character issue to take effect. Bush tried unsuccessfully to convince voters that Clinton was unfit for the presidency.[16] But his strategy failed and Clinton survived.

A "NEW PROGRESSIVE" TAKES COMMAND

Despite the fact that Clinton ran as a New Democrat, it soon became clear that he intended to govern as a new progressive. Clinton surrounded himself with advisors, including his wife, who urged him to push aggressively for a progressive agenda.[17] Clinton put national health-care reform at the top of his agenda and temporized on his promised middle-class tax cut.

Clinton soon found that the expectations of progressives far exceeded his ability to deliver. While he needed to hit the ground running to have any chance of implementing his agenda, like most new presidents Clinton badly underestimated the difficulty of putting together an effective staff.

Although he included the "best and the brightest" on his staff, only a handful had any practical experience governing.[18] Clinton had badly overestimated the ability of his crew to handle even routine White House operations and mobilize public support for his progressive reform agenda.

The Clinton transition team tried to get off to a good start. Clinton made it clear that he would augment his ethics arsenal by subjecting transition employees and appointees to stringent new ethics guidelines.

As governor, Clinton never made public ethics reform a top priority. Perhaps this was because, unlike many other states during the 1980s, Arkansas experienced few public corruption scandals. But although Clinton had promised to make political reform a top priority of his new administration, nothing in his background indicated that he was prepared to combat the powerful elites. In fact, presidential candidate Clinton and the Democratic Party had collected a record sum of money from special interests.[19]

On November 13, 1992, transition director Warren Christopher announced a new code of ethics for members of the Clinton transition.[20] The guidelines required transition employees to sign a pledge not to lobby any federal agency in which "he or she had substantial responsibility during the transition for six months after[ward]."[21] The guidelines also required employees to disqualify themselves from any matters in which they held a financial interest. With the exception of the six-month revolving-door rule, the Clinton rules differed little from those adopted by Bush in 1988. However, they were touted as a major improvement.

In early December, it was announced that Clinton planned to issue a new executive order requiring appointees to comply with strict new ethics rules.[22] On January 21, 1993, President Clinton issued the promised order imposed on former high-level officials: (1) a five-year lobbying ban, (2) a total prohibition against engaging in activity on behalf of a foreign power after leaving federal service and (3) a five-year ban against representing a foreign government or corporation within five years of participation in a trade negotiation for the U.S. government.[23]

To Clinton's surprise, not everyone saw the order as a major improvement to existing ethics guidelines. The directive did nothing to stop former high-level officials from becoming high-paid lobbyists since it did not prevent them from developing strategies or directing the lobbying activities of others. The 1989 ethics reform law already prohibited very senior federal officials from lobbying their own agencies or other very senior federal officials for one year after leaving government.[24]

Clinton ostensibly issued the order to stop former high-level federal officials from working as lobbyists for foreign governments or foreign corporations. Ross Perot had attacked George Bush on this issue during the 1992 campaign.[25] Clinton clearly expected accolades for his initiative, but the media response was less than hoped and reporters pressed the White

House to explain just how the order would reduce the massive amount of lobbying conducted in Washington.[26]

Clinton soon learned that merely issuing a new directive did not guarantee all his appointees would always exercise good judgment. Robert E. Rubin, Clinton's top economic advisor, wrote his former Wall Street clients informing them of his new position and urging them to stay in contact with him.[27] After the disclosure, Rubin assured the media that he had not sent the letters in an effort to cash in on his influential position. But the Rubin letters turned out to be only one of several ethics-related controversies that highlighted major ethics problems in the Clinton administration.

CARNAGE ON THE ETHICS FRONT

The Clinton transition had faced the enormous task of checking the backgrounds of hundreds of high-level appointees, only to discover that the clearance process was less than foolproof. In early January 1993, President Clinton nominated Zoe Baird for attorney general. Reports soon surfaced that Baird and her husband had employed illegal aliens and failed to pay Social Security withholding taxes. This violation of law led to calls for her to withdraw from consideration for the highest law enforcement position in the administration. The White House initially downplayed the controversy and allowed the Bairds to pay the back taxes, hoping that would end the matter. But faced with lingering questions over Clinton's character, the White House panicked and Baird withdrew from consideration for the post.[28]

Immediately after Baird's withdrawal, Clinton nominated Judge Kimba Wood for the post.[29] When reports appeared that she also had employed an illegal alien as a nanny,[30] she withdrew her name from consideration.[31] Clinton's third choice, Miami prosecutor Janet Reno, survived the confirmation process.

During the 1992 campaign, candidate Clinton had promised to guarantee every American affordable quality health care. However, he had no particular plan. To accomplish health-care reform, President Clinton established a task force to develop a detailed plan. A controversy errupted over the announcement that the task force planned to conduct its deliberations in secret.[32] The Justice Department defended the position on secrecy and the courts ruled in favor of the administration.[33]

The White House also argued that the Freedom of Information Act did not require it to release either working papers or even the names of task force members.[34] The task force claimed it needed secrecy to protect members from lobbyists and other special interests and that the public could always comment once the task force had completed its work.

Critics refused to accept this decision, and citing the Federal Advisory Committee Act,[35] filed suit to force disclosure of members' names and deliberations so the public could evaluate what influence special interests may have exercised in the process.

Through the rest of 1993 and into 1994, the White House fought these demands.[36] By the summer of 1994, when it became clear that his health-care reform plan had little hope of passing,[37] Clinton began to search for a face-saving way out of this public relations disaster.[38] During August 1994, the White House agreed to release the names of task force members and a record of deliberations.[39]

Ira Magaziner, the director of the ill-fated project, came under investigation for possible perjury in relation to the task force activities.[40] A preliminary Justice Department investigation resulted in a finding by Attorney General Janet Reno that insufficient evidence existed to call for the appointment of an independent counsel to investigate the matter further.[41]

Travelgate, a postinauguration scandal, proved highly damaging to the Clinton presidency as well. White House mismanagement of this scandal revived heretofore flagging interest in the Whitewater controversy, may have been a factor in the untoward death of Vincent Foster, raised questions of the possible obstruction of justice and exposed the "Filegate" quagmire. Travelgate per se involved questions of greed and the improper use of federal law enforcement.

The Travelgate story is familiar by now. In May 1993, the White House announced the firing of the entire travel office staff after an internal investigation found "mismanagement, over-billing and shoddy accounting methods."[42] The seven career White House employees who operated the office all served at the pleasure of the president.

The motivation for the firing remains in dispute. Throughout the controversy, the White House argued that it took the action in good faith after consultation with the FBI "to reform and reorganize the White House Travel Office as a consequence of the financial mismanagement exposed by an internal review and an external audit."[43] Critics of the firings maintained that the White House fired the employees so the function could be given as patronage to an Arkansas firm.[44]

The controversy refused to die. Reporters soon learned that White House officials had not followed established procedures in requesting an FBI investigation.[45] Critics blamed the White House for attempting to use the FBI to buttress its own findings. Washington quickly remembered that the Nixon White House had misused the FBI in an attempt to cover up the Watergate burglary. This adverse association led the White House to deny any presidential involvement in the firings.[46]

By late May it had become clear that the White House faced no choice but to back away from its initial allegations. Five of the fired employees were placed on leave with pay,[47] while Chief of Staff Thomas McLarty conducted an internal review of the events leading up to the firings.[48] On July 3, 1993, McLarty reprimanded four members of his staff for their actions.[49] His report found no evidence, however, that the firings had anything to do with patronage. A month later, five of the former travel office employees were advised that they were no longer under investigation for possible criminal wrongdoing.[50]

However, the cost of the fiasco continued to grow. In addition to paying the salaries of the five vindicated employees, Congress appropriated another $150,000 to pay their legal fees.[51] Moreover, Billy Ray Dale, the former director of the office, was indicted on embezzlement charges,[52] which he fought for almost a year before his speedy acquital once the question got to a federal jury on November 17, 1995.[53]

The resonant "not guilty" verdict set off another round of Travelgate inquiries. A memorandum by David Watkins, former White House director of administration, indicated the direct involvement of Hillary Clinton in the firings and created the impression that she had ordered them.[54] Watkins, in subsequent congressional testimony, told a House committee that he felt tremendous pressure from the Clintons to fire the travel office staff.[55] In March 1996, Hillary Clinton denied any involvement in the firings, but did acknowledge being told of "managerial problems in the office by then deputy White House counsel Vincent Foster and businessman Harry Thomason, a close Clinton friend."[56] After a request from the Department of Justice, a federal judicial panel in late March 1996 directed Whitewater independent counsel Kenneth Starr to investigate whether individuals had lied about Mrs. Clinton's involvement in the White House travel office firings.[57]

Travelgate had cost the Clinton White House dearly. Even if the firings had nothing to do with replacing travel office employees with friends of the Clintons, the handling of the firings demonstrated that the White House just did not understand how to conduct public business.

The late 1993 departure of two high-level Clinton officials then raised doubts concerning the sincerity of Clinton's campaign criticism of the revolving door.

The *New York Times*, on November 24, 1993, reported that Howard Paster and Roy Neal had left the White House to move into private-sector positions that involved a significant amount of lobbying.[58] Howard Paster left the White House to become the new president of Hill & Knowlton Worldwide, a major Washington public relations firm.[59] Roy Neal left to become the head of the United States Telephone Association, "the lobbying operation for the regional and local telephone companies."[60]

The Clinton White House attempted to put the best light on these departures. Both men, according to the White House, complied fully with all ethics rules and regulations. Both had made a personal decision to return to the private sector.[61] Despite the strong defense of Neal and Paster, their departures made it abundantly clear that the Clinton ethics guidelines had done little to slow the revolving door. Even though the rule prohibited former high-level officials from lobbying their former agency or other high-level officials for five years, the market for government insiders remained strong.

A PROLIFERATION OF OTHER SCANDALS

If the above controversies had not provided the Clinton White House with enough problems, the second half of 1993 saw a series of new public integrity problems. The August 1993 death of Vincent Foster was a turning point. Prior to that event, many media observers had attributed White House problems to inexperienced staff. Foster's death suggested more culpable explanations. However, some Clinton administration scandals involved conduct that occurred before Clinton became president.

The untimely death of Ronald Brown on a Bosnian mountainside ended an investigation into his business dealings prior to becoming secretary of commerce. For an administration that had pledged to reduce the power of special interests in Washington, Brown's selection for his post seemed conspicuously inconsistent.

Before Brown assumed federal office, he had worked as an influential Washington lobbyist. Brown's clients included the government of Haiti and a number of Japanese companies.[62] Like a number of Clinton appointees, Brown took extensive steps to adjust his financial holdings to comply with conflict-of-interest rules and regulations prior to becoming secretary of commerce. He sold off a large number of financial assets,[63] and like other high-level Clinton appointees, he had used a certificate of divestiture to avoid capital gains tax on certain investments.[64]

In 1993, the Justice Department investigated an allegation that Brown had been paid $700,000 by a Vietnamese businessman to persuade federal officials to remove the trade embargo against Vietnam.[65] The attorney general rejected calls for an independent counsel and the Justice Department found no credible evidence to support the allegation.[66]

But the 1994 election gave Republicans control of the Congress and the House Government Operations Committee soon began examining Brown's finances in detail.[67] By December 1995, attention had focused on Brown's business relationship with Nolanda Hill, whose firm Corridor Broadcasting had defaulted on a large S&L loan.[68]

Brown's business relationship with Hill had nothing to do with Corridor or the Sunbelt Savings Association. Together, Brown and Hill had established First International Communications. Like other financial holdings owned by Brown, he ended the partnership when he was nominated for secretary of commerce. On December 15, 1993, Hill paid Brown between $250,000 and $500,000 for his interest in First International.[69] But on January 23, 1995, Committee Chairman William F. Clinger (Rep.–PA) questioned the propriety of accepting a full buyout from an individual who had defaulted on loans that contributed to the failure of Sunbelt Savings.[70] Representative Clinger subsequently accused Brown of failing to disclose some $135,000 of income received from First International.[71] Moreover, Brown did not report a $78,000 loan Hill had forgiven him.[72] These disclosures led to the appointment of veteran Miami lawyer Daniel S. Pearson as independent counsel to determine "whether Brown improperly accepted nearly $500,000 from a business partner and filed inaccurate financial disclosure statements."[73]

Despite the investigation, Clinton's support for Brown never waivered. Brown continued his duties until his death prompted Pearson to end his investigation.[74]

In early August 1994, the Justice Department requested the appointment of an independent counsel to investigate the gift-acceptance practices of Agriculture Secretary Mike Espy.[75] Over the next month or so, a steady stream of media stories reported numerous gifts apparently accepted by Espy, including free seats at the Tyson Foods skybox at Soldier Field in Chicago[76] and free tickets from an Atlanta museum to attend the 1994 Super Bowl.[77] On September 10, 1994, Los Angeles attorney Donald C. Smaltz was appointed independent counsel for the Espy investigation.[78] Shortly thereafter, the press reported that Espy had billed the government for twenty trips to his home state of Mississippi during his first twenty months in office.[79] Any hope that Espy had of keeping his job ended when stories appeared that the Agriculture Department had leased a Jeep Cherokee for Espy that Espy garaged at the airport in Jackson, Mississippi.[80] Espy repaid the government $7,500,[81] and resigned his cabinet post to devote his full attention to his legal problem.[82]

The Ethics in Government Reform Act of 1989 permits the respective branches to draft different gift-acceptance rules. The Espy affair, and the forced resignation of White House administrator David Watkins in May 1994 for using an official helicopter to fly to a Maryland golf course,[83] led the White House to tighten its free travel rules by prohibiting "Cabinet Secretaries and other Presidential appointees in executive branch agencies and the White House from accepting travel services or accommodations from any company or association of companies regulated by or doing business with the agency in question, regardless of whether full reimbursement is made."[84] But issuance of the directive did little to abate the growing storm over public service ethics as practiced by the Clinton administration.

WHITEWATER: *GUERRE À OUTRANCE*

It is beyond the purpose of this book to chronicle either the evolution or the details of Arkansas scandals such as Whitewater or Troopergate. The name *Whitewater* is drawn from a relatively minor real estate venture in which the Clintons had invested a small amount of capital for an equal partnership. The project ended up being financed by an S&L that cost American taxpayers millions of dollars when it failed. The scandal involves this venture and a host of related allegations that then Governor Clinton had improperly used his office and connections, including the state police, to promote his political power and personal self-interest. Over time, Whitewater evolved to include possible White House efforts to obstruct justice by limiting the scope of earlier investigations into the Clintons' activities during his tenure as governor of Arkansas and aspects of Travelgate and Filegate.

The Whitewater scandal officially began in March 1992 with the publication of a *New York Times* article discussing the Clintons' involvement in an Ozark real estate venture.[85] While campaigning in Texas, Clinton told reporters that he did nothing improper when he and his wife entered into the Whitewater Development real estate partnership with savings and loan owner James B. McDougal, explaining that they had lost money.[86] A *New York Times* editorial, however, questioned Clinton's understanding of ethics since he saw no conflict of interest in the venture and asked for a fuller explanation of his Whitewater involvement.[87]

To diffuse this controversy, Clinton announced that Denver lawyer James Lyons would conduct a full review of the Whitewater land deal and prepare a full accounting for the public.[88] On March 23, James Lyons reported that the Clintons had lost $68,900 in the investment. Whitewater soon slipped from the headlines following release of Lyons's report.

The 1993 suicide of White House counsel Vincent Foster constituted the single most significant event that converted Whitewater from a minor embarrassment into a major scandal. The search for the cause of the suicide led many to take a much harder look at the Whitewater investment and Arkansas government under Clinton. A week after the suicide, the White House reported that staff members had removed Foster's working files from his office and had distributed them among the president's legal advisors.[89]

Whitewater thus became entangled with the much larger issue of fixing the blame for the failure of thousands of S&Ls. Whitewater also contributed to a growing perception that Clinton had deceived the nation with respect to his commitment to political reform. It appeared inconsistent for an individual to run on a platform attacking Republicans for fostering a culture of greed while he and his wife apparently had attempted to exploit a situation for personal gain.

In early December 1993, the Whitewater scandal intensified when the White House confirmed that staff had removed Whitewater files from Foster's office and turned them over to the Clintons' personal lawyer.[90] The White House had not earlier admitted that Whitewater files had been included among Vince Foster's papers. This disclosure prompted the *New York Times* and a number of other newspapers to call for the release of the documents in question to end any speculation concerning a coverup.[91] The White House failed to respond adequately.

The Whitewater scandal is impossible to understand outside the context of the ongoing public integrity war and the struggle between movement conservatives and new progressives for control of government. Movement conservatives needed Whitewater to demonstrate the moral bankrupcy of new progressives. They saw Whitewater and the other Clinton scandals as an opportunity to show how Clinton had deceived voters. For movement conservatives, Whitewater had evolved into a crusade against big government. They felt Clinton had deceived the nation into believing he stood for change when, in fact, he sought to protect his own corrupt status quo.

Besides providing movement conservatives with an avenue to attack big government and the administrative state, Whitewater also evolved into a battle over the independence of the public integrity bureaucracy, which since Watergate had acquired an unprecedented level of independence from political control. Individuals investigated for public corruption investigations inevitablity tried to blame their predictiment on an abuse of discretion by unaccountable members of the bureaucracy. As in the earlier Iran-*Contra* case, Clinton's defenders attacked his public and official tormentors. The intensity of the personal assaults on independent counsel Kenneth Starr led him to take the highly unusual step of defending the integrity of his investigation in the pages of the *Washington Post*.[92]

Historians gave Harry Truman a C grade as president, in part because he allowed personal friendship to interfere with his judgment. However, over time, history books have placed less and less emphasis on the Truman scandals. Much like the reaction of Truman to the scandals that tainted his administration, Clinton has expressed puzzlement over how Whitewater has become such a preoccupation. Nothing in Truman's background could have prepared him for the ethical bloodletting that occurred during his second term. Progressives pounded him from the left and conservatives hit from the right. In contrast, Clinton was governor when federal authorities prosecuted record numbers of state and local officials on charges of public corruption and many states enacted ethics laws designed to tighen conflict-of-interest restrictions. Moreover, he knew that new progressives had spent much of the 1980s attacking the influence of special interests in Republican administrations.

Clinton apparently took a calculated risk that the public had tired of the public integrity war. He read America much better than most political experts and pundits. Even after the Democratic Party suffered its worst defeat in forty years, he sensed that a majority of Americans would reject the fine print of the Contract with America. Clinton understood that, while character mattered, issues and ideology mattered more.

Even after Watergate, the country had continued its conservative migration. Ronald Reagan remained an extremely popular president despite major public corruption scandals involving the Department of Defense and the Department of Housing and Urban Development. Voters sent Michael Dukakis back to Boston after he failed to convince them that George Bush's involvement with Iran-*Contra* made him unsuitable to serve as president.

But the fact that Clinton understood that public integrity allegations do not necessarily mean the end of a national political leader does not explain why he failed so miserably at public integrity management.

STALEMATE IN A WAR OF ATTRITION

Between Watergate and Whitewater, neither major combatant has significantly expanded its base of support. Movement conservative attacks on big government have not significantly reduced public support for middle-class programs such as Medicare, Social Security and student loans. New progressives, on the other hand, have failed miserably to convince voters to demand a massive redistribution of wealth within the United States. And allegations of wrongdoing have failed to persuade independent voters to choose one or the other side. Yet neither side has shown any inclination to stop demonizing its foes.

NOTES

1. See Elizabeth Drew, *On the Edge* (New York: Simon & Schuster, 1994); Elizabeth Drew, *Showdown: The Struggle Between the Gingrich Congress and the Clinton White House* (New York: Simon & Schuster, 1996); Gregory Walden, *On Best Behavior: The Clinton Administration and Ethics in Government* (Indianapolis: Hudson Institute, 1996); Bob Woodward, *The Agenda: Inside the Clinton White House* (New York: Simon & Schuster, 1994).

2. See James B. Stewart, *Blood Sport: the President and His Adversaries* (New York: Simon & Schuster, 1996).

3. Douglas Harbrecht, "Bill Clinton: Can He Make it out of Arkansas?" *Business Week*, July 8, 1991, p. 43

4. For a discussion of reform initiatives undertaken by Governor Clinton during the 1980s, see Ellie McGrath, "No More Dragging up the Rear," *Time*, December 26, 1983, p. 77; Shawn Doherty "The Statehouse Action and Innovation," *Newsweek*, March 24, 1986, pp. 30–32; Sandra R. Gregg, "The Yuppies of Dixie," *U.S. News & World Report*, March 28, 1988, p. 24.

5. Margaret B. Carlson, "The Neoliberal Blues," *Time*, April 2, 1990, p. 21.

6. Rhodes Cook, "Arkansan Travels Well Nationally as Campaign Heads for Test," *Congressional Quarterly Weekly Report*, January 11, 1992, pp. 58–65.

7. Howard Fineman, "Second Thoughts on 'Character Cops,'" *Newsweek*, August 12, 1991, pp. 24–25.

8. Scott Shepard, "Clinton Seeks to Put Adultery Rumors to Rest," *Atlanta Constitution*, September 17, 1991, p. E3; Jeffrey Stinson, "Clinton Gets Jump on Personal Issues," *USA Today*, September 17, 1991, p. A32.

9. Dan Balz, "Clinton Concedes Marital 'Wrongdoing,' " *Washington Post*, January 27, 1992, p. A1.

10. "Tabloid Prints New Bill Clinton Infidelity Charges," *Nightline-ABC*, Program number 2784, January 23, 1992.

11. Reese Cleghorn, "Bimboni Plagues and Ethics: What Next?" *Washington Journalism Review* 14 (March 1992): 4; Todd Gitlin, "Media Lemmings Run Amok?" *Washington Journalism Review* 14 (April 1992): 28–32.

12. Jeffrey H. Birnbaum, "Campaign 92: Clinton Received a Vietnam Draft Deferment for an ROTC Program that He Never Joined," *Wall Street Journal*, February 6, 1992, p. A16.

13. Maureen Dowd, "How a Battered Clinton Has Stayed Alive," *New York Times*, March 16, 1992, p. A1.

14. Steve Daley and Thomas Hardy, "Primary Takes Nasty Turn: Brown Blasts Clinton, Wife over Ethics," *Chicago Tribune*, March 16, 1992, p. 1.

15. Rhodes Cook, "Clinton Can't Shake Doubters Despite Strong Performance," *Congressional Quarterly Weekly Report*, April 11, 1992, pp. 965–72.

16. Andrew Rosenthal, "Bush Campaign Issues Stinging Attack," *New York Times*, August 3, 1992, p. A14.

17. Bob Woodward, *The Agenda: Inside the Clinton White House* (New York: Simon & Schuster, 1994).

18. See Jeffrey B. Trammell and Gary B. Osifchin, *The Clinton 500: The New Team Running America* (Washington DC: Almanac Publishing, 1994).

19. Greg B. Smith, "Clinton Talks Reform; Takes Big Donations," *San Francisco Chronicle*, April 19, 1992, p. A1.

20. Thomas L. Friedman, "Clinton Issues Ethics Policies for Transition Team," *New York Times*, November 14, 1992, p. A1.

21. Ibid., p. A8.

22. "Ethics in the Clinton Administration," Editorial *New York Times*, December 14, 1992, p. A16.

23. Bill Clinton, Office of the Press Secretary, Executive Committments By Executive Branch Appointees, Executive Order 12834, January 20, 1993.

24. Robert Roberts, "Regulatory Bias and Conflict of Interest Regulation." In *Handbook of Regulation and Administrative Law*, eds. David H. Rosenbloom and Richard D. Schwartz (New York: Marcel Dekker, 1994), p. 496.

25. Hobart Rowen, "Foreign Lobbies, Fairness and the 'Revolving Door,' " *Washington Post*, October 25, 1992, p. H1.

26. Sheila Kaplan, "The Revolving Door Still Spins," *Washington Post*, January 31, 1993, p. C5.

27. Keith Bradsher, "A Clinton Aide's Farewell to Clients: Keep in Touch," *New York Times*, February 5, 1993, p. A1.

28. Adam Nagourney, "Baird Abandons Cabinet Bid," *USA Today*, January 22, 1993, p. A1.

29. Richard L. Berke, "Clinton Chooses New York Judge for Justice Post," *New York Times*, February 5, 1993, p. A1.

30. Jerry Seper and Paul Bedard, " 'Baird Problem' Forces Wood out," *Washington Times*, February 6, 1993, p. A1.

31. Jill Smolowe, "Rush to Judgement," *Time*, February 15, 1993, pp. 30–31.

32. Paul Bedard, "Health Care Panel Shuts Door Tighter," *Washington Times*, March 10, 1993, p. A1.

35. Michael York, "Health Task Force Closed Doors Backed," *Washington Post*, June 23, 1993, p. A15.

34. Michael Duffy, "Operation Hillary," *Time*, March 22, 1993, pp. 36–38.

35. Robert Pear, "Justice Department Defends Setup of Care Panel," *New York Times*, July 26, 1994, p. A16.

36. Paul Craig Roberts, "First Lady's Secrets Are in the Dock," *Los Angeles Times*, July 31, 1994, p. M5.

37. Karen Tumulty and Edwin Chey, "Blame for Health Plan's Collapse Falls Everywhere," *Los Angeles Times*, August 28, 1994, p. A1.

38. Robert Pear, "White House Seeks Settlement of Health Suit," *New York Times*, August 10, 1994, p. A16.

39. "Administration Agrees to Make Public Files of Health Task Force," *New York Times*, August 18, 1994, p. A21; Robert Pear, "Now it Can Be Told; the Task Force Was Bold, Naive and Collegial," *New York Times*, September 18, 1994, p. 4.

40. David Johnston, "Ruling on Top Health Care Aide Brings Worry for Administration," *New York Times*, December 23, 1993, p. A20.

41. David Johnston, "Reno Rejects G.O.P. Request for Prosecutor," *New York Times*, March 5, 1995, p. A1; Toni Lacy, "Clinton Health Aide Won't Face Charges in Task Force Dispute," *Washington Post*, August 4, 1995, p. A2.

42. Michael K. Frisby, "Clinton Fires White House Travel Office, FBI Is Probing Allegations of Kickbacks," *Wall Street Journal*, May 20, 1993, p. A1.

43. White House, Statement of George Stephanopoulos, May 21, 1993.

44. Ann Devoy, "Staff Denies Clinton Ally Had Role in Firing," *Washington Post*, May 21, 1993, p. A7.

45. Thomas L. Friedman, "White House Asked Aid of F.B.I. in Dismissals," *New York Times*, May 25, 1993, Sec. 8, p. 18; Michael Kranish, "Aides Asked FBI to Skirt its Policy," *Boston Globe*, May 25, 1993, p. 1.

46. Thomas Friedman, "White House Retreats on Ouster at Travel Office, Reinstating 5," *New York Times*, May 26, 1993, p. A1.

47. Ruth Ann Marcus, "White House Backs Off on Firing 5," *Washington Post*, May 26, 1993, p. A1.

48. Ibid.

49. John M. Broder, "White House Reprimands 4 in Travel Staff Flap," *Los Angeles Times*, July 3, 1993, p. A1.

50. Gwen Ifill, "5 from Travel Office Get Partial Vindication," *New York Times*, July 3, 1993, p. A1.

51. Ann Devoy, "Costs of Clinton Travel Firings Still Growing," *Washington Post*, October 8, 1994, p. A1.

52. Toni Locy, "Travel Unit's Ousted Head is Indicted," *Washington Post*, December 8, 1994, p. A1.

53. "White House Travel Chief Found Innocent of Charges," *Wall Street Journal*, November 17, 1995, p. A20.

54. "Excerpt from a Memo on the White House Travel Office," *New York Times*, January 5, 1996, p. D20.

55. Toni Locy and Susan Schmidt, "Ex-Aide Tells of Pressure for Travel Office Firings," *Washington Post*, January 18, 1996, p. A6.

56. David Johnston, "Mrs. Clinton Responds in Travel Office Inquiry," *New York Times*, March 22, 1996, p. A23.

57. "World-wide: A Federal Judicial Panel," *Wall Street Journal*, March 25, 1996, p. A1.

58. Gwen Ifill, "2 Clinton Aides Are Leaving on a Winning Streak," *New York Times*, December 8, 1993, p. D20.

59. Marshall Ingwerson, "Revolving-Door Standard Raises Tough Issues for Administration," *Christian Science Monitor*, December 16, 1993, p. 1.

60. Ibid.

61. Paul Richter and David Lauter, "White House Defends Ethics Policy as Officials Take Private-Sector Jobs," *Los Angeles Times*, December 8, 1994, p. B28.

62. Bob Davis, "Brown Nominee for Cabinet Post Defends Past Work," *Wall Street Journal*, January 7, 1993, p. A16.

63. Byron York, "Ron Brown's Booty," *American Spectator*, June 1995, p. 37.

64. Certificate of Divestiture No. 93–09, February 1993.

65. Joe Davidson, "Brown Faces Ethics Questions on Vietnam Ties: House Member May Call for Special Prosecutor," *Wall Street Journal*, September 30, 1993, p. A20.

66. Neil A. Lewis, "Inquiry Clears Commerce Chief on Vietnam Bribery Accusation," *New York Times*, February 3, 1994, p. A8.

67. Keith Bradsher, "Commerce Chief is Accused of Misleading Panel on Investment," *New York Times*, January 24, 1995, p. A16.

68. Jerry Knight, "Senator Seeks FDIC Probe of Hill Loan Default; Target is Ex-Partner of Commerce Secretary Brown," *Washington Post*, January 21, 1995, p. C1.

69. Ibid.

70. Bradsher, "Commerce Chief is Accused," p. A16.

71. Keith Bradsher, "Commerce Chief is Accused of Failing to Disclose Income," *New York Times*, January 27, 1995, p. A1.

72. Keith Bradsher, "Congress Investigating Forgiveness of Loan to Commerce Head," *New York Times*, January 29, 1995, p. A21.

73. Keith Bradsher, "Justice Officials Start Preliminary Inquiry of Commerce Secretary," *New York Times*, February 17, 1995, p. A19; David Johnston, "A Miami Lawyer is Chosen to Investigate Commerce Secretary's Finances," *New York Times*, July 7, 1995, p. A14.

74. Sharon Walsh, "Special Prosecutor to Drop Brown Probe," *Washington Post*, April 5, 1996, p. A23;

75. Pierre Thomas, "Espy Probe May Get Independent Counsel," *Washington Post*, August 8, 1994, p. A5. See also David Johnston, "Agriculture Chief Questioned on Gifts," *New York Times*, June 9, 1994, p. A12; Bruce Ingersoll and Viveca Novack, "Justice Department Won't Charge Espy in Closing Probe of Possible Gift," *Wall Street Journal*, June 10, 1994, p. A12.

76. Richard Cohen, "Gift Seat in Tyson Skybox," *Washington Post*, August 11, 1994, p. A31.

77. "Agriculture Chief Was Given Tickets," *New York Times*, August 25, 1994, p. B7.

78. Pierce Thomas and Howard Schneider, "Los Angeles Attorney Chosen to Head Investigation of Espy," *Washington Post*, September 10, 1994, p. A3.

79. Sharon LaFraniere and Susan Schmidt, "Espy Billed U.S. for Monthly Trips Home," *Washington Post*, September 17, 1994, p. A1.

80. Bruce Ingersoll and Viveca Novack, "Secretary Espy Drove U.S. Leased Auto for Personal Use, Violating Strict Rules," *Wall Street Journal*, September 20, 1994, p. A26.

81. Alan C. Miller, "Espy Repays $7,500 for Gifts and Expenses," *Los Angeles Times*, September 20, 1994, p. A10.

82. Ann Devoy and Susan Schmidt, "Agriculture Secretary Espy Resigns," *Washington Post*, October 4, 1994, p. A1.

83. William Neikirk, "Use of Chopper for Golf Costs Clinton Aide his Job," *Chicago Tribune*, May 27, 1994, p. A1.

84. White House, Office of the Press Secretary, August 11, 1994; also see Ruth Ann Marcus and Sharon LaFraniere, "White House Bans Gifts, Free Travel for Appointees," *Washington Post*, August 12, 1994, p. A14.

85. Jeff Gerth, "Clintons Joined S&L Operator in Ozark Real Estate Venture," *New York Times*, March 8, 1992, p. A1.

86. Gwen Ifill, "Clinton Defends Real-Estate Deal," *New York Times*, March 9, 1992, p. A13.

87. "Governor Clinton Misses the Point," Editorial *New York Times*, March 12, 1992, p. A22.

88. David Maraniss and Michael Weisskoff, "Lawyer Will Review Arkansas Land Deal," *Washington Post*, March 12, 1992, p. A1.

89. Gwen Ifill, "Files of Dead Clinton Aide Are Dispensed to Legal Staff," *New York Times*, August 12, 1993, p. A16.

90. Bruce Ingersoll, "File on Business Dealings of Clintons is Being Sought in Foster Suicide Case," *Wall Street Journal*, December 20, 1993, p. A14; Michael Isikoff, "Whitewater Files Were Found in Foster's Office, White House Confirms," *Washington Post*, December 22, 1993, p. A16.

91. "Release the Whitewater Files," Editorial *New York Times*, December 23, 1993, p. A16.

92. R. H. Melton, "Starr Rebuts Column Critical of Whitewater Case," *Washington Post*, April 11, 1996, p. A6.

Chapter 13

It's Not Character, Stupid!

Throughout the 1992 presidential campaign, the Clinton campaign followed the motto "It's the Economy, Stupid!" Day after day the Clinton campaign pounded President George Bush on the slow growth of the nation's economy. Despite persistent efforts by the Bush campaign to attack the character of Bill Clinton, the Clinton campaign succeeded in keeping the focus of the campaign on the economy.

GOVERNMENT MAKES A COMEBACK: PRESIDENT FIX-IT

By early 1996, it became clear that the Republican Party planned to try to convince the American public that Bill Clinton and Hillary Rodham Clinton lacked the character to reside in the White House for another four years. To counter the expected attacks, the Clinton campaign adopted a two-prong strategy for maintaining control of the agenda and avoid drawing the president directly into a debate over character. President Clinton announced a series of initiatives that demonstrated the ability of government to deal with important issues without increasing the federal budget deficit. At the same time, administration and campaign officials responded immediately to any attack against the integrity of Bill Clinton or members of his administration.

On June 24, President Clinton proposed legislation to amend the Family and Medical Leave Act of 1993 to allow workers to take "as many as 80 hours of 'flex time' in lieu of overtime pay." The legislation would allow workers to use the compensatory time for a wide range of nonmedical purposes, such as attending PTA meetings.[1] A day later, Clinton proposed a Victim's Rights Constitutional Amendment.[2] On July 3, he announced that the Department of Education would "spend $10 million in discretionary funds to pay for anti-truancy pilot programs in 25 school districts."[3] "Recalling the muckraking food-industry exposes of almost a century ago," on July 6 President Clinton "announced a new system for guarding against deadly bacteria in meat and poultry."[4] On July 9, he announced a $2 million pilot program "to help track down those who sell guns to young people."[5] On July 23, in a San Francisco speech, Clinton told the assembled, "What we in the government should be doing is empowering you to make the most of your own lives, to meet the challenges, to protect your values."[6] On July 29, Clinton convened a White House conference on children's television. He made it clear that he wanted the broadcast industry to increase the amount of children's programming.

Not everyone applauded the strategy. Columnist Maureen Dowd wrote, "Instead of the Great Society, Clinton now brings us the Itsy-Bitsy Society. Instead of a rendezvous with destiny, he has an appointment with detail. From grand, epic-making schemes of social engineering, he has come around to suggestions that we cross a few t's and dot a couple of i's."[7]

Despite criticism, the polls indicated that the strategy worked remarkably well. The fact that Bill Clinton did not face any opposition for the Democratic nomination meant that the Clinton campaign could devote all its energy to presenting the image of a president who understood the problems of average Americans, but who also had no plans of returning to an era of big government and high taxes. A June 27, 1996, NBC-*Wall Street Journal* poll found that 62 percent of those surveyed believed issues mattered more than character.[8]

The Character Issue and Campaign '96

Throughout the spring and summer of 1996, Bob Dole and the Republican Party tried to ignite a character backlash against Bill Clinton. Republican Senator John McCain, in mid-April, told Reuters news service, "one of President Clinton's weaknesses is when we get into the trust factor. Do you trust President Clinton? Large numbers of Americans simply do not."[9] The Republican National Committee unleashed an attack ad in late May that slammed Clinton "for trying to use the Soldiers and Sailors Relief Act of 1940 to defer Paula Jones' sexual harassment lawsuit."[10]

On May 28, a Little Rock, Arkansas, jury "convicted Clinton's former business partners, James B. and Susan McDougal, and the man who succeeded him as governor of Arkansas, Jim Guy Tucker(D)"[11] on various bank fraud charges. Many Republicans believed these convictions would turn the campaign around by focusing renewed attention on the character issue.[12]

In a June 2 speech, Bob Dole told a luncheon of Republican Party leaders: "I want to be President because I want to return integrity to our government—a mission that's more important this week than even a week ago."[13]

But a June 21 *USA Today*-CNN-Gallup poll found that 57 percent of those questioned planned to vote for Bill Clinton and only 38 percent planned to vote for Republican candidate Bob Dole. Sixty-two percent of those polled said that Bob Dole had the personal characteristics of honesty and trustworthiness, while only 45 percent believed that Bill Clinton had such characteristics. Fifty-seven percent of Americans believed that Hillary Rodham Clinton had participated in a coverup in matters related to Whitewater.[14] Yet 64 percent believed Bill Clinton cared about people like them, while only 47 percent believed Bob Dole cared about them.

By late June, Clinton faced yet another integrity crisis. A House Committee investigation into the 1993 firing of White House travel office employees learned that the White House Office of Personnel Security had improperly requested FBI files on 407 individuals as part of updating White House pass files.[15] Attorney General Janet Reno subsequently asked Whitewater independent counsel Kenneth Starr to investigate the request, and the FBI file fiasco gave Republicans new hope that the tide might turn against Clinton.[16]

But like the Whitewater convictions, the FBI file controversy had no impact on support for Clinton. A July 12 CNN-*Time* poll gave Clinton a 53 percent to 38 percent lead.[17]

In a rare public comment on the character issue on July 15, 1996, Bill Clinton said that "every reading of the evidence fails to demonstrate any wrongdoing by either one of us."[18] President Clinton also assailed the Whitewater investigation as a "highly politicized operation" that had "no precedent that I know of, ever."[19] He said that he believed character was a legitimate issue in the campaign, but that character can be demonstrated "most effectively by what you fight for and for whom you fight."[20]

Drug Abuse and the War on Crime

In 1988, the Republican Party had successfully portrayed Michael Dukakis as soft on crime. On July 15, 1996, stories began to appear that "the Clinton administration allowed 21 employees to work at the White House, even though their background checks indicated recent drug use."[21] As a condition of giving the individuals security clearances, the Secret Service required that they submit to special drug testing. Secret Service officials subsequently told a House committee investigating the FBI White House file flap "that more than three dozen White House employees had used cocaine, crack and other illegal hallucinogenic drugs before they were hired and were given security clearances despite concerns about safety at the presidential mansion."[22]

Republicans and the Dole campaign seized on the White House drug-testing disclosures as evidence that the White House did not take the use of illegal drugs seriously. But like previous Clinton administration public integrity questions, the controversy failed to catch on as a major campaign issue. Likewise, the character issue failed to catch fire, and by the early August convention, the Dole campaign was forced to shift its focus to tax reform and the regulatory burden on small businesses.

As with the Democratic Party's strategy of attacking the character of Reagan administration officials in 1984 and 1988, the Dole campaign badly misjudged the impact that character issues would have on swing voters. Although voters cared about the character of candidates for president, the Republican Congress had struck fear into the hearts of key voting blocks. Efforts by Republicans in Congress to slow the growth in Medicare expenses panicked older voters. Likewise, many women voters viewed the Republican agenda as hostile to women.

A July 23, 1996, CNN-*USA Today*-Gallup poll asked voters who they thought was better on key issues. On issues of great importance to swing voters, Clinton held a large lead over Bob Dole. Clinton held a 59 percent to 22 percent lead on the environment; a 56 percent to 28 percent lead on education; a 51 percent to 27 percent lead on abortion and a 44 percent to 35 percent lead on the crime issue.[23] And Clinton held a 41 percent to 30 percent lead on the economy.[24]

A BORN-AGAIN MOVEMENT CONSERVATIVE

By early August, conventional wisdom held that Bill Clinton had a secure lead in the polls and that Bob Dole had little chance of catching up. Floundering in the polls, the Dole campaign took two gigantic risks. Throwing away decades of opposition to supply-side economics, Dole announced his support of a 15 percent cut in federal taxes. As Ronald Reagan had argued in 1980, Dole maintained that the tax cut would stimulate economic growth and produce more federal revenue. Dole also argued that hundreds of billions of dollars in savings could be found in the federal budget without tampering with Social Security or Medicare. The choice of Jack Kemp as Dole's running mate added a vigorous campaigner who had the ability to articulate a broad Republican vision. A *Newsweek* poll, taken shortly after the end of the Republican convention, had Bill Clinton with 44 percent of the vote, Bob Dole with 42 percent of the vote. The Dole convention bounce and its bold strategy made clear that Clinton's reelection campaign would not be a cake walk.

On Sunday, August 18, Bill Clinton appeared on *60 Minutes* with Dan Rather. After Rather recounted the string of personal barbs made by Republican speakers at the convention, Clinton responded, "I don't believe frankly that the Republicans could do anything to damage my character. They may be able to attack my reputation, but God is the ultimate judge of people's character and He knows all facts . . . and there's no angle there."[25] Clinton also took time to defend his White House staff. Bob Dole, during his convention acceptance speech, had described the Clinton White House as a "corps of the elite who never grew up, never did anything real, never sacrificed."[26]

The high-risk strategy adopted by the Dole campaign caught the Clinton campaign off-guard. Clinton understood that key swing voters wanted to keep certain federal government services, but they also believed that there was a tremendous amount of waste, fraud and abuse in federal programs. The Clinton campaign realized it faced a difficult time explaining to these cynical swing voters that they could not have both a large tax cut and popular federal programs. Their campaign hinged on convincing voters that a Republican Congress and a Republican president had a secret agenda that only Bill Clinton had the ability to stop. That secret agenda included destroying Medicare, Social Security, student loans, and environmental regulation.

Bob Dole, the Better Man for a Better America

Despite Dole's decision to pledge an income tax cut of 15 percent for every American family, the campaign attempted to keep the character issue alive. Its slogan, "The Better Man for a Better America," left little to the imagination.[27] Yet the Dole campaign did not repeat the mistake of the 1992 Bush campaign, which had made character the central theme of its strategy to defeat Bill Clinton.

Shortly before the beginning of the Democratic convention, the Dole campaign received help from an unlikely source for its character attack. The Department of Health and Human Services, on August 20, 1996, released a report showing that illicit drug use by twelve- to seventeen-year-olds had increased from 5.3 percent to 10.9 percent between 1992 and 1995.[28] At a campaign stop, Bob Dole said that the survey marked "nothing short of a national tragedy."[29] Making reference to the controversy over drug testing of Clinton White House employees, the Dole campaign worked hard to persuade the American people that Clinton did not regard illegal drug use as a major national problem. "We shouldn't be surprised that Clinton is losing the war on drugs," commented Republican National Committee Chairman Haley Barbour. "From the beginning, he has treated illegal drug use with a wink and nod in his policies, appointments, and attitude of his administration."[30]

A day after release of the report, the White House leaked to the media Bill Clinton's decision to authorize the Food and Drug Administration to treat nicotine in cigarettes as a drug. On Friday, August 23, Clinton approved sweeping new FDA regulations banning most cigarette vending machines, sharply limiting cigarette advertising and requiring cigarette companies to spend $150 million a year on advertising to dissuade young people from smoking.

The same week saw Clinton sign the insurance portability bill and landmark welfare reform agenda. These stories quickly crowded out the stories of increasing illegal drug use by young people.

BETWEEN HOPE AND HISTORY

A few days before the start of the Democratic convention, Bill Clinton's book *Between Hope and History* began appearing in bookstores across the country. He used the book to more clearly define his view of the role of government in American society: "Americans don't want our government gutted," he said. "My vision does not seek to promote government, but to perfect it, to make it a better servant of our people."[31] Following this theme, on Saturday, August 24, 1995, President Clinton announced the establishment of a national registry of sex offenders.

Shortly after the announcement, Clinton began his train trip from Huntington, West Virginia, to the Democratic Party convention in Chicago. At each stop along the way, Clinton took time to stress the role of government in making lives better and the danger to key programs if Bob Dole took the White House, with Newt Gingrich as Speaker of the House.

Dick Morris and the Blip on the Radar Screen

The Democratic convention went flawlessly until the *Star* tabloid released a story that Clinton political consultant Dick Morris had "cavorted with a $200-an-hour hooker in a Washington hotel—even letting her listen secretly to telephone conversations he had with the president."[32] With the story coming on the same day as President Clinton's acceptance speech, political pundits pondered how the public would react to the latest Clinton integrity problem. An *ABC News* tracking released on the Saturday after the end of the convention found that "Clinton was favored by 54 percent, compared with Dole's 34 percent and 8 percent for Reform Party presidential candidate Ross Perot."[33] The departure of Dick Morris apparently had no impact on key swing voters.

Enemy Identification

Despite the fact that Bill Clinton held a twelve-point lead in most polls during the first week of September,[34] the Clinton campaign continued to view the independent counsel investigation of Kenneth Starr as a major threat. A week before the Hartford, Connecticut, presidential debate, the *Washington Post* ran a story entitled "Clinton Steps Up Effort to Portray Whitewater Prosecutor as Partisan."[35] But this decision to take off the gloves regarding the Whitewater investigation backfired. It seemed that Bill Clinton was running against Kenneth Starr, not against Bob Dole.

Liberal *Washington Post* columnist Richard Cohen criticized White House efforts to discredit the independent counsel investigation and called for Hillary Rodham Clinton to address the findings of a Federal Deposit Insurance Corporation Report "suggesting that Hillary Clinton was involved in a 'sham' real estate transaction back when she was a lawyer in private practice."[36] In a PBS interview the week of September 24, Bill Clinton told Jim Lehrer that there was a lot of evidence to support the argument that politics motivated the independent counsel investigation. But a September 27, 1996, *Washington Post* editorial rejected Clinton's assertion: "We have seen no evidence of any impropriety in the conduct of the special prosecutor's office itself."[37] According to the *Post*, "Mr. Starr and his team seem to be following precisely the mandate they were set by a panel of federal judges at the request of Mr. Clinton's attorney general, Janet Reno."[38]

Conservative *New York Times* political commentator William Safire unleashed an equally critical attack on the Clinton campaign strategy against Kenneth Starr: "Here's how to succeed in obstructing justice: (1) publicly disparage all investigators as partisan miscreants, as Clinton now does, (2) encourage co-conspirators to resist prosecutorial pressure by arranging for hush money and (3) hint at post-election pardons."[39] Referring to the authority of a president to issue anticipatory pardons, Safire moved to discredit any argument Clinton might make to issue anticipatory pardons to Whitewater figures: "Does anyone doubt that if indictments appear likely, the president would repeat his phony claim that 'it's obvious' that partisan plotters are out to get him—and would protect himself by a parade of pardons?" Late September polls, however, failed to provide evidence that the morality issue had changed voters' minds. When asked which candidate they think would do the better job of dealing with the country's moral problems, Clinton received the support of 39 percent of likely voters, Bob Dole 38 percent and Ross Perot 8 percent.

However, the Clinton campaign had made its first major blunder of the campaign. Key swing voters had not found the character issue compelling enough to switch from Bill Clinton to Bob Dole. But the issue of Bill Clinton's granting pardons in anticipation of indictments, or even after indictments, cast an entirely new light on the character issue. The memory of Watergate reared its ugly head. Despite the ideological nature of the public integrity war, the Clinton campaign failed to understand that a professional

public integrity bureaucracy had established itself on the political landscape.

A SECOND FRONT

The Dole campaign had pinned its hope on the 15 percent tax cut, but
the failure of that proposal to shake lose voters forced a reconsideration
of the character issue.

On October 6, Bob Dole and Bill Clinton squared off in a long-
anticipated debate. An ABC poll taken immediately after the debate reported that 50 percent of viewers thought Clinton won and 29 percent
percent gave the nod to Bob Dole.[40] Toward the end of the debate, mod-
erator Jim Lehrer asked the candidates, "Are there also significant differences in the more personal areas relevant to this election?"[41] The questions
provided Dole with an opportunity to ask Bill Clinton about the pardons.
In a carefully worded response, Clinton stressed that he would "not give
any special treatment and [he would] strictly adhere to the law, and that
is what every president has done, as far as I know in the past. But whatever
other presidents have done, this is something I take seriously and that's my
position."[42] Dole, in response, argued that the president never should have
commented on the pardon issue in the first place.

On the whole, Dole had declined to press the character issue in the first
debate. The failure of that first presidential debate, and the vice-presidential
debate as well, to reduce Clinton's lead in the polls led criticism to mount
in Republican circles. Dole needed to take off the gloves and begin pound-
ing Clinton on the character issue.[43] In an October 11 campaign speech in
Kettering, Ohio, Bob Dole portrayed President Clinton as a "slick-talking
politician who breaks his promises and is an unacceptable role model for
the nation's young people."[44] Far behind in the polls, Dole found that he
had little choice but to launch the character issue as a second front.[45]

The October 16 San Diego presidential debate provided another chance
for Dole to raise the character question in front of millions of Americans.
He wasted little time alleging that the Democratic administration was guilty
of "endless violations of public trust."[46] To the surprise of most observers,
Clinton did not respond to Dole's character attacks and continued to press
home that his administration had protected the public from disastrous cuts
in programs such as Medicare and student loans. Clinton waited until his
closing statement to address his critic. "No attack ever created a job or
educated a child or helped a family make ends meet," the president said.
"No insult ever cleaned up a toxic waste dump or helped an elderly person."[47] Thus, Clinton succeeded in raising the specter of a mean-spirited
Bob Dole. A CNN-*USA Today*-Gallup poll taken immediately after the
debate found that 59 percent of the American people believed Bill Clinton

did a better job in the debate and 58 percent believed that Bob Dole "was more unfair in criticizing his opponent."[48]

Mired in the Mud

In the week following the San Diego debate, the Dole campaign unleashed one of the most vigorous character assaults in recent presidential election history. "More investigations, more prosecutions, and more convictions, and the list goes on and on," pounded one postdebate Dole ad.[49] The disclosure "that an Indonesian couple with ties to the financial conglomerate Lippo Group made a $450,00 donation to the Democrats" led the Dole campaign to accuse the Democrats of permitting foreigners to buy influence and compared it to Watergate.[50] The Clinton campaign countered with disclosure of a Pat Buchanan memo indicating that in February 1970 freshman Senator Bob Dole had urged Republicans to initiate "politically inspired investigations" of misdeeds by prior Democratic administrations.[51] *Newsweek* then released a survey that found that 59 percent of registered voters thought Dole was "more negative or nasty" than Clinton. More disturbing for the Dole campaign, it found that 48 percent of those surveyed said Clinton had the better personal character to be president, compared to 36 percent for Dole.[52,53]

In the final weeks of the campaign, Dole intensified his character attacks against Bill Clinton, with charges that a liberal media refused to tell the American public the truth about the ethics of Bill Clinton.[54] Dole expressed disbelief that the American public could consider allowing Bill Clinton to stay in the White House for another four years. He warned the nation that "the Clinton administration's ethical problems could bring about a traumatic second term for the president reminiscent of Watergate."[55] Yet into the final week of the campaign, Clinton held a double-digit lead in the polls. Then in his final push, Dole barnstormed across the nation for ninety-six hours, attacking the ethics of the Clinton administration. "I think the American people are starting to say, 'What's going on here?' 'What's going on in this White House?' Every week, every week, every week, every week?" hammered Bob Dole.[56]

To the surprise of almost no one, Bill Clinton won a second term with 379 electoral votes and 49 percent of the popular vote.[57] Voters, however, kept Republicans in control of both the House and the Senate.[58] Exit polls revealed that 60 percent of all voters felt that Clinton did not tell the truth about Whitewater, while 89 percent of Clinton voters believed he had told the truth.[59] Fifty-four percent of all voters had concerns regarding his honesty and trustworthiness, while 88 percent of Clinton voters believed the man was honest and trustworthy.[60]

NO LIGHT AT THE END OF THE TUNNEL

In the aftermath of the Watergate scandal, it appeared that Watergate-inspired reforms might help repair the damage done to public trust in government. But growing divisions over the role of government quickly shattered this dream. The public integrity war has profoundly changed the character of American politics and government. A constant barrage of allegations has made it next to impossible for most Americans to distinguish between legitimate charges of improper conduct and those motivated by ideology. Forty-nine percent of eligible voters—the lowest figure since 1924—turned out to vote in the 1996 Presidential election.

The public integrity war has helped to transform the political landscape into a battlefield where honesty in government is simply another political issue. The day after the 1996 presidential election, the *Washington Post* ran a front-page story entitled "Clashing Coalitions Produce Split in Government Power: 2 Constituencies in Opposition Ideologically, Demographically."[61] The Republican coalition, "more male-dominated, more pessimistic, more Protestant, more conservative and more likely to own a gun," placed a much higher priority on honesty in government than did members of the Democratic coalition, who are "more apt to be female, Catholic, single," and "ideologically moderate to liberal."[62] Members of the clashing coalitions, in fact, regard the role of government not the integrity of public officals as their primary concern.

Light At the End of the Tunnel?

Throughout the modern public integrity war, proposals for massive political reform have followed each new series of scandals. Almost simultaneous with the swearing in of William Jefferson Clinton for a second term as president of the United States, Speaker of the House Newt Gingrich accepted a reprimand from the House and a $300,000 penalty for violating House ethics rules related to using tax exempt donations to fund a television course.[63] Despite the prospect of a number of ongoing ethics investigations related to Whitewater, Paula Corbin Jones and questionable fund-raising efforts by the Democratic National Committee during the 1996 presidential campaign, President Clinton embarked upon a campaign cast himself as the mediator between the clashing coalitions: "We need a new government for a new century humble enough not to try to solve all our problems for us, but strong enough to give us the tools to solve our problems ourselves."[64] The conciliatory tone did nothing to slow the ongoing ethics investigations.[65]

Although numerous public officials have found their lives turned upside down by the public integrity war, the American public has turned out the be the greatest loser. Sadly, a large percentage of the public has come to accept apparent unethical behavior by public officials as the rule rather than the exception. The restoration of public trust in government will take much more than the passage of a new campaign finance law or the tightening of existing ethics laws and rules. It will take a realization that neither movement conservatives nor new progressives have much hope of forcing each other into an unconditional surrender.

The vast majority of public servants work hard and strive to comply with the numerous ethics regulations spawned by the public integrity wars. Ethics rules and regulations, however, play a small role in the moral development of public servants. Too many public servants, however, have learned to rationalize questionable conduct as necessary to prevent "evil forces" from taking or remaining in power.

The public integrity war is not a story of saints and sinners. It is a story of how easily the passion for policies and programs can cloud one's judgement. Congress can do little to legisolate the end to the public integrity war. New presidential directives on government ethics will only complicate the problem. The public integrity war will only end when we stop viewing political opponents as mortal enemies. Only then will we regain the ability to distinguish between individuals who have truly violated the public trust and those individuals simply caught up in the battles of the public integrity war.

NOTES

1. Melissa Healy, "Clinton Proposes Allowing More Time Off for Workers," *Los Angeles Times*, June 25, 1996, p. A1.

2. John Broder, "Clinton Calls for Victims' Rights in Constitution," *Los Angeles Times*, June 26, 1996, p. A1.

3. John Broder, "Clinton Announces Effort to Curb School Truancy," *Los Angeles Times*, July 4, 1996, p. A16.

4. Stanley Meisler, "Clinton Upgrades Meat, Poultry Rules," *Los Angeles Times*, July 7, 1996, p. A1.

5. Paul Richter and Greg Krikorian, "Clinton Takes Aim at Rogue Gun Dealers," *Los Angeles Times,* July 9, 1996, p. A11.

6. Kevin Merida, "Clinton Pushes Low-Cost Initiatives: President Offers Noncontroversial Proposals on Campaign Swing," *Washington Post*, July 24, 1996, p. A8.

7. Maureen Dowd, "Mr. Fix-It of Politics: Truant Officer Clinton, President Pothole, Handy William," *Richmond Times-Dispatch*, July 28, 1996, G7.

8. "Poll Finds Voters Care Most About Issues, Not Character," *All Politics*, June 27, 1996, URL: http://allpolitics.com/news/9606/27/poll/

9. "Do You Trust Bill Clinton?" *All Politics*, April 18, 1996, URL: http://allpolitics.com/news/9604/18/character/index.shtml

10. "Campaign '96 Ads, Stripes," *All Politics*, January 17, 1996, URL: http://allpolitics.com/candidates/campaign.96/index4.html

11. Ann Devoy and Dan Balz, "Jurors Keep Issue Alive for Clinton," *Washington Post*, May 29, 1996, p. A1.

12. Dan Balz, "Character Issue Is Focus for Dole at GOP Luncheon: Kansan Hints at Whitewater in Attack on Clinton's Integrity," *Washington Post*, April 21, 1996, p. A19.

13. Ibid.

14. Richard Benedetto, "Character Bullets Are Bouncing off Clinton," *USA Today*, June 21, 1996, p. 6A.

15. John F. Harris and George Lardner, Jr., "Reno Seeks Starr Probe of FBI Files," *Washington Post*, June 21, 1996, p. A1.

16. John M. Broder and Ronald Brownstein, "Specter of Past Disarray Besets White House," *Los Angeles Times*, June 24, 1996, p. A1.

17. "Clinton Holds A 15–Point Lead," *All Politics*, July 12, 1996, URL: http://allpolitics.com/news/9607/12/poll/index.shtml

18. "Clinton Unrattled By Suspicions in Polls," *Richmond Times-Dispatch*. July 16, 1996, p. A3.

19. Paul Richter, "Clinton Assails Starr Over Whitewater Probe," *Los Angeles Times*, July 16, 1996, A8.

20. John F. Harris, "Clinton: Judge Character by Actions, Not Allegations," *Washington Post*, July 16, 1996, p. A5.

21. "21 White House Employees in Drug Testing Because of Backgrounds," *Associated Press*, July 15, 1996, URL: http://www.politicsnow.com/news/July96/15/ap0715drugtesting/index.htm

22. Richard A. Serrano, "Panel Hears Drug History of 36 Clinton Staffers," *Los Angeles Times*, July 18, 1996, p. A11.

23. Poll Track: Report from the Nation, July 23, 1996, URL: http://www.politicsnow.com/resource/polltrak/index.htm

24. Ibid.

25. John F. Harris, "President Promises Convention Will Be About Ideas, Not Insults," *Washington Post*, August 18, 1996, p. A8.

26. Ibid.

27. "Ad Watch," *USA Today*, August 21, 1996, p. A4.

28. Robert Sure, "Teens' Use of Drugs Still Rising," *Washington Post*, August 21, 1996, p. A1.

29. Ibid.

30. Ibid., p. 10.

31. John F. Harris. "Clinton's Book Declares Need for Active Government," *Washington Post*, August 22, 1996, p. A8.

32. Jerry Seper, "Morris Is but the Latest Bump in Clinton's Road," *Washington Times-Whitewater-Current*, August 30–Sept. 1, 1996, URL: http://www.washtimes.com/whitewater/ww.current.html

33. John F. Harris and Dan Balz, "Democrats Revive Campaign Busing: Poll Suggest Convention Helped Clinton," *Washington Post*, August 31, 1996, p. A1.

34. A September 6, 1996, CNN-*Time* poll gave Clinton a 52 percent to 38 percent lead over Bob Dole. All Politics, URL: http://allpolitics.com/polls/national/cnn.time/090696.shtml

35. R. H. Melton, "Clinton Steps Up Effort to Portray Whitewater Prosecutor as Partisan," *Washington Post*, September 27, 1996, p. A22.

36. Richard Cohen, "Blaming the Prosecutor: Mrs. Clinton's explanation is simply not convincing," *Washington Post*, Thursday, September 26, 1996, p. A31.

37. "Isn't It Obvious?" *Washington Post*, September 27, 1996, p. A24.

38. Ibid.

39. William Safire, "The Road to National Nightmare," *Daily News-Record*, September 28, 1996, p. A6.

40. Gary Langer, "In Debate No. 1: A Clinton Win by 21 Points," *ABC News, PoliticsNow—News*, October 6, 1996, URL: http://www.politicsnow.com/news/ Oct96/06/abc1006poll/

41. *All Politics—Presidential Debates*—Transcripts, October 6, 1996, URL: http://allpolitics.com/debates/transcripts/index14.shtml

42. Ibid.

43. Dan Balz, "Silence on Character Issue Puzzles Some Republicans: Ticket Faulted for Avoiding Clinton Ethics," *Washington Post*, October 11, 1996, p. A1.

44. Edward Walsh, "Dole Lashes Clinton on Trust Issue," *Washington Post*, October 12, 1996, p. A1.

45. Edward Walsh and Paul Duggan, "Dole Campaign to Open Second Front on Character Theme," *Washington Post*, October 13, 1996, p. A26.

46. R. Morris Barrett, "The Debates '96: No Fireworks, No Flames," *All Politics*, October 17, 1996, URL: http://allpolitics.com/news/9610/16/analysis/in-dex.shtml

47. Ibid., p. 2.

48. Justin C. Oppmann, "Flash Point Suggest Clinton Reigns," *All Politics*, October 16, 1996, URL: http://allpolitics.com/news/9610/16/instapoll/, pp. 1–3.

49. "Riady2," *PoliticsNow*—Campaign '96—White House—Presidential Ad Watch—Bill Clinton. January 17, 1997.

50. "Dole Keeps Heat on Clinton's Ethics," *MSNBC*, October 19, 1996, URL: http://www.msnbc.com/news/35871.asp

51. George Lardner, Jr., "Dole Pushed Nixon Probe of Democrats," *Washington Post*, October 19, 1996, p. A12.

52. " 'Wake Up' Frustrated Dole Says on Stump," October 24, 1996. The Associated Press. URL: http://search.politicsnow.com/PN/news/Oct96/24/ap1024dole/ index.htm

53. "Poll: Clinton has character to be president," *USA Today, Election '96*, October 19, 1996, URL: http://167.8.29.8/elect/eq/eq149.htm

54. Blaine Harden, "A Seething Dole Intensifies Attack: Candidate Lobs FBI Files Accusations," *Washington Post*, October 26, 1996, p. A1.

55. Dan Balz and Blaine Harden, "Dole Hammers Clinton on Ethics, Slow Economic Growth," *Washington Post*, October 31, 1996, p. A15.

56. Katharine Q. Seelye, "On the Final Weekend, a Restrained Clinton and Insistent Dole: Ethics Pushed in Challenger's 4-Day Tour." *New York Times,* November 3, 1996, p. A1.

57. Election results, *New York Times: Politics*, November 6, 1996, URL: http:// www.nytimes.com/specials/election/BC-US-Pres-State-by-State-1.html.

58. Senate: 55 Republican, 45 Democratic; House: Republican 204, Democratic, 207.

59. Presidential Election Exit Polls Results-Part 1, *All Politics*, CNN-Time, November 6, 1996, URL: http://allpolitics.com/elections/natl.exit.poll/index2.html

60. Ibid.

61. Thomas B. Edsall and Mario A. Brossard, "Clashing Coalitions Produce Split in Government Power," *Washington Post*, November 7, 1996, p. A1.

62. Ibid.

63. Marc Lacey and Janet Hook, "Gringrich Nulls Options for Paying Penalty," *Los Angeles Times*, January 23, 1997, p. A1.

64. "Inaugural '97 William J. Clinton, President of the United States," *All Politics*, January 20, 1997, URL: http://allpolitics.com/news/9701/201/transcripts/

65. Elizabeth Shogen, "Controversies to Haunt Clinton in Second Term," *Los Angeles Times*, January 23, 1997, p. A1.

Bibliography

"A September 6, 1996, CNN/Time Poll gave Clinton a 52% to 38% lead over Bob Dole." *All Politics*, URL: http://allpolitics.com/pols/national/cnn.time/090696.shtml

Abels, Jules. *The Truman Scandals.* Chicago: Regnery, 1956.

"Ad Watch." *USA Today*, 21 August 1996, p. A4.

Adams, Bruce, and Kathryn Kavanagh-Baran. *Promise and Performance: Carter Builds a New Administration.* Lexington, MA: Lexington Books, 1979.

Administrative Conference of the United States. *Presidential Transition Worker's Code of Ethical Conduct.* Washington, DC: The Conference, 1988.

Administrative Conference of the United States. Office of the Chairman, Administrative Conference of the United States. *Sourcebook on Governmental Ethics for Presidential Appointees.* Washington, DC: Administrative Conference, December 1988.

Aldrich, Gary W. *Unlimited Access: An FBI Agent Inside the Clinton White House.* Washington, DC: Regnery, 1996.

Allen, Robert S. and William V. Shannon. *The Truman Merry-Go-Round.* New York: The Vanguard Press, 1950.

Alston, Chuck. "Common Cause: A Watchdog That Barks at Its Friends." *Congressional Quarterly Weekly Report*, August 26, 1989, p. 2204.

American Civil Liberities Union. *Why President Nixon Should Be Impeached.* Washington, DC: Public Affairs Press, 1973.

"Americans Still Preceive Politicans as Dishonest." *The Gallup Report* (November 1986): 28.

"An Ethics Test for Mr. Bush." Editorial. *Washington Post*, April 12, 1989, p. A22.

Anderson, Jack and Dale Van Atta. "For 'Parity,' Some Ethics Rules Relaxed." *Washington Post*, January 9, 1990, p. B8.

Andrews, Edmund L. "GOP Falters on Pro-Business Laws." *New York Times*, December 23, 1995, p. A39.

Art, Robert J. *The TFX Decision: McNamara and the Military*. Boston: Little Brown, 1968.

Babcock, Charles. "Behind Charges: 279 Pages of Detail: New Disclosures Include Oil Well Investment; Further Probe Planned." *Washington Post*, April 18, 1989, A12.

Babcock, Charles, Ann Devoy and Lucy Shackelford. "Sununu: Frequent Flier on Military Aircraft: Trips to Ski Resorts, Home, and Fund-Raisers." *Washington Post*, April 21, 1991, p. A1.

Balz, Dan. "Character Issue is Focus for Dole at GOP Luncheon: Kansan Hints at Whitewater in Attack on Clinton's Integrity." *Washington Post*, April 21, 1996, p. A19.

———. "Silence on Character Issue Puzzles Some Republicans: Ticket Faulted for Avoiding Clinton Ethics." *Washington Post*, October 11, 1996, p. A1.

———. "Clinton Concedes Marital 'Wrongdoing.' " *Washington Post*, January 27, 1992, p. A1.

Balz, Dan and Blaine Harden. "Dole Hammers Clinton on Ethics, Slow Economic Growth." *Washington Post*, October 31, 1996, p. A15.

Barnes, Fred. "Shooting Starr." *Weekly Standard*, April 15, 1996, pp. 11–12.

Barr, Stephen. "White House Shifts Role in Rule-Making." *Washington Post*, October 1, 1993, pp. A1, A22.

Barrett, R. Morris. "The Debates '96, No Fireworks, No Flames," *All Politics*, October 17, 1996, URL: http://allpolitics.com/news/9610/16/analysis/index.shtml

Beale, Sara Sun. "Federalizing Crime: Assessing the Impact on the Federal Courts." *Annals of The American Academy of Political and Social Science* 543 (January, 1996), pp. 39–51.

Beckwith, David. "Picking on the Prosecutor." *Time*, March 9, 1987, p. 31.

Bedard, Paul. "Health Care Panel Shuts Door Tighter." *Washington Times*, March 10, 1993, p. A1.

Benedetto, Richard. "Character Bullets Are Bouncing off Clinton." *USA Today*, June 21, 1996, p. 6A.

Benedetto, Richard. "Most Disapprove of Iran-Contra Pardon." *USA Today*. December 30, 1992. p. A4.

Benson, George C., Steven A. Maaranen and Alan Heslop. *Political Corruption in America*. Lexington, MA: Lexington Books, 1978.

Berke, Richard L. "Clinton Chooses New York Judge for Justice Post," *New York Times*, February 5, 1993, p. A1.

Binstein, Michael. *Greed, Keating, Congress and the S & L Debate*. New York: Putnam's, 1991.

———. *Trust me: Charles Keating and the Missing Billions*. New York: Random House, 1993.

Birnbaum, Jeffrey H. "Campaign 92: Clinton Received a Vietnam Draft Deferment for an ROTC Program that he Never Joined." *Wall Street Journal*, Eastern edition, February 6, 1992, p. A16.

————. *Madhouse: The Private Turmoil of Working for the President*. New York: Times Books, 1996.

Blecker, Robert I. "Beyond 1984: Undercover in America: Serpico to Abscam." *New York Law School Review* 28(1989):823–1024.

Bonafede, Don. "Ethics and the 88 Race." *National Journal*, 8 August 1987, p. 1968–71.

Booe, Martin. "Kentuckians Amazed that $400 Can Buy a Lawmaker." *Los Angeles Times*, April 13, 1990, p. A5.

Boorstin, Daniel J. *The Americans: The Colonial Experience*. New York: Random House, 1958.

————. *Hidden History*. New York: Harper & Row, 1987.

————. *The Lost World of Thomas Jefferson*. New York: Henry Holt, 1948.

Bowen, Howard R. "How Public Spirited Is American Business?" *Annals of the American Academy Of Political And Social Science* 280 (March 1952): 82–89.

Bowman, Ann and Richard C. Kearney. *State & Local Government*. Boston: Houghton Mifflin, 1990.

Bradsher, Keith. "A Clinton Aide's Farewell to Clients: Keep in Touch." *New York Times*, February 5, 1993, p. A1.

————. "Commerce Chief Is Accused of Misleading Panel on Investment." *New York Times*, January 24, 1995, p. A16.

————. "Commerce Chief is Accused of Failing to Disclose Income." *New York Times*, January 27, 1995, p. A1.

————. "Congress Investigating Forgiveness of Loan to Commerce Head." *New York Times*, January 29, 1995, p. A21.

————. "Justice Officials Start Preliminary Inquiry of Commerce Secretary." *New York Times*, February 17, 1995, p. A19.

Breger, Marshall J. "Can Corporate Masters Afford to Become Public Servants?" *Business and Society Review* 71 (Fall 1989): 42–46.

Broder, John. "Clinton Announces Effort to Curb School Truancy." *Los Angeles Times*, July 4, 1996, p. A16.

Broder, John. "Clinton Calls for Victims' Rights in Constitution." *Los Angeles Times*, June 26, 1996, p. A1.

Broder, John M. "White House Reprimands 4 in Travel Staff Flap." *Los Angeles Times*, July 3, 1993, p. A1.

Broder, John and Ronald Brownstein. "Specter of Past Disarray Besets White House." *Los Angeles Times*, June 24, 1996, p. A1.

Brownstein, Ronald. "Agency Ethics Officers Fear Meese Ruling Could Weaken Conflict Laws." *National Journal*, March 23, 1985, 639–42.

Burch, Philip H., Jr. *Elites In American History: The New Deal to the Carter Administration*. New York: Holmes & Meier, 1990.

"Campaign '96 Ads, Stripes." *All Politics*, Candidates, Primary Season, January 17, 1996, URL: http://allpolitics.com/candidates/campaign.96/index4.html

Campbell, Joseph. *The Power of Myth with Bill Moyers*. Ed. Betty Sue Flowers. New York: Doubleday, 1988.

Carlson, Margaret B. "The Neoliberal Blues." *Time*, April 2, 1990, 21.

Carlson, Margaret. "Washington Diary; Star Wars." *Time*, May 6, 1996, p. 20.

Caro, Robert A. *The Years of Lyndon Johnson: Means of Ascent.* New York: Alfred A. Knopf, 1982.

"Carolina Inquiry Indicts 18th Lawmaker." *New York Times*, August 22, 1991, p. A24.

Carroll, James D. and Robert N. Roberts. "If Men Were Angels: Assessing the Ethics in Government Act of 1978." *Policy Studies* 17 (Winter 1988–89): 435–47.

Chandler, Alfred D., Jr. "Government Versus Business: An American Phenomenon." In *Business and Public Policy*, Ed. John T. Dunlop. Cambridge: Harvard University Press, 1980, pp. 1–11.

Clayton, Cornell W., ed. *Government Lawyers: The Federal Legal Bureaucracy and Presidental Politics.* Lawrence: University Press of Kansas, 1995.

Cleghorn, Reese. "Bimboni Plagues and Ethics: What Next?" *Washington Journalism Review* 14 (March 1992): 4.

"Clinton Holds A 15–Point Lead." *All Politics*, July 12, 1996, URL: http://allpolitics.com/news/9607/12/poll/index.shtml

"Clinton Looks to Heighten Scrutiny of Lobbyists." *Inside Politics*, CNN, Program 904, August 4, 1995.

"Clinton raps lobbies' role in regulatory legislation." *Wall Street Journal*, April 24, 1995, p. B9.

Cloud, David S. "Bush's Package on Ethics, Pay Seeks Uniform Standards." *Congressional Quarterly Weekly Report*, April 15, 1989, p. 817.

COGEL *Blue Book*, 9th Ed. *Campaign Finance, Ethics, Lobby Law & Judicial Conduct.* Lexington, KY: Council of State Governments, 1993.

Cohen, Bob. "Anatomy of a Pardon: Why Weinberger Walked." *Newsweek.* January 11, 1993, pp. 22–23.

Cohen, Richard. "Blaming the Prosecutor: Mrs. Clinton's Explanation is Simply not Convincing." *Washington Post*, September 26, 1996, p. A31.

Cohen, Richard. "Gift Seat in Tyson Skybox." *Washington Post*, August 11, 1994, p. A31.

Cohen, Richard. "Will the 96th Become the 'Oversight Congress?' " *National Journal*, January 13, 1979, p. 44.

Cohodas, Nadine. "Congress Weighing Revisions in Special Prosecutor Law." *Congressional Quarterly Weekly Report*, April 24, 1982, p. 907.

"Commentary: Sparring Over Whitewater," *TimesFax*, June 19, 1996, p. A8.

"Common Cause 1970–1990." *Common Cause Magazine* (Fall 1992): 1–40.

Common Cause. *Serving Two Masters: A Common Cause Study of Conflicts of Interest in the Executive Branch.* Washington, DC: Common Cause, October 1976.

Common Cause. *Employment Backgrounds of ERDA and NRC Officials.* Washington, DC: Common Cause, 1976.

Congressional Ethics: History, Facts, and Controversy. Washington, DC: Congressional Quarterly, 1992.

Congressional Quarterly. *Watergate: Chronology of a Crisis.* Washington: Congressional Quarterly, 1974.

Cook, Rhodes. "Arkansan Travels Well Nationally as Campaign Heads for Test." *Congressional Quarterly Weekly Report*, January 11, 1992, p. 58–65.

Cook, Rhodes. "Clinton Can't Shake Doubters Despite Strong Performance." *Congressional Quarterly Weekly Report*, April 11, 1992, pp. 965–72.

Cooper, Ann. "Carter Signs Government-Wide Ethics Bill." *Congressional Quarterly Weekly Report*, October 28, 1978, pp. 3126–127.

CQ Researcher. "Political Scandals." *Congressional Quarterly*, May 27, 1994, pp. 457–79.

CQ Researcher. "Politicians and Privacy." *Congressional Quarterly*, April 17, 1992, pp. 338–59.

Crock, Stan Carey. "A GOP Jihad Against Red Tape." *Business Week*, 28 November 1994, 48–49.

Crook & Crony Government: The Story of Democrat Fraud and Graft: Document and Index. Washington, DC: Republican National Committee, 1952.

Cuff, Robert D. *The War Industries Board: Business-Government Relations during World War I*. Baltimore, MD: Johns Hopkins University Press, 1973.

Cushman John H., Jr. "Republicans Plan Sweeping Barriers to New U.S. Rules." *New York Times*, December 25, 1994, p. A1.

Daley, Steve and Thomas Hardy. "Primary Takes Nasty Turn: Brown Blasts Clinton, Wife over Ethics." *Chicago Tribune*, March 16, 1992, p. 1.

Darley, Roger. "Personal Conflict of Interest Digest." *Public Contract Law Journal* 20 (1991): 302–25.

Davidson, Joe. "Brown Faces Ethics Questions on Vietnam Ties." *Wall Street Journal*, September 30, 1993, p. A20.

Davis, Bob. "Brown Nominee for Cabinet Post Defends Past Work." *Wall Street Journal*, January 7, 1993, p. A16.

Davis, Bob and Bruce Ingersoll. "Clinton's Team Moves to Extend Regulation to a Variety of Industries." *Wall Street Journal* April 13, 1993, p. A1.

Davis, Kenneth Culp. *Administrative Law: Cases-Text-Problems*. St. Paul, MN: West Publishing Company, 1977.

Davis, Richard. *The Press and American Politics: The News Mediator*. New York and London: Longman, 1992.

Dean, John. *Blind Ambition*. New York: Simon & Schuster, 1976.

Dempsey, Paul Stephen. "Deregulation and Reregulation: Policy, Politics, and Economics." In *Handbook of Regulation and Administrative Law*. Ed. David H. Rosenbloom and Richard D. Schwartz. New York: Marcel Dekker, 1994, pp. 175–206.

Devoy, Ann. "Bush Offers Proposal on Ethics, Pay." *Washington Post*, April 13, 1989, p. A1.

———. "Costs of Clinton Travel Firing Still Growing." *Washington Post*, December 8, 1994, p. A1.

———. "Staff Denies Clinton Ally Had Role in Firing." *Washington Post*, May 21, 1993, p. A7.

Devoy, Ann and Dan Balz. "Jurors Keep Issue Alive for Clinton." *Washington Post*, May 29, 1996, p. A1.

Devoy, Ann and Charles Babcock. "Sununu Travel Rules Tightened." *Washington Post*, June 22, 1991, p. A1.

Devoy, Ann and Susan Schmidt. "Agriculture Secretary Espy Resigns." *Washington Post*, October 4, 1994, p. A1.

Dewar, Helen. "House Passes Strict Ban On Gifts From Lobbyists: Rules Cover Meals, Expense-Paid Travel." *Washington Post*, November 17, 1995, p. A1.

Dewar, Helen and Michael Weisskopf. "House Gives Final Approval to Lobbyist Disclosure Bill." *Washington Post*, November 30, 1995, p. A1.

Dionne, E. J. Jr. *They Only Look Dead: Why Progressives Will Dominate the New Political Era*. New York: Simon & Schuster, 1996.

"Do You Trust Bill Clinton?" *All Politics*, April 18, 1996, URL: http://allpolitics.com/news/9604/18/character/index.shtml

Doherty, Shawn. "The Statehouse Action and Innovation." *Newsweek*, March 24, 1986, 30–32.

"Dole Keeps Heat on Clinton's Ethics." *MSNBC*, October 19, 1996, URL: http://www.msnbc.com/news/35871.asp

Douglas, Paul. *Ethics in Government*. Cambridge, MA: Harvard University Press, 1952.

Douglas, Paul H. "Improvement of Ethical Standards in the Federal Government: Problems and Prospects." *Annals of the American Academy of Political And Social Science* 280 (March 1952): 149–57.

Dowd, Maureen. "How a Battered Clinton Has Stayed Alive." *New York Times*, March 16, 1992, p. A1.

———. "Mr. Fix-It of Politics: Truant Officer Clinton, President Pothole, Handy William." *Richmond Times-Dispatch*, July 28, 1996, p. G7.

Drew, Elizabeth. *On the Edge*. New York: Simon & Schuster, 1994.

———. *Portrait of an Election: The 1980 Presidential Campaign*. London: Routledge & Paul, 1981.

———. *Showdown: The Struggle Between the Gingrich Congress and the Clinton White House*. New York: Simon & Schuster, 1996.

Ducat, Craig R. and Harold W. Chase. *Constitutional Interpretation*, 5th ed. St. Paul, MN: West Publishing, 1992.

Duffy, Michael. "Need Friends in High Places." *Time*, 4 November 1991.

———. "Operation Hillary." *Time*, March 22, 1993, 36–38.

Dunar, Andrew J. *The Truman Scandals And The Politics of Morality*. Columbia: University of Missouri Press, 1984.

Eastland, Terry. "An Agressive Approach to Ethics." *Washington Post*, February 1, 1989, p. A23.

Edmondson, June E. "And Gifts and Travel for All: A Summary and Explanation of the Ethics Reform Act of 1989." *Federal Bar News & Journal* 37 (September 1990): 402–6.

Edsall, Thomas B. and Mario A. Brossard, "Clashing Coalitions Produce Split in Government Power." *Washington Post*, November 7, 1996, p. A1.

Ehrenhalt, Alan. "Justice and Ambition: U.S. Attorneys Can Do What They Want in Prosecuting Public Corruption. Is that Wise?" *Governing* 2 (September 1989): 38–44.

Eisner, Marc Allen. "Economic Regulatory Policies: Regulation and Deregulation in Historical Context." In *Handbook of Regulation and Administrative Law*. Ed. David H. Rosenbloom and Richard D. Schwartz. New York: Marcel Dekker, 1994.

Emery, Fred. *Watergate: The Corruption of American Politics and the Fall of Richard Nixon*, 1st ed. New York: Times Books, 1994.

"Espy undoing: Law of 'The Jungle' era." *Chicago Tribune* October 9, 1994, p. 25.

"Ethical Standards in American Public Life." *Annals of the American Academy of Political And Social Science* (1952): 1–157.

"Ethics in the Clinton Administration." Editorial. *New York Times*, December 14, 1992, p. A16.

"Ethics Investigations." *Journal of Law & Politics* 11 (Summer 1995): 409–608.

"Ethics Office is Reviewing Sununu's Travel." *New York Times*, May 23, 1991, p. A22.

Etzioni, Amitai. *Capital Corruption: The Attack On American Democracy.* New York: Harcourt Brace Jovanovich, 1984.

Fell, Anne. "Heroes, Rogues and Milestones." *Ethics: Easier Said Than Done*, Issue 13/14 (1991): 52–54.

Fesler, James W. *Public Administration: Theory and Practice.* Englewood Cliffs, NJ: Prentice-Hall, 1980.

Fineman, Howard. "Second Thoughts on 'Character Cops'," *Newsweek*, August 12, 1991, pp. 24–25.

Fish, Carl Russell. *The Civil Service And The Patronage.* New York: Russell & Russell. 1963.

Fitzgibbons, Tim. "Whitewater Chronology." Washingtonpost.com, January 5, 1997. URL: http://www.washingtonpost.com/wp-srv/national/longterm/wwtr/chron.htm

Fly, Richard. "Introducing Dan Quayle, Competitiveness Czar." *Business Week*, February 27, 1989, p. 37.

Ford, Frederick W. Acting Assistant Attorney General, Office of Legal Counsel. *Memorandum For the Attorney General, Re: Conflict of Interest Statute,* December 10, 1964.

"Four of 'Keating Five' Escape Punishment." *Congressional Quarterly Almanac* (1991): 37E.

Francke, Warren. "The Evolving Watchdog: The Media's Role in Governmental Ethics." *Annals of the American Academy of Political And Social Science* 537 (January 1995):109–21.

Frederickson, H. George and David G. Frederickson, "Public Perceptions of Ethics in Government." *Annals of the American Academy of Political and Social Science* 537 (January 1995): 163–72.

Freedman, James O. *Crisis and Legitimacy: The Administrative Process and American Government.* Cambridge: Cambridge University Press, 1978.

Friedman, Thomas L. "Clinton Issues Ethics Policies for Transition Team." *New York Times*, November 14, 1992, p. A1.

———. "White House Asked Aid of F.B.I. in Dismissals." *New York Times*, May 25, 1993, Sec. 8, p. 18.

———. "White House Retreats On Ouster At Travel Office, Reinstating 5." *New York Times*, May 26, 1993, p. A1.

Frier, David. *Conflict of Interest in the Eisenhower Administration.* Ames: Iowa State University Press, 1969.

Frisby, Michael K. "Clinton Fires White House Travel Office, FBI is Probing Allegations of Kickbacks." *Wall Street Journal*, May 20, 1993, p. A1.

Fritschler, Lee. *How Washington Works: The Executive's Guide to Government.* New York: Harper Business, 1987.

Garment, Suzanne. *Scandal: The Crisis of Mistrust in American Politics.* New York: Random House, 1991.

Gerlach, Wendy L. "Amendment of the Post-Employment Laws." *Arizona Law Review* 33 (1991): 401–26.

Germond, Jack. *Blue Smoke and Mirrors: How Reagan Won and Why Carter Lost the Election of 1980.* New York: Viking, 1981.

Gerth, Jeff. "Clintons Joined S&L Operator in Ozark Real Estate Venture." *New York Times,* March 8, 1992, p. A1.

Gilman, Stuart C. "Presidential Ethics and the Ethics of the Presidency." *Annals of the American Academy of Political and Social Science* 537 (January 1995): 58–75.

Ginsberg, Benjamin and Martin Shefter. *Politics by Other Means: The Declining Importance of Elections in America.* New York: Basic Books, 1990.

Giobbe, Dorothy. "Pentagon Papers' Strategist," *Editor & Publisher,* January 27, 1996, p. 9.

Gitlin, Todd. "Media Lemmings Run Amok?" *Washington Journalism Review* 14 (April 1992): 28–32.

Goodgame, Dan. "Fly Free or Die." *Time.* May 13, 1991, 16–18.

Goodsell, Charles T. *The Case for Bureaucracy: A Public Administration Polemic,* 3rd ed. Chatham, NJ: Chatham House, 1994.

"Governor Clinton Misses the Point." Editorial. *New York Times,* March 12, 1992, p. A22.

Grant, Linda. "Shutting Down the Regulatory Machine." *U.S. News & World Report,* February 13, 1995, p. 70.

Green, Mark, ed. *The Monopoly Makers: Ralph Nader's Study Group Report on Regulation and Competition.* New York: Grossman, 1973.

Greenfield, Meg. "Right and Wrong in Washington: Why Do Our Officials Need Specialists to Tell the Difference?" *Washington Post,* February 6, 1995, p. A7.

Gregg, Sandra R. "The Yuppies of Dixie." *U.S. News & World Report,* March 28, 1988, p. 24.

Gugliotta, Guy. "Are the Rules Awry, or Rhetoric Just Wry?" *Washington Post,* May 16, 1995, p. A15.

Harbrecht, Douglas. "Bill Clinton: Can He Make it out of Arkansas?" *Business Week,* July 8, 1991, p. 43.

Harden, Blaine. "A Seething Dole Intensifies Attack: Candidate Lobs FBI Files Accusations." *Washington Post,* October 26, 1996, p. A1.

Harder, Philip J. *Standards of Conduct for Presidential Transition Workers, Report to the Administrative Conference of the United States.* Washington, DC: The Conference, 1988.

Harris, John F. "Clinton's Book Declares Need for Active Government." *Washington Post,* 22 August 1996, A8.

———. "Clinton Defends Ethics Record." *Washington Post,* March 4, 1995, p. A10.

——. "Clinton: Judge Character by Actions, Not Allegations." *Washington Post*, July 16, 1996, p. A5.

——. "Law Aspiring to Shed Light on Lobbyists Leaves Some Gray Areas." *Washington Post*, 20 December 1995, A4.

——. "President Promises Convention Will Be About Ideas, Not Insults," *Washington Post*, 18 August 1996, p. A8.

Harris, John F., and George Lardner, Jr. "Reno Seeks Probe of FBI files." *Washington Post*, June 21, 1996, p. A1.

Haverman, Judith. "Ethics Pledge to Be Transition Hallmark: Bush to Impose Strict Conflict-of-Interest, Financial Disclosure Rules on Staff." *Washington Post*, November 16, 1988, p. A17.

Healy, Melissa. "Clinton Proposes Allowing More Time Off for Workers." *Los Angeles Times*, June 25, 1996, p. A1.

Hedges, Michael. "Walsh Says Pardon Hid Truth." *Washington Times*, February 9, 1993, pp. A1, A4.

Hoffman, David. "Bush Calls for 'Strict' Ethics Code for White House." *Washington Post*, March 8, 1988, p. A9.

Hoffman, David. "Bush Pledges Staff 'Code of Conduct': Congress Again Pressed to Adopt Comparable Ethics Standards." *Washington Post*, July 27, 1988, p. A4.

——. "Bush Retreats on Hill Honoraria Ban: Ethics Commission's Proposal to be Left out of Legislative Package." *Washington Post*, April 11, 1989, p. A6.

Hofstadter, Richard. *The Age of Reform: From Bryan To F.D.R.* New York: Vintage Books, 1955.

——. *The American Political Tradition & the Men Who Made It.* New York: Vintage Books, 1973.

"Honesty and Behavior Standards: Americans Chide Counterparts for Dishonesty, Unethical Behavior." *The Gallup Report* (May 1986): 12–13.

"Honesty in Government Stirs Great Concern in Huge Majority of Voters." *The Gallup Report* (March 1988): 26

Hoogenboom, Ari. *Outlawing the Spoils: A History of the Civil Service Reform Movement 1865–1883.* Urbana: University of Illinois Press, 1961.

Hook, Janet. "Passion, Defiance, Tears. Jim Wright Bows Out." *Congressional Quarterly Weekly Report*, June 3, 1989, p. 128–29.

Huddleson, Mark W., and Joseph C. Sands. "Enforcing Administrative Ethics." *Annals of the American Academy of Political and Social Science* 537 (January 1995): 139–50.

Idelson, Holly, "Bush Leaves Partisan Mark with Surprise Pardons: Weinberger, Five Others." *Congressional Quarterly Weekly Report.* January 2, 1993, 31–32.

Ifill, Gwen. "Clinton Defends Real-Estate Deal." *New York Times*, March 9, 1992, p. A13.

——. "Files of Dead Clinton Aide Are Dispensed to Legal Staff." *New York Times*, August 12, 1993, p. A16.

——. "5 from Travel Office Get Partial Vindication." *New York Times*, July 3, 1993, p. A1.

————. "Scandals Cast New light on Statehouse." *Washington Post* February 24, 1991, p. A3.

————. "2 Clinton Aides Are Leaving on a Winning Streak." *New York Times*, December 8, 1993, p. D20.

Ingersoll, Bruce. "File on Business Dealings of Clintons Is Being Sought in Foster Suicide Case." *Wall Street Journal*, December 20, 1993, p. A14.

Ingersoll, Bruce and Viveca Novack. "Justice Department Won't Charge Espy in Closing Probe of Possible Gift." *Wall Street Journal*, June 10, 1994, p. A12.

————. "Secretary Espy Drove U.S. Leased Auto for Personal Use, Violating Strict Rules." *Wall Street Journal*, September 20, 1994, p. A26.

Ingwerson, Marshall. "Revolving-Door Standard Raises Tough Issues for Administration." *Christian Science Monitor*, December 16, 1993, p. 1.

Isikoff, Michael. "Whitewater Files Were Found in Foster's Office, White House Confirms." *Washington Post*, December 22, 1993, p. A16.

"Isn't It Obvious?" *Washington Post*, Editorial, September 27, 1996, p. A24.

Jackson, Robert L. and Ronald J. Ostlaw. "Key Democrats Backed Pardon of Weinberger." *Los Angeles Times*, December 26, 1992, p. A1.

Jackson, Walter J. "The Ethics in Government Act, Conflict of Interest Laws and Presidential Recruitment." *Public Administration Review* 41 (November/December 1981): 659–65.

————. "Number 51, The Social Foundations of Political Freedom." In *The Federalist Papers, Alexander Hamilton, John Jay, James Madison*. Ed. Andrew Macke. New York: Washington Square Books, 1964, p. 122.

Johnson, Christopher. "Whitewater: A Special Report." Washingtonpost.com. October 10, 1996, URL: http://www.washingtonpost.com/wp.srv/national/longterm/wwtr/front.htm

Johnson, Haynes and David S. Broder. *The System: The American Way of Politics at the Breaking Point*. Boston: Little, Brown, 1996.

Johnson, Thomas H. *The Oxford Companion to American History* New York: Oxford University Press, 1966.

Johnston, David. "A Miami Lawyer Is Chosen to Investigate Commerce Secretary's Finances." *New York Times*, July 7, 1995, p. A14.

————. "Agriculture Chief Questioned on Gifts." *New York Times*, June 9, 1994, p. A12.

————. "Mrs. Clinton Responds in Travel Office Inquiry." *New York Times*, March 22, 1996, p. A23.

————. "Reno Rejects G.O.P. Request for Prosecutor." *New York Times*, March 5, 1995, p. A1.

————. "Ruling on Top Health Care Aide Brings Worry for Administration." *New York Times*, December 23, 1993, p. A20.

Josephson, Michael. "The Ethics of Politics: The Best of Times, the Worst of Times." *Ethics* 13/14 (1991): 39.

Kamerck, Elaine Crulla. "A Third World State Muddles Clinton's Path." *Los Angeles Times*, March 26, 1992, p. B7.

Kaplan, Sheila. "The Revolving Door Still Spins." *Washington Post*, January 31, 1993, p. C5.

"Kennedy Promises," *Congressional Quarterly Weekly Report*, January 13, 1961, A41.

Kenworthy, Tom. "House Committee Charges Wright with 69 Ethics-Rule Violations: Improper Gifts, 'Scheme' to Evade Income Limit by Book Sales Cited." *Washington Post*, April 18, 1989, pp. A1, A10.

"Key Players in the Keating Five Case." *Congressional Quarterly Almanac* (1990): 79.

Knight, Jerry. "Senator Seeks FDIC Probe of Hill Loan Default; Target is Ex-Partner of Commerce Secretary Brown." *Washington Post*, January 21, 1995, p. C1.

Kohlmeier, Louis M., Jr. *The Regulators: Watchdog Agencies and the Public Interest*. New York: Harper & Row, 1969.

Kranish, Michael. "Aides Asked FBI to Skirt its Policy." *Boston Globe*, May 25, 1993, p. A1.

Kristol, Irving. "Post-Watergate Morality: Too Good for Our Good?" *New York Times Magazine*, November 14, 1976, pp. 35, 50–51, 53, 55.

Kurtz, Howard. "The Big Sleazy: Is Clinton's Low-Rent as Reagan's?" *Washington Post*, March 26, 1995, pp. C1–2.

———. *Media Circus: The Trouble With America's Newspapers*. New York: Times Books, 1992.

———. "Reagan's People: Issues of Propriety: Deaver Case Revives Questions About Senior Officials' Conduct." *Washington Post*, April 27, 1986, pp. A1, A11–13.

Kutler, Stanley I. *The Wars of Watergate: The Last Crisis of Richard Nixon*. New York: Knopf, 1990.

Kuzma, Susan M. "Bribery and Gratuities." Appendix A. In U.S. Department of Justice. *Prosecution of Public Corruption Cases*. Washington, DC: Department of Justice, February 1988.

LaFraniere, Sharon and Susan Schmidt. "Espy Billed U.S. for Monthly Trips Home." *Washington Post*, September 17, 1994, p. A1.

Lanoutee, William J. "The Revolving Door—It's Tricky To Stop It." *National Journal* 9 (November 1977): 1796–1803.

Lardner, George, Jr. "Dole Pushed Nixon Probe of Democrats." *Washington Post*, October 19, 1996, p. A12.

Lauter, David. "Sununu Using Corporate Jets for Free Travel." *Los Angeles Times*, June 18, 1991, p. A1.

"Legal Travel? Then It's a Rotten Law." Editorial. *New York Times*, July 1, 1991, p. A12.

Leone, Richard C. "Public Interest Advocacy and the Regulatory Process." *Annals of The American Academy of Political and Social Sciences* 400 (March 1972): 46–58.

Lewis, Carol W. "Ethics Codes and Ethics Agencies: Current Practices and Emerging Trends." In *Ethics and Public Administration*, Ed. H. George Frederickson. Armonk, NY: M. E. Sharpe, 1993.

Lewis, Neil A. "Inquiry Clears Commerce Chief on Vietnam Bribery Accusation." *New York Times*, February 3, 1994, p. A8.

Link, Arthur. *Progressivism*. Arlington Heights, IL: Harlan Davidson, 1983.

Locke, Hubert G. "Ethics in American Government: A Look Backward." *Annals of the American Academy of Political and Social Science* 537 (January 1995): 14–24.

Locy, Toni. "Clinton Health Aid Won't Face Charges in Task Force Dispute." *Washington Post*, August 4, 1995, p. A2.

———. "Ex-officer Says Greed Guided Him into Net of Drug Sting." *Washington Post*, October 20, 1994, p. C1.

———. "Fees Paid in Passport Inquiry." *Washington Post*, June 1, 1996, p. A6.

———. "Reagan to Receive $562,111 for Iran-Contra Legal Costs." *Washington Post*, September 4, 1996, p. A24.

———. "Travel Unit's Ousted Head Is Indicted." *Washington Post*, December 8, 1994, p. A1.

Locy, Toni and Susan Schmidt. "Ex-aide Tells of Pressure for Travel Office Firings." *Washington Post*, January 18, 1996, p. A6.

Maass, Arthur. "Bad Federal Policy." *Spectrum* 66 (Winter, 1993): 17–26.

———. "U.S. Prosecution of State and Local Officials for Political Corruption." *Publius: The Journal of Federalism* 17 (Summer 1987).

MacDougall, Malcolm D. *We Almost Made It.* New York: Crown, 1977.

MacKenzie, G. Calvin. *The Politics of Presidential Appointments.* New York: Free Press, 1980.

MacKenzie, G. Calvin. *Presidential Transitions and the Ethics in Government Act,* In *Sourcebook on Government Ethics for Presidential Appointees.* Washington, D.C.: Office of the Chairman, Administrative Conference of the United States, 1988, pp. 1–19.

Macy, John W., Jr. *Public Service: The Human Side of Government.* New York: Harper & Row, 1971.

Madison, Christopher. "Ethics as Usual?" *National Journal*, July 8, 1989, pp. 1743–44.

Madison, James. "Federalist 51." *The Federalist Papers.* Ed. Andrew Macke. New York: Pocket Books, 1964, p. 121.

Magnuson, Ed. "A Mixed Verdict for Meese." *Time.* August 1, 1988, p. 24.

Magnusson, Paul. "Quayle's Pet Project Is Looking More like a Liability." *Business Week*, December 23, 1991, p. 39.

Malone, Julia. "Sununu's Travel Data Released." *Atlanta Constitution*, April 24, 1991, p. 1.

Manning, Bayless. "The Purity Potlatch: An Essay on Conflict of Interests, American Government, and Moral Escalation," *Federal Bar Journal* 24 (Summer 1964): 243–49.

Maraniss, David and Michael Weisskoff. "Lawyer Will Review Arkansas Land Deal." *Washington Post*, March 12, 1992, p. A1.

Marcus, Ruth Ann. "White House Back Off on Firing 5." *Washington Post*, 26 May 1993, A1.

Marcus, Ruth Ann and Sharon LaFraniere. "White House Bans Gifts, Free Travel For Appointees." *Washington Post*, August 12, 1994, p. A14.

McAllister, Bill. "Deaver Found Guilty of Lying about Lobbying: Former Reagan Aide Acquitted on 2 Counts." *Washington Post*, December 18, 1987, p. A1.

McAllister, Bill. "Seymour 'Loose Money,' Law Ethics Plague Capital." *Washington Post*, December 18, 1987, p. A1.

McCardle, Carl W. "The Public Service as a Springboard for Private Profit," *Annals Of The Academy of Political and Social Science* 280 (March 1952): 77–81.

McCulloch, David. *Truman.* New York: Simon & Schuster, 1992.

McGrath, Ellie. "No More Dragging up the Rear." *Time*, December 26, 1983, p. 77.

Meier, Kenneth J. and Thomas M. Holbrook. " 'I Seen My Opportunities and I Took 'Em': Political Corruption in the American States." *Journal of Politics* 54 (February 1992): 135–55.

Meisler, Stanley. "Clinton Upgrades Meat, Poultry Rules." *Los Angeles Times*, July 7, 1996, p. A1.

Melton, R.H. "Clinton Steps Up Effort to Portray Whitewater Prosecutor as Partisan." *Washington Post*, September 27, 1996, p. A22.

Melton, R.H. "Starr Rebuts Column Critical of Whitewater Case." *Washington Post*, April 11, 1996, p. A6.

Melton, R. H. and Michael Haddigan. "Three Guilty in Arkansas Fraud Trial." *Washington Post*, May 29, 1996, p. A1.

Merida, Kevin. "Clinton Pushes Low-Cost Initiatives: President Offers Noncontroversial Proposals on Campaign Swing." *Washington Post*, July 24, 1996, p. A8.

Miller, Alan C. "Espy Repays $7,500 for Gifts and Expenses." *Los Angeles Times*, September 20, 1994, p. A10.

Miller, Nathan. *Stealing From America: A History of Corruption from Jamestown to Reagan.* New York: Paragon House, 1992.

Moore, John W. "Grass-roots Graft," *National Journal*, August 19, 1987, pp. 1962–67.

Moore, John W. "Hands Off: To Avoid Conflict-of-Interest Questions, Many of President Bush's Appointees Are Holding on to Corporate Stocks but Disqualifying Themselves from Issues Involving Specific Firms." *National Journal*, July 1, 1989, p. 1678–83.

Morgan, Dan and Walter Pincus. "Regan Says President Knew Of Cover Story: Account of Arms Sale Differs From Reagan's." *Washington Post*, July 31, 1988, p. A1.

Morgan, Peter. "Broader Costs of the New Prosecutorial Ethics." *Journal of Law and Politics* 11 (Summer 1995): 543–47.

Morin, Richard and Mario A. Brossard. "Dole's Resignation Doesn't Resonate with Voters, Poll Suggests." *Washington Post*, May 24, 1996, p. A12.

Morison, Samuel Eliot and Henry Steele Commager. *The Growth of the American Republic* New York: Oxford University Press, 1962.

Morley, Jefferson. "Reagan vs. Walsh." *Nation.* April 23, 1988, pp. 556–57.

Morris, Roger. *Partners in Power: The Clintons and Their America.* New York: Henry Holt, 1996.

Mosher, Frederick. *Democracy and Public Service.* 2nd ed. New York: Oxford University Press, 1982.

———. *The GAO: Quest for Accountability in American Government.* Boulder, CO: Westview Press, 1979.

———. *Watergate: Implications for Responsible Government: A Special Report at the Request of the Senate Select Committee on Presidential Campaign Activities.* New York: Basic Books, 1974.

"Most See Federal Bureaucrats as Overpaid, Lazy, Pampered." *Gallup Opinion Poll, Report No. 146* (September 1977): 20–24.

Nagourney, Adam. "Baird Abandons Cabinet Bid." *USA Today,* January 22, 1993, p. A1.

National Commission on the Public Service. *Committing to Excellence: Recruiting and Retaining a Quality Public Service.* Washington, DC: National Commission on the Public Service, 1989.

Neikirk, William. "Use of Chopper for Golf Costs Clinton Aide His Job." *Chicago Tribune,* May 27, 1994, p. A1.

Nixon, Richard. *In the Arena: A Memoir of Victory, Defeat, and Renewal.* New York: Simon and Schuster, 1990.

"Nofziger's turn." *Time,* February 22, 1988, p. 31.

Nord, David Paul. "The Nineteenth-Century Origins of Modern American Journalism." In *Three Hundred Years of the American Newspaper.* Ed. John B. Hench. Worcester, MA: American Antiquarian Society, 1991.

Norton, Robert H. "Who Wants to Work in Washington." *Fortune,* August 14, 1989, pp. 77–80.

Oppmann, Justin C. "Flash Point Suggest Clinton Reigns." *All Politics,* October 16, 1996, URL: http://allpolitics.com/news/9610/16/instapoll/

"Panel Probes Senators' Aid to Keating." *Congressional Quarterly Almanac* (1990): 519.

Parlstein, Michael and Walt Philbin. "Nine Cops Charged in Drug Sting." *New Orleans Times-Picayune,* December 8, 1994, p. A1.

Pear, Robert. "Justice Department Defends Setup of Care Panel." *New York Times,* July 26, 1994, p. A16.

———. "Now it Can Be Told; The Task Force was Bold, Naive and Collegial." *New York Times,* September 18, 1994, p. 4.

———. "White House Seeks Settlement of Health Suit." *New York Times,* August 10, 1994, p. A16.

Perkins, Roswell B. "The Federal Conflict of Interest Law." *Harvard Law Review* 76 (April 1963): 1113–69.

Phillips, Cabell. *The Truman Presidency.* New York: Macmillan Company, 1966.

Phillips, Don. "Congress Aims to Pass Pay and Ethics Bill Before Thanksgiving," *Washington Post,* November 14, 1989, p. A9.

———. "Pay and Ethics Legislation." *Washington Post,* November 21, 1989, p. A23.

———. "Stepping Into the Ethics Thicket: Reluctant Congress Moves Toward Possible Revision of Laws," *Washington Post,* April 27, 1989, p. A21.

Phillips, Don and Tom Kenworthy. "Pay-Ethics Plan Delayed By Demands From Bush." *Washington Post,* November 15, 1989, p. A7.

Phillips, Kevin. *Arrogant Capital.* Boston, MA: Little, Brown and Company, 1994.

"Politicians and Privacy." *Congressional Quarterly,* April 7, 1992, p. 352.

"Poll: Clinton has Character to be President." *USA Today, Election '96,* October 19, 1996. URL: http://167.8.29.8/elect/eq/eq149.htm

"Poll Finds Voters Care Most About Issues, Not Character." *All Politics*, June 27, 1996, URL: http://allpolitics.com/news/9606/27/poll/

"Poor tutor." *Houston Chronicle*, August 30, 1994, p. A12.

"Post Office Probe Hints at Larger Scandal." *Congressional Quarterly Almanac* (1992): 47

Presidential Appointee Project. *Leadership in Jeopardy: The Fraying of the Presidential Appointments System*. Washington, DC: National Academy of Public Administration, 1985.

"Presidential Election Exit Polls Results-Part 1," *All Politics*, CNN-Time, November 6, 1996 URL: http://allpolitics.com/elections/natl.exit.poll/index2.html

Priest, Dana. "Suddenly Being Taken Seriously at Office of Government Ethics: For Low Key Agency, Overseeing Standards Is Field with Growth." *Washington Post*, January 15, 1992, p. A21.

"Professional: Pharmacists, Clergy Rated Highest for 'Honesty' and 'Ethical Standards.'" *Gallup Report* (December 1988): 3.

Public Integrity Research Corporation Home Page. January 20, 1997, URL: http://www.pihome.com:80/pirc/pirc1.html

Public Papers and Addresses of Franklin D. Roosevelt. Comp. Samuel Irving Rosenman. New York: Macmillan Company, 1941.

"Public Says 48 cents of each Federal Tax Dollar is Wasted." *Gallup Opinion Index*, December 1979: 15–16.

"Qualified Rollover Can Also Avoid Conflict of Interest." *Journal of Taxation* 73 (September 1990): 138.

"Quayle Council Repels Attack on Role of Regulatory Agencies." *Chemical Marketing Reporter*, December 16, 1991, p. 22.

Rabkin, Jeremy. "White House Lawyering: Law, Ethics, and Political Judgements." In *Government Lawyers: The Federal Legal Bureaucracy and Presidential Politics*. Ed. Cornell W. Clayton. Lawrence, KS: University Press of Kansas, 1995.

Raum, Tom. "Clinton Shrugs W'Water Polls." *Associated Press*, July 15, 1996, *PoliticsNow*, URL: http://www.politicsnow. com/egibin . . . rch?APO+%28 character%29%3Aall

Reid, T.R. "Dukakis Vows Strict Rules On Lobbying: Democrat Slams Bush Over 'Sleaze Factor.'" *Washington Post*, September 29, 1988, p. A18.

"Release the Whitewater Files." Editorial. *New York Times*, December 23, 1993, p. A16.

Report of Independent Counsel Concerning Edwin Meese III, before Senior Circuit Judge Robb, Washington, DC: Division for the Purpose of Appointing Independent Counsels, U.S. Court of Appeals for the District of Columbia Circuit, 1989.

"Revolving Door Proposal Strikes a Nerve." *Broadcasting* 20 (February 1978): 44

Reynolds, Harry W., Jr. "Educating Public Administrators About Ethics." *Annals of the American Academy of Political and Social Science* 537 (January 1995): 126–35.

Richter, Paul. "Clinton Assails Starr Over Whitewater Probe." *Los Angeles Times*, July 16, 1996, p. A8.

Richter, Paul and Greg Krikorian. "Clinton Takes Aim at Rogue Gun Dealers." *Los Angeles Times*, July 9, 1996, p. A11.

Richter, Paul and David Lauter. "White House Defends Ethics Policy as Officials Take Private-Sector Jobs." *Los Angeles Times*, December 8, 1994, p. B28.

Riehle, Thomas. "Scandals, Etc. from A to Z," *National Journal* January 14, 1984, 92–93.

Roberts, Paul Craig. "First Lady's Secrets Are in the Dock." *Los Angeles Times*, July 31, 1994, p. M5.

Roberts, Robert. "Lord, Protect Me From the Appearance of Wrongdoing." In *Public Personnel Policy: The Politics of Civil Service*. Ed. David H. Rosenbloom. Port Washington, NY: Associated Faculty Press, 1985.

Roberts, Robert. "Regulatory Bias And Conflict of Interest Regulation." In *Handbook of Regulation and Administrative Law*, Ed. David H. Rosenbloom and Richard D. Schwartz. New York: Marcel Dekker, 1994.

Roberts, Robert. *Report to the Administrative Conference of the United States. A Federal Guide To Federal Ethics Laws For Presidential Appointees*. Washington, DC: Office of the Chairman Administrative Conference of the United States, December 1988.

Roberts, Robert. *White House Ethics*. Westport, CT: Greenwood Press, 1988.

Roberts, Robert and Marion T. Doss. "Public Service and Private Hospitality," *Public Administration Review* 52 (May/June 1992): 260–69.

———. "The Federalization of 'Grass Roots' Corruption," *Spectrum* 66 (Winter 1993): 9–12.

———. "Recruitment of American Presidential Nominees: Divestiture and Deferred Taxation of Gain." *Journal of Social, Political and Economic Studies* 21 (Spring 1996): 49–63.

Rosenbaum, David E. "Clinton May Gain As Counsel Bill Clears Congress." *New York Times*, June 22, 1994, p. A1.

Rosenbloom, David H. "The Evolution of the Administrative State and Transformation of Administrative Law." In *Handbook of Regulation and Administrative Law*. Ed. David H. Rosenbloom and Richard D. Schwartz. New York: Marcel Dekker, 1994, 3–36.

Rosenthal, Andrew. "Bush Campaign Issues Stinging Attack." *New York Times*, August 3, 1992, p. A14.

Ross, Shelly. *Fall from Grace: Sex, Scandal, and Corruption in American Politics from 1702 to the Present*. New York: Ballantine Books, 1988.

Rowe, Robert. *The Bobby Baker Story*. New York: Parallax, 1967.

Rowen, Hobart. "Foreign Lobbies, Fairness and the 'Revolving Door,' " *Washington Post*, October 25, 1992, p. H1.

Rudman, Warren. *Combat: Twelve Years in the U.S. Senate*. New York: Random House, 1996.

Ruff, Charles E. "Federal Prosecution of Local Corruption: A Study in the Making of Law Enforcement Policy." *Georgetown Law Journal* 65 (June 1977): 1171–228.

Sabato, Larry J. *Feeding Frenzy*. New York: Free Press, 1991.

Safire, William. "The Road to National Nightmare." *Daily News-Record*, September 28, 1996, p. A6.

Salant, Jonathan D. "Clinton Order." *Congressional Quarterly Weekly Report*, August 5, 1995, p. 2334.

Schlesinger, Arthur M., Jr., ed., *History of Presidential Elections. 1789–1968*. New York: Chelsea House, 1971.

Schreiber, G. R. *The Bobby Baker Affair*. Chicago: Regnery, 1964.

Seidman, Harold and Robert Gilmour. *Politics, Position and Power*, 4th ed. New York: Oxford University Press, 1986.

Seper, Jerry. "Morris Is but the Latest Bump in Clinton's Road." *Washington Times-Whitewater-Current*, August 30–September 1, 1996, URL: http://www.washtimes.com/whitewater/ww.current.html

Seper, Jerry and Paul Bedard. " 'Baird Problem' Forces Wood out." *Washington Times*, February 6, 1993, p. A1.

Serrano, Richard A. "Panel Hears Drug History of 36 Clinton Staffers." *Los Angeles Times*, July 18, 1996, p. A11.

Shannon, Albert. *The Organization and Administration of the Union Army: 1861–1865*. Gloucester, MA: Peter Smith, 1965.

Shepard, Scott. "Clinton Seeks to Put Adultery Rumors to Rest," *Atlanta Constitution*, September 17, 1991, p. E3.

Siemer, Deannne C. "Enforcement of the Federal Ethics Laws as Applied to Executive Branch Personnel." In *Sourcebook on Government Ethics for Presidential Appointees*. Washington, DC: Office of the Chairman, Administrative Conference of the United States, 1988.

Sittig, Robert F. "Campaign Reform: Interest Groups, Parties, and Candidates." *Annals of the American Academy of Political and Social Science* 537 (January 1995): 85–95.

Smith, Greg B. "Clinton Talks Reform; Takes Big Donations." *San Francisco Chronicle*, April 19, 1992, p. A1.

Smith, William French. *Corporate Political Contributions: The Law and the Practice*. Washington: National Association of Manufacturers, 1973.

Smolowe, Jill. "Rush to Judgement." *Time*, February 15, 1993, pp. 30–31.

Smothers, Ronald. "5 South Carolina State Officials Indicted in Corruption Inquiry." *New York Times*, August 25, 1990, p. A1.

Sobieraj, Sandra. "Dole Urges America To 'Wake Up.' " *PoliticsNow*, October 24, 1996, URL: http://pnl.politicsnow.com/APO/19961024/V000395–102496–idx.html

Solomon, Burt. "The Lingering Ethical Quandaries of Nice People With Old Money." *National Journal*, February 25, 1989, p. 483.

"Special prosecutors, Down But Not Out." *U.S. News & World Report*, December 21, 1992, p. 26

Sproat, John G. *"The Best Men:" Liberal Reformers in the Gilded Age*. Chicago: University of Chicago Press, 1982.

Stewart, James B. *Blood Sport: The President and His Adversaries*. New York: Simon & Schuster, 1996.

Stinson, Jeffrey. "Clinton Gets Jump on Personal Issues." *USA Today*, September 17, 1991, p. A32.

Strine, James Michael. "The Office of Legal Counsel: Legal Professionals in a Political System." Ph.D Thesis, Johns Hopkins University, 1992. U.M.I. no. 92–29411.

Summers, Mark Wahlgren. *The Era of Good Stealing*. New York: Oxford University Press, 1993.

———. *The Plundering Generation: Corruption and Crisis of the Union 1849–1861*. New York: Oxford University, Press, 1987.

Sure, Robert. "Teens' Use of Drugs Still Rising." *Washington Post*, August 21, 1996, p. A1.

"Tabloid Prints New Bill Clinton Infidelity Charges." Nightline-ABC, Program number 2784, January 23, 1992.

"Tax Notes: Executive Officials May Be Entitled to Deferral of Gain." *The Army Lawyer* (July 1990): 52.

Taylor, Paul. "Bush Endorses Widened, Strengthened Ethics Bill: 'I'll Be Speaking Out . . . to Get It Passed.' " *Washington Post*, May 3, 1988, p. A7.

Terry, Dan. "30 in Cleveland Police Held in Federal Gambling Inquiry." *New York Times*, May 31, 1991, p. A21.

Thomas, Pierce and Howard Schneider, "Los Angeles Attorney Chosen To Head Investigation of Espy." *Washington Post*, September 10, 1994, p. A3.

Thomas, Pierre. "Espy Probe May Get Independent Counsel." *Washington Post*, August 8, 1994, p. A5.

To Serve with Honor: Report of the President's Commission on Federal Ethics Law Reform. Washington, DC: Government Printing Office, March 1989.

Tolchin, Martin. "Bush Lambastes House and Senate." *New York Times*, October 25, 1991, p. A1.

Tolchin, Martin. "Nofziger Wins Court Reversal of Conviction." *New York Times*. June 28, 1989, p. A1.

"Tower Nomination: Majority Opposes Tower Confirmation." *Gallup Report* (March/April 1989): 17.

Trammell, Jeffrey B. and Gary B. Osifchin. *The Clinton 500: The New Team Running America*. Washington, DC: Almanac Publishing, 1994.

"Tripping Down Special-Prosecutor Memory Lane," *Time*, August 22, 1994, p. 16.

Tumulty, Karen and Edwin Chey. "Blame for Health Plan's Collapse Falls Everywhere." *Los Angeles Times*, August 28, 1994, p. A1.

Twentieth Century Fund. *Obstacle Course: The Report of the Twentieth Century Fund Task Force on the Presidential Appointment Process*. New York: Twentieth Century Fund, 1996.

"21 White House Employees in Drug Testing Because of Backgrounds." *Associated Press*, July 15, 1996, URL: http://www.politicsnow.com/news/July96/15/ap0715drugtesting/index.htm

U.S. Congress, House Committee on Merchant Marine and Fisheries. *Investigation of Shipyard Profits*. Washington, D.C.: Government Printing Office, 1946.

U.S. Department of Justice. Criminal Division. *Prosecution of Public Corruption Cases*, 1988.

U.S. Department of Justice. Ford, Frederick W. Acting Assistant Attorney General. Office of Legal Counsel. Memorandum For the Attorney General Re: Conflict of Interest Statutes, December 10, 1956.

U.S. Department of Justice. Public Integrity Section. Criminal Division, *Report to*

Congress on the Operations of the Public Integrity Section for 1992. Washington, DC: U.S. Department of Justice, 1992.

U.S. Office of Government Ethics. *Take the High Road: An Ethics Booklet for Executive Branch Employees.* Washington, DC: United States Government Printing Office, 1992.

U.S. Office of Government Ethics Home Page: January 20, 1997, URL: http://www.access.gpo.gov/usoge/index.html

U.S. President. Bush, George. White House. Office of Press Secretary. Remarks by the President To American Society of Newspaper Editors, April 12, 1989 (Unpublished).

U.S. President. Bush, George. White House. Office of Press Secretary. The Government-Wide Ethics Act of 1989-President Bush's Ethics Reform Proposals. April 12, 1989 (Unpublished).

U.S. President. Clinton, William Jefferson. Remarks on Regulatory Reform in Arlington, Virginia. *Weekly Compilation of Presidential Documents* 31, March 30, 1995, p. 426

U.S. President. Clinton, William Jefferson. The White House, Office of the Press Secretary, Executive Committments By Executive Branch Appointees, Executive Order 12834, January 20, 1993 (Unpublished).

U.S. President. Clinton, William Jefferson. The White House, Office of the Press Secretary, Radio Address By The President To The Nation: The Oval Office, July 22, 1995, p. 1. Texas A & M Presidential Archives. URL: http://library.whitehouse.gov/Retrive.cgi?dbtype = audio & id = 78 & query = bipartisan+commission

U.S. President. Clinton, William Jefferson. The White House, Office of the Press Secretary, Remarks of the President on Political Reform. August 4, 1995. p. 2 (Unpublished).

U.S. President. Kennedy, John F. House Document. No. 145, 87th Cong. 1st Sess. *Message from the President to the United States Congress Relative to Ethical Conduct in Government*, April 27, 1961.

U.S. President. Roosevelt, Franklin D. Memorandum. Franklin D. Roosevelt for the United States Civil Service Commission. June 11, 1935. Official File. Franklin D. Roosevelt Library.

U.S. President, Truman, Harry S. Message to Congress. *Ethics in Government*, September 27, 1951.

U.S. Senate. Committee on Labor and Public Welfare. *Report of the Subcommittee on Labor and Public Welfare on Ethical Standards in Government*, 82nd. Cong. 1st. Sess., 1951.

U.S. War Production Board. *Policies and procedures on Dollar-a-Year and Without Compensation Employees of the War Production and Predecessor Agencies,* May 1940 to March 1944. Washington, DC: War Production Board, 1944.

United States v. Mississippi Valley Generating Co., 364 U.S. 520 (1961).

Van Riper, Paul P. "Americanizing a Foreign Invention: The Pendleton Act of 1883." In *Classics of Public Personnel Policy*, Ed. Frank J. Thompson. Oak Park, IL: Moore, 1979.

———. *History of the United States Civil Service.* Evanston, IL: Row, Peterson, 1958.

———. "Spoils as Dysfunctional and Functional." In *People in the Public Service*, Ed. Robert Golembiewski and Michael Cohen, Itasca, IL: F. E. Peacock, 1976, pp. 519–31.

" 'Wake Up' Frustrated Dole Says On Stump." *The Associated Press*, October 24, 1996, URL: http://search.politicsnow.com/PN/news/Oct96/24/ap1024dole/index.htm

Walden, Gregory. *On Best Behavior: The Clinton Administration and Ethics in Government*. Indianapolis: Hudson Institute, 1996.

Walsh, Edward. "Dole Lashes Clinton on Trust Issue." *Washington Post*, October 12, 1996, p. A1.

Walsh, Edward and Paul Duggan. "Dole Campaign to Open Second Front on Character Theme." *Washington Post*, October 13, 1996, p. A26.

Walsh, Kenneth T. "Regulation Returns." *U.S. News & World Report*, December 28, 1992, p. 52.

Walsh, Sharon. "Special Prosecutor To Drop Brown Probe." *Washington Post*, April 5, 1996, p. A23.

Wang, Jennifer. "Raising the Stakes at the White House: Legal and Ethical Duties of the White House," *Georgetown Journal of Legal Ethics* 8 (1994): 115–35.

Warren, Kenneth F. *Administrative Law in the Political System*, 2d.ed. St. Paul, MN: West Publishing Company, 1988.

———. *Administrative Law in the Political System*, 3d.ed. St. Paul, MN.: West Publishing Company, 1996.

"Watergate: Chronology of a Crisis." *Congressional Quarterly*, 1975.

Watson, Richard L., Jr. *The Development of National Power: The United States 1900–1919*. Boston: Houghton Mifflin, 1976.

Weinberg, Arthur. *The Muckrakers: The Era in Journalism that Moved America to Reform, 1902–1912*. New York: Simon and Schuster, 1961.

Wertheimer, Fred. "20 Years: Common Cause: Advancing Honesty and Fairness in our Political System." *Common Cause Magazine* (Fall 1992): 2–5.

"Where Mr. Espy got his bad habits." *St. Louis Post-Dispatch* September 9, 1994, p. C6.

White, Leonard D. *The Jacksonians*. New York: MacMillan, 1954.

———. *The Jeffersonians*. New York: MacMillan 1959.

———. *The Republican Era*. New York: Henry Holt, 1948.

"White House Travel Chief Found Innocent of Charges." *Wall Street Journal*, November 17, 1995, p. A20.

Wildavsky, Aaron. *Dixon-Yates: A Study in Power Politics*. Westport, CT: Greenwood Press, 1976.

Wilkins, Lee. "Journalists and the Character of Public Officials/Figures." *Journal of Mass Media Ethics* 9 (1994): 157–60.

Williams, Henry A. "How to Report the Lewd and Unproven." *Time*, May 16, 1994, p. 46.

Wilson, James Q. "Corruption: The Shame of the States." In *Political Corruption: Readings in Comparative Analysis*. Ed. Arnold J. Heidenheimer, New Brunswick, NJ: Transaction Books, 1970, pp. 298–306.

Wilson, James Q. "The Changing FBI—The Road to Abscam." *Public Interest* (Spring 1990): 3–14.

Wilson, Woodrow. "The Study of Administration." *Political Science Quarterly* 2 (June 1887): 201.

Woll, Peter. *American Bureaucracy*, 2d ed. New York: W. W. Norton 1977.

Woodward, Bob. *The Agenda: Inside the Clinton White House*. New York: Simon & Schuster, 1994.

————. *The Choice: Inside the Clinton and Dole Campaigns*. New York: Simon & Shuster, 1996.

Woodward, C. Van, ed. *Responses of the President to Charges of Misconduct*. New York: Delacorte, 1974.

York, Byron. "Ron Brown's Booty." *American Spectator* (June 1995): 37.

York, Michael. "Health Task Force Closed Doors Backed." *Washington Post*, June 23, 1993, p. A15.

Index

About the Authors

ROBERT N. ROBERTS is Professor of Political Science and Law at James Madison University. He has written extensively on the subjects of public service ethics, political ethics, and employee rights and responsibilities.

MARION T. DOSS, JR. is Professor of Political Science and Law at James Madison University. A combat veteran of the Vietnam War, his professional interests include the areas of criminal law, legal issues related to law enforcement, public service and corruption, criminal justice education, and counterintelligence. He has published a number of articles, many in collaboration with Robert N. Roberts.

ISBN 0-275-95597-4

90000>

EAN

9 780275 955977

HARDCOVER BAR CODE